P9-DEQ-007

The Vocabulary-Enriched Classroom

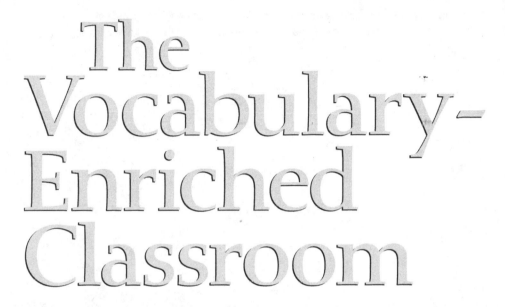

Practices for Improving the Reading Performance of All Students in Grades 3 and Up

Cathy Collins Block & John N. Mangieri

SCHOLASTIC

NEW YORK • TORONTO • LONDON • AUCKLAND • SYDNEY
MEXICO CITY • NEW DELHI • HONG KONG • BUENOS AIRES

Dedication

To Judy deTuncq, a cherished friend who has been an invaluable source of support to
our work and whose contributions to the field of education are outstanding.

Credit:
Page 92: From Hailstones and Halibut Bones
by Mary O'Neill and Leonard Weisgard.
Copyright©1961 by Mary LeDuc O'Neill. Used by permission of
Random House Children's Books, a division of Random House, Inc.

Scholastic Inc. grants teachers permission to photocopy the reproducible pages from this book for classroom use.
No other part of this publication may be reproduced in whole or in part, or stored in a retrieval system, or
transmitted in any form or by any means, electronic, mechanical, photocopying, recording, or otherwise, without
written permission of the publisher. For information regarding permission, write to
Scholastic Inc., 557 Broadway, New York, NY 10012.

Cover design by Maria Lilja
Interior design by Holly Grundon
Interior photos by Ed Lallo
ISBN 0-439-73093-7
Copyright © 2006 by Cathy Collins Block and John N. Mangieri

All rights reserved. Published by Scholastic Inc.
Printed in the U.S.A.
4 5 6 7 8 9 10 23 12 11 10 09

Table of Contents

Acknowledgments 4

Introduction 6

Chapter 1:   **Vocabulary Instruction: The New Look** 8
             of Research-Based Best Practices
             Cathy Collins Block and John N. Mangieri

Chapter 2:   **Developing Vocabulary by Learning** 18
             Words Through Context
             Linda B. Gambrell and Kathy N. Headley

Chapter 3:   **Developing Vocabulary Through Word Building** 36
             Timothy Rasinski

Chapter 4:   **Developing Vocabulary by Learning** 54
             Content-Area Words
             Robert J. Rickelman and D. Bruce Taylor

Chapter 5:   **Helping Students Learn Unusual Words:** 74
             Homophones, Idioms, and Figurative Language
             Jerry L. Johns and Janet L. Pariza

Chapter 6:   **Effective Vocabulary Instruction for Struggling Readers** . . 98
             Diane Lapp, James Flood, and Sharon Flood

Chapter 7:   **Effective Vocabulary Instruction for** 118
             English-Language Learners
             Michael F. Graves and Jill Fitzgerald

Chapter 8:   **Effective Vocabulary Instruction for Gifted Students** . . . 138
             David Lund

Chapter 9:   **Vocabulary Assessment: A Key to** 164
             Planning Vocabulary Instruction
             Rita M. Bean and Allison Swan

Chapter 10: **Preparing Today's Generation of** 188
             Students for Tomorrow
             Arthur L. Costa and Rebecca Reagan

References Cited 214

Index 222

Acknowledgments

We sincerely hope that *The Vocabulary-Enriched Classroom* will not be merely "another book" for you. Rather, we hope it makes a significant impact on you, personally as well as professionally, as you teach vocabulary to children.

The book was written with the objective of identifying the excellent vocabulary research that has been conducted in recent years and translating important findings into easy-to-implement teaching strategies.

To achieve this, we enlisted the assistance of many of our country's foremost literacy experts. Their knowledge of research-based vocabulary practices that produce high vocabulary performance on the part of students has been invaluable to us. You will find their words to be not only informative but also interesting. To these dedicated professionals, we offer thanks for being a part of our book and for the contributions they have made over the years to the body of knowledge about literacy development.

We would like to recommend two things. First, please read *The Vocabulary-Enriched Classroom* in its entirety rather than merely focusing on topics of special interest to you. The book's content was designed to address comprehensively the many diverse but interrelated ingredients that are significant to the acquisition and retention of vocabulary. So, to gain a complete understanding of that process, you should read the entire book. Second, we sincerely hope that you will read this book with an open mind. If you do, you will discover that it is based on research conducted in schools with students of diverse backgrounds and reading abilities. The strategies we present have been clearly and repeatedly shown to lead to high reading performance among students. They are also popular with students.

Although the book was written by multiple authors, you will note a common thread throughout its chapters: the recommendation to abandon instruction that relies on memorization and rote learning. As an alternative, we show you how to teach strategies that your students will find interesting and challenging, and that will lead them to greater success not only in literacy achievement and vocabulary development but also in content-area mastery.

We would also like to thank three other individuals. Our heartfelt gratitude is given to Terry Cooper, vice president and general manager of Scholastic Teaching Resources, who agreed to publish this book and whose advice was instrumental in planning and organizing it. In addition, we would like to thank Margery Rosnick, acquisitions editor, and Ray Coutu, development editor, whose considerable expertise was crucial to the writing of this book. They worked tirelessly to assure that its message would be clearly conveyed.

We are also grateful to Charles Lincoln, the principal of Oakmont Elementary School, and to the teachers who allowed us to photograph them and their students for this book: Rose Hernandez, Juan Marquez, Mary Daniels, Alice Cedillo, Alison Adkins, Gena Chaucer, Stephanie Whitting, Wendy Taube, Gayle Biemeret, and Juan Puente.

Finally, we thank you for taking the time from your busy life to read this book. We wish you the very best in your efforts to provide students with quality vocabulary instruction and to promote their literacy success.

Cathy Collins Block
John N. Mangieri

Introduction

The *Vocabulary-Enriched Classroom* examines vocabulary development from in-depth and wide-ranging perspectives. As such, there are many ways to read it, including

- focusing on a certain aspect of vocabulary instruction, such as research-based strategies. The book offers numerous research-based strategies that can produce significant increases in vocabulary performance, and you may decide to study and use them all, without delving into other aspects.

- learning about vocabulary acquisition and retention in a more comprehensive fashion. You could read to gain an understanding of why some students possess inadequate reading vocabularies, how words can be effectively acquired and retained, and many other topics related to this complex facet of literacy.

- combining these approaches. By doing that, you will gain an in-depth understanding of both vocabulary development and high-quality vocabulary instruction.

Regardless of the approach you choose, we hope the book is instrumental in helping you carry out successful vocabulary instruction.

We present topics in a sequence that will enable you to understand basic vocabulary principles before teaching them to students with diverse needs. However, you need not read the book from cover to cover. Depending on what *you* wish to derive from it, you may want to read the chapters in a sequence that *you* establish and that will best suit *your* objectives.

You have another decision to make: whether to read the book on your own, with another professional, or as part of a professional book club. While the first two options should be self-explanatory, the following may help you better understand the third.

In *Literacy and the Youngest Learner* (2005), Susan Bennett-Armistead, Nell Duke, and Annie Moses offer excellent ideas on the planning and implementation of book clubs:

1. **Think carefully about the size of the club**—Groups of four to five members make participation (and scheduling) manageable.

2. **Create a diverse group**—The club should include professionals who teach different grade levels. This will ensure an examination of the topic through a developmental lens.

3. **Set shared goals early on**—By asking and answering questions such as What do we want to get out of this club? What contribution will each of us make? and What can be expected from others?, you will set a strong direction for the club and provide guidelines on how it should operate.

4. **Hear from everyone**—Since everyone has a response to share, do what you can to encourage full participation at each session.

5. **Make connections to practice**—Implement in your classroom what you are learning. Think about what others in the club have said about the book's content. Use or adapt their ideas into your teaching practices.

Whether you decide to read our book alone, with a colleague, or as part of a book club, we urge you to use its content as a framework from which to reexamine your literacy-instruction practices. Many effective strategies are contained in its pages. There's a great deal of research-based information about today's elementary and middle school students and the manner in which they learn. Using some or all of the book's material can significantly improve the quality of your vocabulary instruction and the performance of your students.

To help you make the transition from reading the book to implementing its content, at the end of each chapter we pose discussion questions and provide teaching activities to guide your thinking. These are not intended to test your comprehension of the material, nor do they represent all that could be asked or carried out. Rather, as we stated previously, they are designed to help you take the next step. We also hope that they will be starting points for enhancing your thinking about the book's content.

If you are reading this book with another person or as part of a professional book club, we urge you not only to engage in the activities at the end of each chapter but also to share the actions you take and/or the conclusions you reach, to get multiple perspectives about vocabulary instruction. This will help others to learn from you and for you to do likewise. Interactions like these are important for becoming a more effective teacher of vocabulary.

CHAPTER ONE

Vocabulary Instruction: The New Look of Research–Based Best Practices

Cathy Collins Block, Texas Christian University, and
John N. Mangieri, the Institute for Literacy Enhancement

Vocabulary plays a significant role in students' reading success. Without an understanding of the words in a sentence, paragraph, or passage, comprehension cannot occur, and without comprehension, one is not truly literate. Despite its importance, vocabulary does not receive the same amount of attention in many elementary school classrooms as other components of literacy (Beck & McKeown, 1991; Torgeson, 2004). The teaching of vocabulary isn't examined as often as it should be and what is happening in classrooms today is at odds with what research tells us about best practices (Block & Mangieri, 2003). As a consequence, our teaching often does not address the needs of all students. Instead, only the most able students retain an understanding of the words we teach and only they have the advantage of applying that understanding to their reading.

In this chapter, we present "the state of the union" of vocabulary instruction by addressing two critical questions:

♦ What does research tell us about vocabulary development?

♦ What word-learning beliefs should we embrace in our teaching?

Alice Cedillo performs a Think Aloud to show students how to use word-meaning clues and vocabulary-building strategies to learn many new words.

What Does Research Tell Us About Vocabulary Development?

For decades research has shown that the knowledge, attitudes, beliefs, and practices of teachers are crucial factors in determining students' literacy growth. (See Dykstra & Bond, 1966–1967; Block & Mangieri, 2003.) Students learn to read better when they receive exemplary literacy instruction. Here are some interesting findings:

♦ According to the National Reading Panel (2001), which reviewed research about vocabulary development, both vocabulary instruction and assessment are crucial to students' literacy success.

♦ A lack of vocabulary is a key component underlying failure for many students, especially for those who are economically disadvantaged (Biemiller, 2001; Biemiller & Slonium, 2001; Hart & Risley, 1995; Hirsch, 2001).

♦ Both wide reading and explicit instruction help to build new vocabulary. To be most effective, teachers should teach the most useful words (i.e., high-utility words), and students should have the opportunity to apply their knowledge of these words in multiple subject areas and fictional texts (Beck, Perfetti, & McKeown, 1982; Beck, McKeown, & Kucan, 2002).

♦ Consistent and daily attention to words builds students' literacy growth (Brabham & Lynch-Brown, 2002; Dickinson & Tabors, 2001). The repeated teaching of high-utility words and the application of these words in multiple contexts signifi-cantly increase students' comprehension on standardized literacy tests (Block & Mangieri, 2005b; Gough, Alford, & Holly-Wilcox, 1981; Fry, 2004).

Recently, in cooperation with the Institute for Literacy Enhancement (Block & Mangieri, 2005c), we conducted a study that analyzed the vocabulary practices of 409 exemplary teachers from Colorado, Maryland, New Jersey, North Carolina, Pennsylvania, and Texas. An exemplary teacher was defined as one whose students attained significantly higher levels of literacy success than did students who were taught by other teachers in the same building and who came from the same neighborhoods. Many of them had large classes, not enough materials, and students with diverse learn-ing needs. Here are the ten major findings from this study. In the classrooms of exem-plary literacy teachers:

1. **Students understood that vocabulary is important.** Teachers provided direct, meaningful instruction on a daily basis. They worked cooperatively with students to help them learn, understand, and retain words and apply vocabulary-building strategies while they read. Their commitment to high-quality vocabulary instruction was unflinching, as illustrated in the words of Lynn, a fourth-grade teacher from Maryland: "Words are the essence of what I do. Teaching students how to say them, use them in their speaking and writing, and understand them while reading is what literacy teaching should be all about."

2. **Students learned important, relevant words.** These words came from research-based lists developed by literacy experts such as Dolch, Fry, Kucera-Francis, and Harris-Jacobson and appeared in multiple contexts. Teachers thought deeply about these words before spending valuable instructional time on them. They chose words that they knew students would encounter over and over and that represented a larger family of similar-meaning words. For example, Maria, a fifth-grade teacher in Texas, used a "ten-year test" to decide whether or not to teach a word. She asked herself, "Ten years from now, will my students need to understand this word in a book that they are reading in college or in a document that they must read and sign?" Because of careful thinking like that, students were exposed to important words that they would frequently encounter in print. They had many opportunities to apply their word knowledge while reading. As a consequence, their reading skills improved, as did their attitudes toward reading.

3. **Students learned high-utility words.** The National Reading Panel (2001) reports that the more thoroughly students learn high-utility words (such as *forever*, *generate*, *summary*, and *please*), the better they will be able to comprehend text that contains those words or similar ones. The students in our study were exposed to many, many high-utility words selected from widely referenced lists such as those described in finding number 2.

   Such words are important for another reason. Since they are typically at the core of a family of words, learning one such word unlocks the meaning of many others. For example, when students learn the meaning of the word *generate*, they can more rapidly learn related words such as *generation*, *regenerate*, and *general*.

4. **Students learned and retained words more quickly—and had fun doing it.** Teachers used a wide array of instructional activities, such as word walls, games, crossword puzzles, plays, and word-building lessons. Vocabulary instruction was fun. They also taught students to think about their thinking as they read. For instance, in Paul's sixth-grade classroom in Colorado, students enjoyed trying to discover his "mystery word of the week." Paul gave his students one sentence every day with one word—the mystery word—omitted. The students' challenge was to figure out the one word that would make sense in all the sentences. By the end of the week, students would have five clues. In the week that we observed, students were trying to use these sentence context clues to discover the mystery word *correspondent*.

5. **Students learned vocabulary through their preferred learning style.** Students had numerous opportunities to learn words in meaningful, multimodal ways. Students read (visual), listened (auditory), spoke (oral), wrote (tactile), enacted (kinesthetic), and illustrated (spatial) word meanings. For example, on Monday, students would read aloud new vocabulary words in context, employing visual and auditory learning modalities. On Tuesday, students would write and discuss these new words (oral and tactile learning modalities). On the next day, students would create graphics, such as semantic maps and time lines, and stage plays using these words (kinesthetic and spatial learning modalities). No two days of instruction were the same. All students, regardless of their dominant learning modality, benefited. Rashad, a third-grade teacher in North Carolina, summarized it this way: "I am a tactile learner, and when I was a student, many of my teachers did little to offer instruction in the way I best learned. So that none of my students will be put at such a disadvantage, I teach lessons that use each type of learning style. In that way, I know I have given each student the best opportunity to learn what I am teaching."

6. **Students received multiple exposures to words and their meanings.** Lessons in word meanings were taught incrementally and repeatedly so that students were given the opportunity to learn and apply each new word at least six consecutive times (Block & Mangieri, 2005b). Many English-language learners and struggling readers require and were given even more exposures (Dickinson & Smith, 1994; National Reading

Panel [NRP], 2001). This practice is consistent with the findings of studies that show that most students must experience rich, effective instruction in a word before they can understand its meaning (Beck et al., 2002; Block, 2004; Block & Mangieri, 2005a); such instruction is demonstrated in the multimodal activities described on the previous page. When students understand a newly taught word completely, including all its denotations and connotations, they are more likely to retain it.

7. **Students received context-based vocabulary instruction.** Teachers presented every word in context so that vocabulary and comprehension were built simultaneously. As we mentioned, comprehension cannot occur if a student cannot recognize the words in the text. The benefits of intertwining vocabulary instruction and comprehension instruction (i.e., teaching words in context) is supported by research (Block & Mangieri, 2005b; Stahl, 1998). Further, context-based vocabulary instruction not only improves reading comprehension but also fosters a positive attitude toward reading (Block & Reed, 2004). A cycle of success occurs when students understand a text's words and comprehend its message. This cycle accelerates as students learn more words, comprehend more difficult text, and advance to higher levels of reading ability.

8. **Students were assessed using measures that went beyond asking them merely to give the definition of a word.** Tests required students to use inferential thinking and/or apply the word's meaning to their lives. To do so, most test questions included the word *you*. For example, instead of asking students to give the definition of the word *apartment*, teachers would ask students: "What do you think are the benefits of living in an apartment?" Since students would have to apply the definition of the word *apartment* to their lives in order to answer, this question and similar ones show whether students have truly grasped a word's meaning and can use it in new settings.

9. Students learned the process of building their vocabulary through lessons that combined instruction in word-meaning clues and vocabulary-building strategies. High-quality vocabulary instruction includes both word-meaning clues and vocabulary-building strategies in every lesson. (See Figures 1.1 and 1.2 below.) With such instruction, students learn that word meanings can be derived by selecting the appropriate clues an unknown word contains and coupling that word with the most useful vocabulary-building strategy.

Word-Meaning Clues

1. A word's part of speech serves as a clue to its meaning, especially when the word is a high-utility word (coupled with vocabulary-building strategy number 1 below).

2. A word's prefix, root, and suffix serve as clues to its meaning (coupled with vocabulary-building strategy number 2 below).

3. Many long words or words that occur infrequently have a meaning that describes a specific person, place, or thing relative to a particular content area (coupled with vocabulary-building strategy number 3 below).

4. Unusual letter or sound combinations signal that a word may have come from another language and its spelling or sound patterns retained, so that the word's meaning has to be memorized (coupled with vocabulary-building strategy number 4 below).

Figure 1.1

Vocabulary-Building Strategies

1. Use context clues to determine the meaning of unknown high-utility words.

2. Add the meanings of a word's prefixes and suffixes to the meaning of the root word or base word.

3. Connect the meaning of long, content-specific words to the text's topic.

4. Create mnemonic devices to learn unusual-looking words or words with unusual sounds that are likely to have retained the spelling or sound patterns from their original language.

Figure 1.2

Every word contains a word-meaning clue. This clue helps readers determine what type of word it is, such as a high-utility word, an affixed word, a content-specific word, or an unusual English word. For example, if students recognize that they have seen an unknown word several times before in different types of books, most likely the word is a high-utility word, and the position that word holds in the sentence provides a valuable clue to its meaning. The word's part of speech can also help them deduce its meaning. Then, chances are, when students couple this knowledge with the vocabulary-building strategy of using all the meanings of the other known words in the sentence (context clues), they will be able to determine rapidly the meaning of the unknown word (Block & Mangieri, 1995/1996). This example shows how students can be taught to combine word-meaning clue number 1 with the most useful vocabulary-building strategy for high-utility words (vocabulary-building strategy number 1) to determine a word's meaning.

10. **Students listened to and engaged in Think Alouds.** Teachers used Think Alouds in every vocabulary lesson they taught. Thinking aloud consists of saying the thoughts you have as you are reading a text. It encourages students to think about their own thinking. When it comes to vocabulary instruction, this means thinking about what they are thinking as they try to figure out the meaning of an unknown word, which leads to a deeper understanding and a better retention of vocabulary words (Block & Israel, 2004). By using Think Alouds, teachers model for students how to unlock the meaning of an unknown word.

What can we conclude from the research presented in this section? First, a strong vocabulary is essential to literacy success. Second, important words must be taught explicitly on a repeated basis. Third, these words should be presented to students using a variety of multimodal instructional strategies that will engage higher-level thinking. Fourth, students must learn that words contain clues to their meaning, and that when these clues are coupled with important vocabulary-building strategies, they can independently determine word meanings. Finally, when vocabulary is properly taught, most students will learn and understand words and also improve their comprehension and their attitude toward reading.

In this book, we and other authors describe what exemplary educators do to ensure that all students increase their vocabularies and experience success. If you follow these research-based practices, we're confident that your students will significantly improve not only their vocabulary, but also their comprehension, spelling, and attitude toward reading (Block & Mangieri, 2005b).

What Word-Learning Beliefs Should We Embrace in Our Teaching?

To become proficient readers, students must be able to know how to say words correctly and instantaneously recognize them in print. They must also know the meanings associated with these words in context and develop word consciousness. Exemplary literacy teachers embrace these truths, and their instruction helps students gain competence in *all* of these dimensions of vocabulary development.

So, given what our research and the research of others have shown, what beliefs should guide our vocabulary instruction in order to foster students' acquisition and retention of important words in particular, and word consciousness, positive attitudes toward reading, and reading comprehension in general?

Belief 1: All words are not of equal importance.

The words taught to students should not be selected as the basis of instruction because they are "interesting" or "challenging" or were recommended by a colleague. Rather, students should be taught words that they will encounter frequently in print (Beck et al., 2002; NRP, 2001). Their initial acquisition of these words will be reinforced through subsequent exposures.

Belief 2: Students will retain newly taught words that they truly understand and can use when they speak, listen, read, and write.

High gains in vocabulary growth are not the result of superficial instruction. Instead, they are the result of research-based lessons that help students discern the meaning of important words through a series of structured learning opportunities (Mangieri, 1972). This finding challenges instruction that simply encourages students to pronounce words and give a definition.

Belief 3: Students increase their vocabulary more rapidly when they learn how to use one word-meaning clue with one vocabulary-building strategy each week.

This coupling is crucial to literacy success because students can learn to employ the two strategies together when they confront an unknown word while reading silently alone (Dickinson & Tabors, 2001). Students learn to acquire the words being taught and also independently initiate the thinking processes they'll need to unlock the meaning of unfamiliar terms they'll encounter in the future.

Belief 4: When students understand words frequently used in texts, they develop a positive attitude toward reading (Block & Mangieri, 2005a, 2005b).

A cycle of success is established: students can independently understand important words in a text, which in turn enables comprehension. When students are successful at reading tasks, rather than frustrated by them, they develop a positive attitude toward literacy lessons. Knowledge of important words also increases students' comprehension of the materials that they read each day in all of their content subjects (Block & Mangieri, 2003).

Belief 5: Expert readers know a large number of important words that encompass all parts of speech.

These competencies enable such students to understand not only the words in grade-level texts but also those contained in other material that they may wish to read independently or that they are required to read in content subjects. As our research demonstrates, students taught by teachers who hold this belief were able to determine significantly greater numbers of words in a text with a readability ranking that was one grade level above their own (Block & Mangieri, 2005b).

Summary

In this chapter, we presented "the state of the union" of vocabulary instruction, addressing what research tells us about vocabulary development and what beliefs we should embrace based on that research. In Chapters 2 to 5, you'll find numerous clearly described lessons that will help you put these research findings and beliefs into action.

Discussion Questions and Teaching Activities

1. What instructional behaviors and actions does an exemplary teacher of vocabulary consistently exhibit? How would you rate your present level of performance in terms of them? What factors led you to this conclusion?

2. Design and teach a lesson using one of this chapter's word-meaning clues coupled with its vocabulary-building strategy. Then, teach a lesson in which you utilize a different word-meaning clue and vocabulary-building strategy. Compare the effects of these lessons to those of past ones you have taught.

CHAPTER TWO

Developing Vocabulary by
Learning Words Through Context

Linda B. Gambrell and **Kathy N. Headley,**
both of Clemson University

Michael, a sixth-grade student, came to the word *agape* while reading silently during a guided reading lesson. The word was unfamiliar to him, but on second glance, Michael thought, *Oh,* agape, *I know that word—it means to open widely.* He then reread the sentence, "Agape filled the room as the dying grandmother reached out to comfort her family." Michael had been taught to pay attention to meaning—to monitor comprehension processing—and he quickly realized that "open widely" made no sense. He read on in the passage and found reference to "the love of family" and realized that the word was *a-ga-pe,* a word that he had sung in a church hymn. He remembered that the church hymn was about love of God and realized that in the story, it was love that filled the room.

Michael is skilled at using context clues to problem solve when he encounters unfamiliar words. This is one of the most important skills we can teach in order to promote vocabulary growth in our students.

On the poster:

> Lucinda tied back her long
> hair, with a clean _____
> from the _____ and went back
> to her notebook and pen. She had
> been inspired to write a _____
> in her story. The scene involved her
> _____ of moving across
> the _____ to the United States
> _____ to with her parents
> when she was young. Her parents
> had influenced her through their
> hard work.

Pledge

I pledge a
of the Uni
and to the
it stands,
God, indiv
and justic

Bad B

Stephanie Whitting teaches her fourth graders how to use context clues and parts of speech to learn the meanings of words.

In this chapter, we discuss the connections among vocabulary, comprehension, and context. From there, we address three questions about supporting students in the use of context to build vocabulary:

♦ How does wide reading support vocabulary development in context?

♦ How can teachers more effectively teach students to use context?

♦ What activities, teaching actions, and learning opportunities create a context for building vocabulary?

We then provide research-based teaching ideas that you can implement in your classroom.

Connections Between Vocabulary, Comprehension, and Context

Research indicates that vocabulary knowledge is one of the strongest predictors of reading achievement (National Institute of Child Health and Human Development [NICHD], 2000). As our vocabulary increases, so does our ability to comprehend what we read. Likewise, as our comprehension skills increase, so does our ability to learn new words from context. Because vocabulary and comprehension are so inextricably linked, instruction in both, using narrative and informational text, is a critical part of a well-balanced reading program.

There is general agreement among theorists and researchers that most words are learned from context (Graves, 2000; Hart & Risley, 1995; Nagy, Hermann, & Anderson, 1985; Sternberg, 1983). Using context involves weaving together information from semantic and syntactic sources to unlock the meaning of an unknown or unfamiliar word (Bromley, 2002). Context can be provided by pictures, words, sentences, and
paragraphs that occur before and after the unknown word. Context also refers to clues from the *entire* text that, taken together, reveal the word's meaning. The information derived from the surrounding text helps the reader infer meaning of an individual word and, therefore, better comprehend what is being read. Thus, the meaning of a word can emerge from context, and context can also give the reader a richer, expanded understanding of the word.

There are some situations, however, where context doesn't help the reader figure out the meaning of an unknown word (Bromley, 2002; Robb, 2000)—for example, if the reader's prior knowledge and experience are not adequate enough to make use of the context that may be provided, or if pictures in the text are inaccurate or incomplete, or if the surrounding sentences or paragraph do not contain sufficient information from which to infer the word's meaning. Using context is an extremely powerful tool for vocabulary building; however, students should understand that appropriate context may not always be available or reliable. As stated in Chapter 1, context clues are most valuable when used to learn the meanings of the most frequently occurring words. Sixty-one percent of all English words can be learned using these clues (Block & Mangieri, 2005c).

How Does Wide Reading Support Vocabulary Development in Context?

One way to increase students' vocabulary is to increase the amount of time they spend reading. In fact, some researchers contend that increasing reading time is the most powerful thing we can do to increase vocabulary learning (A. E. Cunningham & Stanovich, 1998; Graves & Watts-Taffe, 2002; Stahl, 1998). According to Graves and Watts-Taffe (2002), teachers should especially encourage their students to read as much and as widely as possible.

Sustained, independent, wide reading provides students with opportunities to learn words from context, and construct meaning using the whole text instead of simply the words in isolation (Harmon, 1999). There is clear evidence that the amount of time spent reading (reading volume) is the major contributor to increased vocabulary development and reading proficiency (Nagy & Anderson, 1984; Stanovich, 1986). According to A. E. Cunningham and Stanovich (1998), reading has cognitive benefits beyond getting meaning from the page. Their research suggests that the very act of reading can help students compensate for modest levels of cognitive ability by increasing their vocabulary and general knowledge. In other words, the more they read, the more their vocabulary increases, and along with increased vocabulary comes increased general knowledge. These increases occur over time as students, reading widely, construct meanings of words they encounter across multiple exposures in various contexts (Harmon, 1999). A. E. Cunningham and Stanovich found that students at all ability levels benefited from time spent reading, especially struggling readers with limited comprehension skills (1998).

How Can Teachers More Effectively Teach Students to Use Context Clues?

Using context is perhaps the most widely recommended and most useful strategy for increasing vocabulary (Graves, 2000, Graves & Watts-Taffe, 2002; Stahl, 1998). Research by Fukkink and de Glopper (1998) and Kuhn and Stahl (1998) documents that teaching students how to use context clues can be done effectively. Knowing and using vocabulary strategies such as this one also helps students become independent thinkers and learners. Research suggests that new words need to be processed deeply and repeatedly for students to internalize and own the new vocabulary (Mason, Stahl, Au, & Hermann, 2003). Strategies that help students connect words with their prior knowledge, emphasize comprehension monitoring, and actively engage students in learning are more likely to result in significant vocabulary growth.

Instruction in using context clues has also been recommended by Graves and Watts-Taffe (2002) as an important part of a carefully planned and comprehensive vocabulary program. Their use can be modeled and taught so that students can apply this strategy in their independent reading. Other teaching techniques that focus on strategies that support the effective use of context include the Vocabulary Cloze Procedure and the Vocabulary Self-Selection Strategy. Both of these promote linking new vocabulary to prior knowledge and active engagement in learning.

What Activities, Teaching Actions, and Learning Opportunities Create a Context for Building Vocabulary?

Context clues that are embedded in a sentence, a paragraph, the whole text, or a picture can help students figure out the meaning of an unknown word. To provide guided instruction in using context clues, collect examples of sentences and short paragraphs that contain challenging words with strong context clues, perhaps from books you are reading aloud to the class or in content-area texts that you are using for daily instruction. Once you have collected good examples, you can use them to carry out the following vocabulary activities with your students: using context clues, the Vocabulary Cloze Procedure, and the Vocabulary Self-Selection Strategy.

Using Context Clues: An Introductory Lesson

1. Select a short paragraph that contains a word that will be challenging, unfamiliar, or unknown to the student. Copy the short paragraph onto a transparency or PowerPoint slide. The following is an example of a short paragraph that contains a challenging word (*traverse*) and some clues to the meaning of the word:

> The travelers set out in early April to traverse the continent. The plan was to leave Bangor, Maine, in early April and arrive in San Diego, California, in late May.

2. Start the lesson by telling students that using context clues is a proven way to increase vocabulary, and that in this lesson, they will be using them to figure out unknown words.

3. Reveal only the first sentence, with the challenging word covered with an index card or sticky note.

> The travelers set out in early April to /   / the continent.

4. Have students read the sentence and guess what the word might be given the context of the sentence. Record the words they suggest on the board for later reference, as in the example below:

> cross   explore   investigate

5. Reveal the second sentence and encourage students to read on.

> The travelers set out in early April to /   / the continent. The plan was to leave Bangor, Maine, in early April and arrive in San Diego, California, in late May.

6. Have the students refine their guesses given the new information provided. Add to the list any additional words provided by the students.

7. Reveal the first letter of the challenging word and have students determine whether any of the words they have guessed begin with that letter.

> The travelers set out in early April to / t   / the
> continent. The plan was to leave Bangor, Maine, in early
> April and arrive in San Diego, California, in late May.

If none of the words on the student-generated list begin with the first letter (*t*, in this example), ask students for words beginning with that letter that make sense. In our example, students may suggest *travel* or *traipse*. If students still have not determined the word through thinking in this way, reveal additional letters of the word (/*trav*/, here) and discuss whether the words they contribute make sense and fit the spelling pattern.

8. Remind students to use the clue the word gives because of its position in the sentence.

9. Once the word has been identified, have students discuss their ideas about the context clues they used to derive the meaning of the word and how they used the clues to figure out the word.

10. Remind students that this is a strategy that good readers use to learn new words. Good readers apply all of the steps above as they read, using known words that occur before and after an unknown word to help them determine its meaning. Sometimes a good reader can figure out the meaning of the word and then pronounce it, because it is a word that he or she has heard before. Sometimes, the word is one that the reader has never seen or heard before. In that case, the reader should ask someone how the word is pronounced or refer to the dictionary for help. Sometimes the dictionary only helps readers come up with an approximate pronunciation of a new word, so tell students it is always a good idea to ask someone if they are still unsure of the pronunciation after consulting a dictionary.

11. In future lessons, select challenging words that are surrounded by a variety of context clues—those that come before the unknown word, after the unknown word, or even in a different part of the text or in a picture in the text. Encourage readers to gather clues by telling them, "Keep reading when you come to an unknown word. You can sometimes figure out the word from clues in the text." For example, a student may get stuck on the word *trounced* in the following sentence:

> The Bulldogs trounced our team in the last inning, and we lost the series.

Reading to the end of the sentence provides a clue. The phrase "we lost the series" tells the reader that the Bulldogs beat, or trounced, the other team. However, sometimes the clue may appear before the unknown word, as in the following version of the sentence:

> Even though our team had not lost a game all season, the Bulldogs trounced us in the last inning of today's game.

By modeling the use of context clues periodically throughout the year, using the Think Aloud procedure, you will reinforce students' understanding of its usefulness. We also encourage having students share examples of times they used context clues to figure out unfamiliar words in their everyday reading.

The Vocabulary Cloze Procedure: Applying and Practicing the Use of Context Clues

The Vocabulary Cloze Procedure helps students become proficient at using context clues. Use it after you've carried out the introductory lesson, so they've had practice applying the strategy. The procedure can be used with narrative or informational text to introduce new vocabulary in a meaningful context. The big idea for using the Vocabulary Cloze Procedure is that there should be some context for providing the meaning of the new vocabulary. Here's how to do it:

1. Select a brief passage that contains a number of challenging words.

2. Replace those words with underlines, but make sure that there are either semantic or syntactic clues to their meanings. The deleted words should be put in a list in scrambled order. Below is an example:

> Ladies and gentlemen, thank you for coming to my lecture. Today, I am going to tell you about a _____ discovery that I made in 1822. At the time, I was a doctor in the English county of Sussex. Although I practiced medicine, my real interest was in geology. Between visits to patients, I would always find time to collect _____ . One spring day, I was visiting a patient with my wife. As I strolled down the lane, I saw a pile of rocks, used by workmen to repair the roads. In one of the rocks, my wife noticed something brown and shiny. Looking closely, she saw that it was a very large tooth. It was worn away on the side from chewing, like the tooth of a plant-eating _____ . I had never seen anything like it. I was excited to learn that the fossil had come from a very old layer of rocks. No mammal fossil had ever been found in such rocks. What a mystery!
>
> fossils   mammal   remarkable

(Adapted from *Dinosaur Detectives* by Peter Chrisp)

3. Have the students brainstorm and discuss words that make sense in the passage, based on the clues provided in the text.

4. Reveal the list of the deleted words and discuss any discrepancies between the students' guesses and the actual words in the text.

5. Acknowledge that the students' guesses are often as appropriate and meaningful as those selected by the author of the text. The focus of this lesson should always be on using the context to generate words that make sense and not on getting the words "right."

6. Encourage students to use this procedure when they are reading independently. They should remember to look for clues in the text that might reveal the meaning of any word that is unfamiliar.

7. Once you've conducted several lessons like this and provided guided practice, give students vocabulary cloze passages to complete independently. Prior to revealing the actual words from the text, students can compare and discuss their guesses with a partner.

According to Blachowicz and Fisher (2002), after students have developed a basic understanding of the variety of ways that semantic (the meaning of other words in a sentence) and syntactic (the role a word performs in a sentence) context reveals the meaning of unfamiliar words, lessons can be created to help them build and test hypotheses about the meaning of other unknown, frequently occurring words. Specifically, students should be encouraged to engage in the following thinking process when they come to an unfamiliar word:

♦ Look—Reread and think about what comes before and after the word.

♦ Reason—Connect what you know about the text with what the author has written.

♦ Predict—Think about a possible meaning for the unfamiliar word by thinking about the role it serves in the sentence.

♦ Resolve—Decide whether you have successfully figured out the word's meaning, or whether you should try again by asking a teacher or friend, or by using a dictionary.

The vocabulary cloze procedure requires the reader to focus on meaning at the word level and at the text level. It is an excellent technique to use for introducing both narrative stories and informational text because it engages the student in making inferences based on context and promotes the linking of vocabulary and prior knowledge.

Vocabulary Self-Selection Strategy

It's a fact of life—being able to make personal choices is more motivating than having to do an assigned, predetermined task. The teacher may know, for example, that a content book contains words that will be unknown or unfamiliar to the class. The teacher can help and motivate students by providing instruction that gives students the opportunity to select unknown or unfamiliar vocabulary they come across. The Vocabulary Self-Selection Strategy (Haggard, 1982), which promotes use of context, does just that.

The strategy requires that each student and the teacher identify two words to bring to the group for discussion. Students collect these words during discussions or while reading novels, stories, textbooks, newspapers, magazines, or Web pages. For the following example, we use Russell Freedman's *Lincoln: A Photobiography* (1987) to illustrate the strategy (Haggard, 1982).

After reading Chapter 7, "Who Is Dead in the White House?," a student might self-select *assassination* and *conspiracy* to record on his My Words: Vocabulary Self-Selection Strategy Sheet. (See Figure 2.1.)

Name: _____   Date: _____

My Words
Vocabulary Self-Selection Strategy Sheet

Selected Words:

1. _____

2. _____

Sentences I heard or read using the selected words:

_____

_____

_____

_____

Definitions: What the words mean:

_____

_____

_____

_____

Memory Help (drawing, word map, mnemonic, etc.):

_____

_____

Ideas for using each word this week:

_____

_____

(Haggard, 1982)

Figure 2.1: My Words: Vocabulary Self-Selection Strategy Sheet

**Figure 2.2:
A filled-in My
Words:
Vocabulary
Self-Selection
Strategy Sheet**

Name: __Caroline__   Date: __11/2__

My Words
Vocabulary Self-Selection Strategy Sheet

Selected Words:

1. __assassination__

2. __conspiracy__

Sentences I heard or read using the selected words:

Lincoln had been living with rumors of abduction and assassination ever since
he was first elected.
Everyone suspected that the attacks were part of a rebel conspiracy to
murder several government officials and capture the city.

Definitions: What the words mean:

killing of a political leader or public figure by a sudden violent attack

an agreement between two or more people to commit an illegal action

Memory Help (drawing, word map, mnemonic, etc.):

drawing of a weapon that might be used in an assassination attempt
drawing of two stick figure people talking with their heads close together.

Ideas for using each word this week:

Read about the assassination of John F. Kennedy.
Learn more about conspiracy in the assassination of John F. Kennedy.

(Haggard, 1982)

Once he writes the words on the sheet, the student copies the text sentences
and either predicts possible meanings from the context or looks in the dictionary for
definitions. Then he lists supports for remembering the words (drawings, word maps,
associations, etc.) and examples of how he himself might use the words. (See Figure
2.2.) Other students reading the same chapter bring their self-selected words, such as
corpse, assassin, vestments, revoke, plagued, or *dirge.* Each student presents his words to
the group and discusses why the words are important to know; the group finally votes on
five to eight of the words that will be learned during that week. Have students write the
group-selected words on the Class Words: Vocabulary Self-Selection Strategy Sheet (see
Figure 2.3) and then guide them through a discussion of the words.

Name: _____

Date: _____

Class Words: Vocabulary Self-Selection Strategy Sheet

Word	Sentence	Definition	Memory Help	How I'll Use It

Figure 2.3: Class Words: Vocabulary Self-Selection Strategy Sheet

Class Words: Vocabulary Self-Selection Strategy Sheet

Name: **Bobby** Date: **11/3**

Word	Sentence	Definition	Memory Help	How I'll Use It
assassination	page 119 paragraph 1	killing of a political leader or public figure	drawing of a weapon	read about Kennedy assassination
conspiracy	page 126 paragraph 1	agreement to do an illegal action	drawing of two or three people talking	read about Kennedy assassination
corpse	page 120 paragraph 2	dead body	television news updates of war losses	study differences in preparing bodies for burial then & now
vestments	page 120 paragraph 2	garments	chart of different items of clothing	What clothing is used for burial in different cultures?
revoke	page 121 paragraph 1	to withdraw or call something back	school rule that seems unfair	interview other students about rules that need changing
plagued	page 121 paragraph 2	bothered by something frequently	homework happens often	develop study plan for doing homework
dirge	page 129 paragraph 1	song of mourning	bugle playing taps	investigate history of military taps

Figure 2.4: A filled-in Class Words: Vocabulary Self-Selection Strategy Sheet

Have students pronounce each word and explore its meaning using the sentence from which it originated. For example, *vestments* appears in the sentence "Before me was a . . . corpse wrapped in funeral vestments" (Freedman, 1987, p. 120) and connects meaningfully to *corpse*. Students may already know that the word *corpse* means a dead body. As you guide the discussion of *corpse* toward the meaning of *vestments*, the verb, "wrapped," offers a hint. So pose the question, *What could the dead body or corpse be wrapped in for the funeral?* Guesses such as "cloth" or "clothes" open opportunities for you to link "garments" to the word *vestments*. Have students write each word's definition and example sentence on their Class Words: Vocabulary Self-Selection Strategy Sheet as the group discussion continues. (See Figure 2.4.) To increase their understanding and retention, ask students to think up ways to remember each word. Student-created memory devices such as drawings, word maps, or mnemonics provide cognitive support. To create a sense of ownership, have each student think of a situation in which he or she may use the word during the week—in assignments, personal writings, games, and so on.

Steps in the Vocabulary Self-Selection Strategy

1. Have students read a text selection and identify two words that they find interesting or challenging.

2. Have each student write these two words on a card so that they can be shared with the class.

3. Ask the class to vote on five to eight words to be learned for the week.

4. Engage the students in a discussion of the words to clarify, elaborate, and extend word meanings.

5. Have students record the words on the My Words sheet and the Class Words sheet, and generate a chart, diagram, picture, and definition to help them remember the words' meanings.

6. As an extension to this activity, ask students to create writing assignments, activities, games, and practice tests based on the selected words.

(adapted from Blachowicz & Fisher, 2002)

You Try It

The Vocabulary Self-Selection Strategy can be used with individual students, small groups, and even the whole class. Begin the lesson by asking students to select five to ten words from the day's reading assignment. Tell them to choose words containing the same type of meaning clues, so that you can focus on a specific vocabulary-building strategy. (See Chapter 1.) After teaching the word-meaning clue and vocabulary-building strategy, direct students to find other words that could be learned using the same clue and strategy. Although you encourage and guide the learning, the student is in charge. This lesson can be modified so that students keep vocabulary logs or maintain a personal My Words notebook, with a separate section to hold the Class Words sheets. You can also display on a classroom wall or bulletin board words chosen by the whole group. Then, based on individual learning rates, students are responsible each week for a few or all of the chosen words. As students discover instances of their selected words (ones that fit the word-meaning clue and vocabulary-building strategy being learned that week) in other texts, have them record the location, sentence, and date beside each collected word. For group words displayed on classroom walls, students can also create colorful word stars with their names, word source, sentence, and date the word was encountered. Tape them alongside the corresponding words.

Students can apply this strategy to trade books and to their basal readers and content-area textbooks. As you are guiding students to preview the story or chapter, words that grab their attention should be recorded immediately and shared with members of the group. From there, students can predict story themes or chapter content. Vocabulary self-selection should continue during reading and after as students share their word choices and choose vocabulary selections with classmates.

Developing a rich vocabulary is an ongoing journey, not a final destination. Students encounter interesting and challenging words every day as they cruise the Internet, shop for electronic games, read directions, and e-mail friends. Their options—and opportunities—are endless, so do whatever you can to entice them to think about and own the words that cross their paths.

Summary

Sustained engagement in reading helps students use context to arrive at word meanings. Its role in building comprehension and vocabulary cannot be overestimated. Providing students with opportunities to engage in self-selected vocabulary-word learning is a powerful means for building skills and knowledge in those areas.

Using context clues to figure out unfamiliar words is perhaps the most important vocabulary-building strategy that a reader can possess, because it can help discern the meanings of most high-utility words, the largest category of English words. It is important that students know and understand why, how, and when to use context to problem solve the meaning of unfamiliar high-utility words. Vocabulary cloze and vocabulary self-selection help students learn how to use context clues independently. Students who master the use of context clues can often efficiently determine the meaning of numerous unfamiliar words without interrupting the comprehension process. They should practice using context clues until it becomes an automatic part of their problem-solving repertoire.

Discussion Questions and Teaching Activities

1. In this chapter, the authors introduce the Vocabulary Cloze Procedure. Construct two cloze assessments, and implement them—one at the beginning of a week and the other at the end. Then answer two questions:

- ◆ What did you learn about individual students' literacy abilities that you did not know previously?

- ◆ How did implementation of the second assessment compare with the first from your standpoint and that of your students?

2. Use the Vocabulary Self-Selection Strategy as described in this chapter with either a group of students or the entire class. Conduct an audit of each student's self-selected words. Organize entries by parts of speech—nouns, verbs, adjectives, etc. Also, assess how many of the words were taught (or are to be taught) in the current year's vocabulary program. What conclusions can be drawn from this audit?

CHAPTER THREE

Developing Vocabulary
Through Word Building

Timothy Rasinski, Kent State University

ave you ever put a word on the classroom board, say, *vacation*, and then asked the students to use the letters in that word to make other words? "Who can come up with the most words made from *vacation*?" You give your students a limited amount of time to make as many words as they can think of, alone, with a partner, or in small groups. You might even give additional points for longer words. Students come up with words such as *cat*, *can*, *oat*, and *van*. More advanced students may make words such as *vacant*, *action*, and *Vatican*. During the activity, students engage in talk about words. When the activity is over, and students have listed on the board some of the words they have made, you elaborate on the words, circling words in the same word families, talking about multiple meanings, pointing out spelling and meaning patterns, and discussing other words that may be related to the ones that were made. This 10- to 20-minute Word Building activity may seem more like a game than instruction. But it requires students to engage in some productive, high-level thinking and learning about words.

Gena Chaucer, a fourth-grade teacher, gives students a picture clue to help them create and learn the word *advertisement*.

Knowledge of words is clearly important in becoming a proficient reader (NRP, 2000). Readers need to know how to decode (sound out) words and understand the meaning of words they decode. Without a solid understanding of most of the words encountered while reading, students will have difficulty constructing an adequate understanding of the text.

In this chapter, I describe how to teach students to use their knowledge of spelling patterns, prefixes, suffixes, root words, and base words to build their vocabularies. I will do this through an instructional approach called Word Building. Specifically, I will

♦ describe Word Building,

♦ give evidence of its effectiveness, and, most important,

♦ share some ways of making Word Building happen in the elementary and middle grades.

Just What Is Word Building?

Word Building is an instructional activity in which students build words from constituent parts or patterns, such as letters, word families, prefixes, suffixes, or Latin or Greek root- or base-word derivations. Working with a given set of word parts, students are guided by the teacher through the process of building the meanings of a larger set of words. The teacher draws attention to various aspects of words worth learning—most particularly, how the spelling and decoding features of words can be combined to build the meanings of affixed words (i.e., category 2 of the word-meaning clues described in Chapter 1).

Is There Evidence That Word Building Is a Productive Way to Teach and Learn About Words?

Word Building activities have been around for many years. Teachers who have employed them know that they build knowledge of and enthusiasm for words. However, in this era of scientifically based reading research, that is not enough. We need empirical evidence that Word Building activities work.

Making Words, an early version of Word Building, developed by Patricia and James Cunningham (1992), involves students manipulating a set of letters in the form of letter tiles, cards, or magnetic letters, under the guidance of a teacher, to make a corpus of words that culminates in a word that uses all the letters from the set. As an integral part of a balanced literacy curriculum, Making Words was found to be remarkably successful in improving young students' reading achievement (P. M. Cunningham, Hall, & Defee, 1998). In their review of phonics instruction programs, Steve Stahl, Ann Duffy-Hester, and Kay Stahl categorize Making Words as a spelling-based phonics approach that "seems to be effective as part of an overall approach to teaching reading" (1998, p. 347). Subsequent to its initial description, a number of variations of Making Words have been developed, implemented, and tested with similarly positive results across a number of measures of progress in learning to read (McCandliss, Beck, Sandak, & Perfetti, 2003, Oswald & Rasinski, 2002; Rasinski, 1999a, 1999b, 2001; Rasinski & Oswald, in press). Later in the chapter, I explain how to carry out Making Words and its alternatives.

How Does Word Building Fit Into the Larger Word-Study Curriculum?

Word Building is a flexible instructional strategy for use with students of all ages in the typical curriculum for word study. It can usually be done in 10 to 20 minutes, which makes it well suited for a variety of instructional contexts. For example, it could be a daily activity done during the word-study component of a reading or language-arts time block. It could also be employed by content-area teachers as a word-study activity connected to some topic under study. Intervention teachers might use it to strengthen students' word knowledge. And it could easily be implemented by parents at home to build word knowledge in an engaging and enjoyable way. Although it is not a curriculum for word study per se, it could be a central instructional activity in language arts and content areas.

Making Words

The activity that I described at the beginning of the chapter is fun, engaging, and productive—if the students are good readers and spellers. If they are not, the activity can be a challenge, to say the least. I recall that when I was a young student and the teacher gave the activity to the class, many of my less able classmates did not partici-pate, acted out after a few minutes, and quit because they were unable to make more than the simplest words on their own.

When Patricia and James Cunningham (1992) developed the Making Words activity, I knew it would be appreciated by students who are not good readers and spellers, because they added the most important ingredient to the activity—the teacher. Rather than allowing students to work on their own, they had students constructing words under the guidance of the teacher, who provided clues and enough support so that even struggling students could be successful.

Here's how Making Words works. You give each student a set of four to ten magnetic letters or small squares of paper, with one of the letters written on each. Then, under your guidance, they slide together and manipulate the letters to make a series of words, usually going from short, easy words to longer, more challenging ones. While they are making words, you elaborate on and point out letter-sound connections, important letter combinations and patterns, and the meanings of words.

Imagine being a first-grade student. The teacher provides you with—*o, p, r, s,* and *t,* and from these you make *rot, pot, top, tops, post, spot,* and *stop.* Through the activity, the teacher is drawing your attention to letters, their sounds, combinations of letters and their sounds, and the meanings of the words you have made. The final word, called the magic or special word of the day, is usually made up of all the letters. In this lesson, the final word is *sport* and your teacher may segue into a story, lesson, or activity related to sports.

After the magic word has been made, you can guide students in making another set of words by replacing some of the letters with new ones. For example, after completing the lesson above, you might guide students in making words such as *past, stomp,* and *stamp* by simply adding the letters *a* and *m* to the activity.

Making and Writing Words

At Kent State University's reading clinic, Making Words is a primary activity for younger students who have difficulties decoding, spelling, and understanding words. For students who have some degree of fluency writing, I have adapted it into an activity I call Making and Writing Words (Rasinski, 1999a). In this version, students build words under the teacher's guidance, as they do in the Cunninghams' version, but instead of manipulating letters, they write the letters and words on a specially designed recording form. (See Figures 3.1 and 3.2 for a blank form you can use in the classroom and a filled-in sample.)

Making and Writing Words has two possible advantages over Making Words. First, instead of having to go through the process of cutting out individual letter cards, organizing them, distributing them, and then collecting them at the end of the lesson, you only have to photocopy enough word-recording forms for the students participating in the lesson.

Making and Writing Words

Vowels		Consonants	
1	6	11	
2	7	12	
3	8	13	
4	9	14	
5	10	15	

Transfer

T-1	T-2	T-3
T-4	T-5	T-6

Figure 3.1

This most certainly saves time and aggravation.

Second, Making and Writing Words requires students to actually write the words down, which can help create a memory trace that will help them remember the words and their spellings.

The lesson itself proceeds in much the same way as Making Words. Since the students are usually older, I tend to focus their attention on the meanings of the words and meaningful letter patterns such as affixes and Latin and Greek derivations.

Here is an example of a Making and Writing Words lesson done around Veterans Day. Using a copy of Figure 3.1, students write the letters *a, e, e* in the vowel box and *n, r, s, t, v* in the consonant box. These are the only letters students use in the initial part of the lesson. (See Figure 3.2.) From this set of letters, the teacher guides the students to make words, providing these clues:

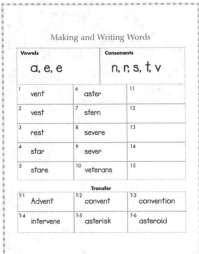

Figure 3.2

In box 1, use four letters to make a word that means a passageway for air or liquids to move from one place to another or to escape from indoors to outdoors.

1. vent

Point out that the word *vent* comes from the French word *vent*, which means "wind." A vent allows air or liquid to come or go.

In box 2, change one letter in box 1 to make a word for a piece of clothing worn on the upper part of the body.

2. vest

In box 3, change one letter in box 2 to make a word that means to be quiet in order to regain strength—something done when tired.

3. rest

Change the vowel in box 3 and rearrange the letters to make a word that describes a celestial object. Our sun is one of these.

4. star

Add one letter to box 4 to make a word that means a hard look at another person or thing.

5. stare

Rearrange the letters in box 5 to make a flower whose petals make it look like the word in box 4. (This is a tough one. You may have to say the word for students.)

6. aster

Draw attention to the fact that *aster* is from the Latin word meaning star and that other words such as *astrology* and *astronaut* have the same origin.

In box 7, use five letters, beginning with *s* and *t* to make a word that means the rear of a boat or ship.

7. stern

Point out that *stern* also means to be very serious, not lighthearted or funny.

Now use six letters to make a word that means something similar to *stern*—to act in a very serious way. You may need to pronounce the word to students and note that it has a silent *e* at the end of the word.

8. severe

Now cut off one letter from box 8 to make a word that means to cut off something. Again, you may need to say the word to the students.

9. sever

Finally, the last word contains all the letters from the set. If students are unable to get it after a few seconds, give them some hints—that it begins with a *v*; that it means a person who once was in the military but is now a civilian; that these people are sometimes called vets. Provide other spelling and meaning clues as necessary.

10. veterans

The next part of the lesson involves making a second set of words based on letter patterns found in the first set, with students being allowed to use all the letters of the alphabet. It may go something like this:

In box T1, add two letters as a prefix to *vent* (box 1) to make a religious season that occurs before Christmas.

T1. Advent

Point out that *Advent* literally means "the coming," the time during which many Christians celebrate the coming of baby Jesus. Point out again that the root *vent* means "wind" in French.

Now add three letters as a prefix to *vent* to make a word that means a place where nuns come to live and pray together.

T2. convent

Now add three letters as a suffix to *convent* to make a word that describes the place where people of the same or similar professions come together to learn more about their profession.

T3. convention

Now take *vent* and change the last letter from *t* to *e*. Add five letters as a prefix to the front of *vene* to make a word that means to come between.

T4. intervene

Point out that the prefix *inter-* means between two things.

Now take *aster*, the word in box 6. Add three letters as a suffix to it to make a word that describes the printing or typing symbol or key that looks like a star. You may have to draw an asterisk and pronounce the word for students.

T5. asterisk

Tell students that the suffix *-isk* means like, therefore *asterisk* means to look like an aster. Finally, add three letters to *aster* to make a word that is a small celestial body or planet that orbits our sun.

T6. asteroid

Tell students that the suffix *-oid* comes from the Greek language and means to form or shape.

If you wish to extend the lesson, have students cut out the boxes containing the words they have made and use the word cards in a variety of ways—they can practice reading the words by themselves or with a partner, use two sets of word cards to play concentration, put the words in alphabetical order, or sort the words according to various features you may want students to note. For example, you could have students sort the words by the presence or absence of a prefix or suffix, by the presence or absence of a silent letter, by parts of speech (noun, verb, and so on), or by theme (for example, the word has something to do with stars and celestial objects).

As they sort, students look at the words critically and from a different point of view with each criterion, which helps them analyze the words deeply and completely and remember them when reading and writing. Making Words and Making and Writing Words are simple but effective activities to help students examine words and learn how they work.

When planning the lesson, choose the last (magic) word first, determine the words that can be made from the last word, and brainstorm appropriate clues for each word. Controlling the lesson's level of difficulty is relatively easy if you focus on the length of the last word. For a less challenging lesson, choose a short last word. For a more challenging lesson, choose a longer one.

Developing a set of words based on the last word is not difficult either. However, it can take time, especially for multisyllabic words. Fortunately, there are several Web sites that can help. (See box below.)

Web Sites for Creating Word Sets Based on Your Final Word

1. **http://www.wordsmith.org/anagram**
   Select "Advanced Anagramming" and click "yes" for "Print candidate word list only."

2. **http://www.wordles.com**
   Select "Words in words."

3. **http://www.scrabble.com**
   Select "USA/Canada" button and then use the Word Builder feature.

At all three Web sites, simply type in your final word and click on the button next to the word. From there a complete set of words that can be made from the letters in the final word will appear. The Wordsmith Web site lists the words from shortest to longest; the Wordles and Scrabble sites lists the words in alphabetical order. The Scrabble site also provides a brief definition for each.

Instead of having vowels and consonants serve as the building blocks for Making and Writing Words, you may want to use individual letters and letter patterns that form word families or affixes. For example, with word families *ort*, *er* and *age*, prefixes *re-*, *de-*, and individual letters *p* and *s*, you could guide students to make *sort*, *port*, *sport*, *deport*, *report*, *porter*, *portage* and other words. Learn more about the activity in an article entitled "Making and Writing Words" in the International Reading Association's electronic journal *Reading Online* (Rasinski, 1999a).

Word Ladders

In Word Ladders, as in Making Words, students are guided to build a series of words as the teacher points out decoding, spelling, and word-meaning clues about the words. However, in word ladders, the letters used for each new word come from the previous word, rather than from a preselected word bank. Students add, subtract, or change one or more letters from the previous word to make new words based on clues from the teacher. Usually, words are listed vertically so that students can easily view each step in the process, and students write the words in a numbered word ladder on a blank sheet of paper. Ideally, the first and last words are related in some way, to add a sense of mystery or interest to the activity; however, this need not be the case. Here is an example of a Word Ladder to be used in October.

What the teacher says:	What students write:
1. Begin with *trick*, a word that means to fool someone.	trick
2. Change one letter to make a large vehicle used for transporting things.	truck
3. Change one letter to form a word that is the name for what trains ride or travel on.	track
4. Change one letter to make a word that means to create a copy of a picture or drawing with a pen or pencil on a transparent sheet placed over the picture or drawing. (At this point, discuss what happened to the short -*a* sound as well as the hard -*k* sound at the end of the word.)	trace

Continued next page

THE VOCABULARY-ENRICHED CLASSROOM

What the teacher says:	What students write:
5. Change one letter to make a word that means a thing that supports a body part, such as a leg or arm, when it is not strong, or that is put on teeth when they need to be straightened.	brace
6. I could change one letter in *trace* to make a girl's name—*Tracy*. But I want you to change another letter in *trace* to make another girl's name. (Point out that *grace* has other meanings—a charming or attractive personal trait and a short prayer made before meals.)	grace
7. Change one letter to make a word that refers to a particular year or level in school or a mark often given on report cards.	grade
8. Change one letter to make a word that means to grind something into small particles, as your mother does when she takes a hunk of cheese and grinds it into small pieces to put on pizza. (Note other meanings for *grate*, such as to cause irritation, a barred frame, a frame covered with strong iron bars or solid strands of wire.)	grate
9. *Grate* is a homophone, one of two words that sound the same but have different meanings and spellings. Normally, when we hear the word we think of something being wonderful or terrific—the word *great*. To make this other word *grate*, you don't have to change any of the letters in *grate*. All you have to do is rearrange the last three. (Note that the spelling and pronunciation of *great* is not in accord with the general phonics rule of giving the long vowel sound to the first vowel when two vowels are side by side. Also, ask student to think of a mnemonic for remembering the difference between the two words. How will you know which version to use when you are writing a story? You might point out the word *rat* in *grate*; this will help students remember that when you grate cheese you might attract some rats!)	great
10. Finally, change one letter in *great* to make a word that goes with the word in step 1. (Note that this word, unlike *great*, does conform to the rule: when two vowels go walking, the first one does the talking and says its name).	treat

In addition to helping students understand word meanings, Word Ladders help students orchestrate the spelling and sounding of letters in words in a simple, quick, engaging way. They also call upon students' visualization learning modality, putting into action the principle from Chapter 1 that vocabulary instruction should call upon multiple modalities. You can use Word Ladders at almost any time during the day, from the word-study block to the few minutes before lunch or at the end of the day. As with the Making Words activities, you can extend and expand on the lesson by having students put the words on cards and sort them in a variety of ways.

In my work with students and teachers, I have discovered that everyone finds Word Ladders to be an enjoyable, challenging way to engage in word study. Although the activity is used most frequently in the primary grades with simple words, it can easily be used in the intermediate grades using structurally and semantically complex words. Here I offer two word ladders that are appropriate for older students.

Word Ladder #1	What the teacher says:	What students write:
1.	Begin with the season marked by snow and cold weather.	winter
2.	Subtract two letters and add one to make a word that means "to come in."	enter
3.	Add one letter to make a word that means the exact middle of something.	center
4.	Add one letter to make the word for a person who lives in an apartment owned by a landlord.	renter
5.	Subtract two letters to make the word for what a renter pays to live in an apartment.	rent
6.	Change one letter to make a word that means the opposite of work.	rest
7.	Add a three-letter suffix to make a word that means being in the state of getting rest.	resting
8.	Subtract two letters to make the word for what a bee or hornet will do when attacking.	sting
9.	Add one letter to make a word that describes a thin strand of cloth cord, often used to tie things together.	string
10.	Change one letter to make the season that comes after the one named in step 1.	spring

Word Ladder #2 **What the teacher says:**	What students write:
1. Begin with a member of the army.	soldier
2. Subtract three letters to make the past tense of *sell*.	sold
3. Change one letter to make a word that means brave or without fear.	bold
4. Change one letter to make a word for a link or tie between two or more things.	bond
5. Change one letter to make the word for a hard part of the body that is beneath the skin and forms its framework or skeleton.	bone
6. Change one letter to make a word that means "finished." (Point out that this word is an exception to the phonics silent *e*, long-vowel-sound rule.)	done
7. Change one letter to make a word that means "to give something to another person."	dole
8. Change one letter to make a word that describes a person from the country of Poland. (Also note other meaning for *pole*.)	Pole
9. Change one letter to make a word for the bottom of a person's foot.	sole
10. Change one letter to make a word that means an act of selling something.	sale
11. Subtract one letter and add one letter to make a homophone of the word in step 10 and a word that describes something used on a boat that moves by the wind.	sail
12. Add two letters to make a member of the navy.	sailor

Word Ladders are easy to implement. Once students have done a few with you, ask them to make their own for their classmates to use. Simply give them the first and last words and ask them to write the steps (for example, "go from *trick* to *treat* in ten steps or fewer"). Be sure to make a ladder based on the two words in advance, to ensure that it's possible to get from point A to point B. Making Word Ladders builds students' word consciousness at a deep level and helps them understand that words with the same prefixes or suffixes will retain the meaning of that word part in their meaning.

Derivational Word Building: "It's Greek to Me"

It has been estimated that more than 75 percent of English words are derived from Latin and Greek roots. Moreover, Latin and Greek words are found extensively in the content areas—particularly science and mathematics. Teaching the Latin and Greek roots, then, is an excellent way to increase students' vocabulary (as well as their decoding and spelling skills).

There are many ways to teach vocabulary through Latin and Greek roots. One of the best is to introduce a root and find and discuss words in English that are derived from it. For example, the Latin root *terra* means "land" or "earth." From this root, English words such as *terrace, territory, terrarium, extraterrestrial, terra-cotta, terra firma, terra nova, Mediterranean,* and *terrier* are derived. For some words, the semantic connection to the concept of earth or land is clear. For others, such as *terrier,* the connection may require some elaboration and research. (In case you're curious, the *terrier* is the original earth dog. It was originally bred to dig for animals that burrow into the earth.) Similarly, the Latin root *spec* means "to see or look." From that root comes these English derivatives: *spectator, spectacles, spectacular, speculate, inspect, inspector,* and *respect.* And from the Greek root *polis,* meaning city, English words such as *metropolis, megalopolis, Minneapolis, Indianapolis, Annapolis,* and *acropolis* are derived. By teaching just one Latin or Greek root, students can learn or reinforce their understanding of many related English words.

Given that Spanish is more closely connected to Latin than English is, the study of Latin roots can be remarkably productive in helping Spanish-speaking English-language learners become fluent. This is true for any ELL whose first language is Latin-based.

The subtitle of this section, "It's Greek to Me," is from Shakespeare. I included it for a couple of reasons. First, and perhaps most obviously, Shakespeare was making reference to the topic of this section—using Latin and Greek to expand students' vocabulary. It is known that Shakespeare was perhaps one of the greatest wordsmiths of all time. He invented (or built) more than 1,700 words that he used in his plays and poems, such as *premeditated, metamorphize, submerge, worthless, lackluster, invulnerable,* and *equivocal.* Many of the words involved combining Latin or Greek roots.

Shakespeare is one master of English we would love all our students to emulate. By encouraging his inventiveness and playfulness with language, we move students in that direction.

How can this be done? The answer is easy. Once students have learned a basic corpus of Latin and Greek roots commonly found in English words, encourage them to build or invent new words, ones that don't really exist outside of your classroom and that are made from the various roots. Of course, you can get your students started by creating a few words on your own and challenging them to come up with meanings for them. Here are a few invented words that teachers and students have built from their study of Latin and Greek roots:

♦   *demophobia:* fear of people

♦   *matermand:* an order given to you by your mother

♦   *aquaphilia:* a love of water

♦   *polyped:* an animal with many feet

♦   *polisophodem:* a city of wise people

Students can create riddles for their invented words. For example, one of our fifth graders invented the word *autophile*. He came into class one day and asked his classmates what they would most likely have in their pockets or purses if they were autophiles—a wad of money, a set of car keys, or a mirror. Universally, his classmates responded with "car keys" They knew that *phil or phile* referred to love, as in *bibliophile*, *Anglophile*, *Francophile*, *philanthropist*, *philosopher*, and *Philadelphia*, so they felt that an *autophile* was a person who loved cars. But this student was able to turn the tables on his classmates and declare that a mirror was the correct answer. He explained that *auto* refers to self. Thus an *autophile* is a person who is in love with himself or herself; a mirror would be a most appropriate instrument for such a person. Of course, that led to a most interesting discussion into why cars are called *automobiles* and how the primary meaning of many words changes over time, as people use them for different purposes and in different ways.

Sourcebooks for Derivational Word Building

English Words From Latin and Greek Elements by D. Ayers, T. Worther, and R. L. Cherry (University of Arizona Press).

Dictionary of Word Roots and Combining Forms by D. Borror (Mayfield).

Instant Vocabulary by I. Ehrlich (Pocket Books).

Word Stems by J. Kennedy (Soho).

NTC's Dictionary of Latin and Greek Origins by R. Moore (McGraw-Hill).

Word Within the Word by M. Thompson (Royal Fireworks).

Word Building using Latin and Greek words is a powerful way to help students develop strong associations between the meanings of the roots and the meanings (and spellings) of words derived from those roots. Because it is so playful and creative, it is sure to capture the interest of all students, from those who are struggling to find ways to increase their vocabularies to those who aren't. Five to ten minutes per day can go a long way toward developing knowledge of and an appreciation for English words. One note of caution, though: be sure to keep these words in a special place and label them as invented. Although they may have real meaning in your classroom, remind students to avoid using them in their writing and speaking in other contexts.

You Try It

The activities I have described in this chapter are excellent ways to build students' vocabulary, their spelling and decoding skills, and, perhaps most important, their enthusiasm for words. Because of the game-like and engaging nature of the activities, teachers and students will want to use them over and over again. One of the best features of these activities is their innate flexibility. They are not inherently connected to any content area or instructional program or philosophy. Any teacher, regardless of her grade level, type of students, content-area specialty, or instructional program, can use these activities regularly to improve students' word knowledge.

Spend a few minutes reflecting on how word-building and word-part activities could fit into your curriculum and instruction. What lessons would you use? When in the school day would you employ them? How often would you use them? How would you group students for these lessons? What are some ways you can expand on and extend the lessons that you develop?

Summary

Developing students' vocabulary is a worthy goal of any instructional program—certainly of reading and language arts, but equally of the content-area curricula, given the sophisticated and specialized vocabulary found in content-area reading materials.

By teaching students how to add the meaning of a prefix or suffix to a root word, and how to build as many words as possible using similar prefixes, suffixes, and root meanings, you invite them to discover independently the meanings of many words as well as their orthographic structures, which is so important for decoding and spelling. I've described four word-building activities that I have used with great success in the Kent State University reading clinic with students experiencing difficulty learning words and reading—Making Words, Making and Writing Words, Word Ladders, and derivational Word Building with word parts. The high level of excitement and enthusiasm for word study that these game-like activities generate convinces me that they will not only lead students to greater depth of knowledge about words but also inspire in them an awareness of and appreciation for the wonderful words that make up the English language.

Discussion Questions and Teaching Activities

1. Try using the Making Words strategy with three groups of students (high-ability, average, and struggling). Afterward, compare and contrast the results of each group.

2. Present the Word Ladders strategy to your students several times. Then, put the students into pairs. We recommend that a high-ability and an average-ability student be grouped together, and that an above-average learner be teamed with a struggling reader. Assign a ladder to each pair and have the students complete only half of it. After teaching this strategy, list the ways it benefits vocabulary learning with the class.

CHAPTER FOUR

Developing Vocabulary by
Learning Content–Area Words

Robert J. Rickelman and **D. Bruce Taylor,**
both of the University of North Carolina at Charlotte

r. Sanchez's sixth-grade mathematics class has been studying the properties of multiplication. Mr. Sanchez writes the names of three properties and three sample problems on the board:

Three Properties of Multiplication:

Associative   Distributive   Commutative

1. $4 \times 8 = 8 \times 4$

2. $(2 \times 3) \times 4 = 2 \times (3 \times 4)$

3. $4 \times (6 + 3) = 4 \times 6 + 4 \times 3$

Joshua and Nicole are having fun working together on Contextual Redefinition, an activity described in this chapter.

Mr. Sanchez:	Let's look at the first problem. This is an example of which multiplication property?
Latasha:	Commutative.
Mr. Sanchez:	Right. Why?
Latasha:	Because when you multiply two numbers together it doesn't matter what order they go in. That's what the commutative property says.
Mark:	I thought that was the distributive property.
Mr. Sanchez:	No, Mark. Latasha's right. It's the commutative property that tells us we can switch or "commute" the numbers when we multiply them. Okay. Let's look at the second example. Mark, do you want to try this one?
Mark:	I thought it was commutative, but it can't be. You know, Mr. Sanchez, I have more trouble with the words than I do with the math.

Mark's last comment highlights the important relationship between vocabulary learning and comprehension in content-area subjects. Research in vocabulary acquisition suggests that students learn between twenty-five hundred and three thousand new words a year (Beck & McKeown, 1991), with a significant amount of these coming from content-area texts. Indeed, vocabulary is fundamental to comprehension (Anderson & Freebody, 1981). Yet, despite research that suggests that students be actively involved in vocabulary learning (Blachowicz & Fisher, 2000), traditional approaches that have students define and learn words in isolation are still used in many classrooms (Nagy & Scott, 2004).

This chapter provides suggestions for alternative strategies that move away from the traditional approach, so that learning vocabulary in the content areas for students like Mark is *meaningful, manageable,* and *lasting.* We begin by showing how teachers can help students in grades 3–8 become involved in vocabulary learning in a *meaningful* way. Active engagement is a key ingredient if students are to connect new vocabulary to concepts they already know. The role of prior knowledge has been well documented as a key to comprehension, including prior knowledge needed for vocabulary learning (Anderson & Freebody, 1981). *Meaningful* also implies that students must be able to place key vocabulary in long-term memory, rather than simply memorizing terms for a test and quickly forgetting them. As explained in Chapter 1, students need to learn that content-area words give a clue to their meaning. By knowing that such words refer to the specific name of a particular thing, event, principle, or phenomenon within a content area, students are more likely to identify such words and build their vocabulary.

We recognize that teachers face enormous demands in a typical day, so we illustrate how they can integrate vocabulary instruction in a *manageable* way that is not complex and time consuming. Instruction that fits with content-specific texts and topics stands the best chance of helping students learn in context.

Finally, what can be done to help students develop *lasting* skills that they can apply across subject areas over time? A strategy that helps Mr. Sanchez's students in mathematics may be useful, but one that can help those students in many subject areas is far more powerful and is more likely to have a lasting impact on their ability to learn.

What Really Works With Students

The three strategies we will describe in this chapter—the Vocabulary Self-Awareness Chart, Contextual Redefinition, and Semantic Feature Analysis—all meet these criteria. They make vocabulary learning more meaningful, manageable, and lasting. Blachowicz and Fisher (2000) identified key aspects of effective vocabulary instruction. They found that students must be active participants immersed in learning, that they must be able to personalize word meanings to their own lives, and that they learn best through repeated exposures from multiple sources. The three strategies that we present move beyond traditionally passive approaches and help students by involving them more in learning.

The Vocabulary Self-Awareness Chart (Goodman, 2001) provides a tool for students to identify words they need to know and to document their ability to define and use those words in a meaningful way. This strategy actively engages students in their vocabulary learning and allows them to personalize word meanings.

Contextual Redefinition (Bean, 1981; J. W. Cunningham, Cunningham, & Arthur, 1981; Tierney, Readence, & Dishner, 1995; Readence, Bean, & Baldwin, 1998; Brassell & Flood, 2004) immerses students in vocabulary learning and helps them unlock the meaning of unknown words by drawing on context and definition. This allows students to make informed guesses from context while providing a tool for checking those guesses, an approach endorsed by the National Reading Panel (2000).

Semantic Feature Analysis (Anders & Bos, 1986; Pittelman, Heimlich, Berglund, & French, 1991) allows students to compare and contrast the characteristics of words in a chart. These features can be defined by the teacher or generated by the students. It is particularly useful for learning concepts and terms in subjects such as mathematics, science, and social studies.

Vocabulary Self-Awareness Chart (VSC)

The Vocabulary Self-Awareness Chart (Goodman, 2001) is, as the name suggests, a chart on which students write words they need to learn in a unit of study. It makes learning more personal and meaningful. Students identify their degree of mastery or knowledge of these words by providing clear examples and definitions. For words that they cannot yet define or for which they cannot offer a clear example, the VSC provides a tool for outlining an effective strategy to discover and learn word meanings. (See Figure 4.1.)

The three steps for using the VSC are simple and flexible enough to allow teachers across subject areas to tailor them to the needs of their students. Below is an abbreviated example of the chart, followed by the steps for using it:

Word	+	□	–	Example	Definition

1. Create a list of words to study. You can determine what words to study on your own or with students, or allow students to create their own lists. For example, you may select five words that all students need to know and invite each student to decide on five additional words he or she wants to learn. Words can also be selected by students working in cooperative groups assigned to different texts or topics, to identify words that are both important and unique to their area of inquiry.

2. Identify level of word knowledge. Regardless of how the words are selected, students should examine the list of words they wrote in the first column of the chart and identify their level of word knowledge by putting a + next to a word for which they can give both an accurate example and definition. This is a word they know well,

Vocabulary Self–Awareness Chart

Word	+	☐	–	Example	Definition

Procedure:

Examine the list of words you have written in the first column.

Put a **+** next to each word you know well, and give an accurate example and definition of the word. Your definition and example must relate to what we are studying.

Put a ☐ next to any words for which you can write only a definition or example, but not both.

Put a **–** next to words that are new to you.

This chart will be used throughout our unit. By the end of the unit you should have the entire chart completed. Since you will be revising this chart, write in pencil.

Figure 4.1

and the definition and example must relate to the context of your lesson. Have students put a ☐ next to any words for which they can write only a definition or an example, but not both. Again, the definition or example must fit with the context of the unit. Have students put a – next to words that are completely new to them. These are words that will require more in-depth study.

3. Develop a plan of study. Put a plan together for learning those words that are new or only partially known to students. Your approach will vary, but it should actively involve students and provide multiple exposures to words and opportunities to read, write, and use the terms in different contexts. Provide whole-class instruction for words that are unfamiliar to many of your students. Have them work in flexible groups to study and teach words to one another. Encourage students to use the VSC for independent word study.

Let's return to the example of Mr. Sanchez's sixth-grade mathematics class to see how the VSC could be used to help. Seeing that some students struggled with words associated with the properties of multiplication, Mr. Sanchez has students write down the terms in the first column of the VSC (step 1) and fill in as much other information into the chart as they can (step 2). Here is Mark's VSC:

Word	+	☐	–	Example	Definition
Associative			–		
Commutative			–		
Distributive		☐		$4 \times (6 + 3) =$ $4 \times 6 + 4 \times 3$	

Although Mark could not give an example or definition for either the associative or commutative properties, he was able to give an example for the distributive property. Here is how Latasha's VSC looks:

Word	+ □ −			Example	Definition
Associative	+			(2 x 3) x 4 = 2 x (3 x 4)	When you multiply 3 or more numbers, it does not matter what order you do it in.
Commutative	+			4 x 8 = 8 x 4	When you multiply numbers, it does not matter what order you do it in.
Distributive			−		

Mr. Sanchez sees from his students' charts that the distributive property is giving them the most trouble, so he writes more examples of this property on the board and works through them with his students:

Three Properties of Multiplication:

Distributive Property

$3 \times (4 + 5) = (3 \times 4) + (3 \times 5) = 12 + 15 = 27$

$2 \times (6 + 10) = (2 \times 6) + (2 \times 10) = 12 + 20 = 32$

$4 \times (8 + 1) = (4 \times 8) + (4 \times 1) = 32 + 4 = 36$

Mr. Sanchez: Look at the first problem here. Do you see how we can "distribute" the three across the four and five? That's why we call it the distributive property. It doesn't matter if we add the four and five first then multiply it by three or distribute the three across the four and five first. Either way the answer is 27.

Mark: So if I add four and five, I get nine. If I multiply that by three, I get 27. Cool.

Mr. Sanchez: Math can be easy, Mark. Let's come up with a definition for the distributive property.

Latasha: How about when you add two numbers together and multiply another number, you can either add and then multiply or multiply each number and then add them?

Mark: That sounds confusing.

Mr. Sanchez: Latasha's got it. Mark, here's another way of stating the distributive property. Your textbook defines it this way: "When a number is multiplied by the sum of two other numbers, the first number can be handed out or distributed to both of those two numbers and multiplied by each of them separately."

Mark: I'm going to write that on my chart.

Following this discussion, Mr. Sanchez has his students work in pairs to come up with examples and definitions for the associative and commutative properties (step 3). Mark and Latasha work together, talking about their charts and why they filled them in the way that they did. When they are done, Mark's chart looks like this:

Word	+	☐	–	Example	Definition
Associative	+			(2 x 3) x 4 = 2 x (3 x 4)	When you multiply three or more numbers, it does not matter what order you do it in.
Commutative	+			4 x 8 = 8 x 4	When you multiply numbers, it does not matter what order you do it in.
Distributive		☐		4 x (6 + 3) = 4 x 6 + 4 x 3	When a number is multiplied by the sum of two other numbers, the first number can be distributed to both of those two numbers and multiplied by each of them separately.

Mark didn't put a + on his VSC for the distributive property yet because although he has a definition written down, he feels that he needs to study it more before he understands it fully. After students are done, Mr. Sanchez asks partners to give examples and to talk about what they have learned and still need to learn:

Mark: I'm doing better with commutative and associative, but I still need to work on the definition of the distributive property.

Latasha: Yeah, that's the one I need to work on, too.

Mr. Sanchez: One thing we may want to do is talk about the order of operations. Let's add that to our VSC. Order of operations can help us better understand the distributive property. Write that down and we can work on that tomorrow in class.

The Vocabulary Self-Awareness Chart gave Mr. Sanchez's students a place to document what they knew and did not know about the properties of multiplication. It served as a starting point for learning key mathematical concepts and important vocabulary and also provided a framework for organizing instruction. Mr. Sanchez was able to see which terms presented the greatest challenge to students. He addressed this with whole-class instruction and drew on both what students knew and what the textbook said about the distributive property. Then students worked in pairs to teach the remaining terms to each other. They were able to take stock of what they had learned during the lesson and note words they needed to study in greater depth. Finally, the VSC pointed Mr. Sanchez to a new concept to teach his students—order of operations. In short, the VSC actively engaged students in word study and provided the teacher with valuable feedback.

Contextual Redefinition

Contextual Redefinition (Readence, Bean, & Baldwin, 2004) is a vocabulary strategy that can be used across different grades and subject areas. It helps students learn to use context to define unknown words. Often students will tell you that when they come to a word in their textbooks that they don't know, they'll stop and look it up in a dictionary. While dictionary skills are certainly important, it takes time to walk over to get the dictionary, locate the word, decide on the correct meaning (if there is more than one), and then go back to the text to see if it fits. By the time students come back to the text, they have generally forgotten what they were reading. If they could quickly figure out the definition, or approximate a good definition, they could return to the text more quickly, enhancing comprehension. They could maintain comprehension and fluency while reading for meaning, which is essential to reading for meaning in content subjects. (For more on Contextual Redefinition, see page 110.)

There are five steps to a Contextual Redefinition lesson:

1. Select eight to ten words that you want students to learn. Because using too many words at one time increases the chances that students will confuse them with one another, choose words that are central to understanding the content.

2. Before class, write (or identify in the text) a contextually rich sentence for each word. Students should be able to accurately define or come up with a good approximation of the meaning of the word using clues from this sentence. Sometimes a sentence might explicitly define the new word ("A **psychrometer** can be used to measure relative humidity"), but more often the actual connection to the target word is less explicit ("The weather **front** brought strong winds and rain to our area").

3. Present the words in isolation, and ask students to define each one using any method they can. They may know some of the words and be able to write an accurate definition. They may have a vague idea of what a word means, or have heard it before, so they might write a definition that is close to being accurate. They may be able to identify a prefix, suffix or root that could give them a clue to the definition. If none of these strategies works, students may have to make a wild guess. They can work individually, in pairs, or in small groups. You might have students begin on their own and then move into pairs. Partners can discuss individual guesses and decide which one they think is the best. Then they can get into small groups and again try to reach a consensus on which of the guesses they think is the most accurate.

4. Present the words to students in the contextually rich sentences written in step 2. After reading these sentences, give students the opportunity to go back and revise their definitions for each word, using the context to help refine them.

5. Assign a volunteer to look up each word in the dictionary to verify the correct meaning. This step is important and should not be omitted, since it allows students to see that they can often use the context to write a definition that is close to (or, at times, the same as) the one found in the dictionary.

If you use Contextual Redefinition in the classroom on a regular basis, students should learn to rely more on using the context to define unknown words, rather than interrupting their reading to use the dictionary. At times, a word may still be difficult to define, even when it appears in a contextually rich sentence. Students may find several different meanings that could make sense from the given context, or they may think they know what a word means but discover they do not as they continue to read. At these times, using the dictionary makes sense.

For example, Ms. Levine's fourth-grade class is studying weather during a science lesson. She does the following, which corresponds to the five-step process outlined above.

1. Based on her reading of the textbook, Ms. Levine decides she wants her students to learn the following words: *transpiration, humidity, cumulus, front,* and *monsoon.*

2. She writes down a contextually rich sentence for each word and underlines the content-specific word. If sentences from the textbook present good opportunities for guessing from the context, she transcribes them directly and underlines the content-specific word. It they don't, she writes her own sentence to provide additional context. Here are her sentences:

Through <u>transpiration</u>, plants give off water into the air through tiny openings in their leaves.

When the weather forecaster said the <u>humidity</u> would be high today, I knew I would sweat when I went outside.

The <u>cumulus</u> clouds reminded me a lot of cotton balls.

Because of the cold <u>front</u> that came through last night, I had to wear a sweater to school today.

I saw on the news that the <u>monsoon</u> that went through India looked a lot like the hurricanes that went through Florida and Louisiana last year.

3. Ms. Levine puts the five words on a handout and asks students to define each one. She reminds students to guess if they have no idea what a word means, but to remember that the words all have something to do with science. After the students have written down their guesses, Ms. Levine asks for volunteers to read their definitions for *transpiration*. She writes down two or three of the suggested meanings for each word. Here are some of the definitions students suggested for all five words:

transpiration—a fatal disease, a church bus, being really hot and fainting

humidity—really hot and sweaty, humming a song, hot weather

cumulus—the highest number, altogether, rain clouds

front—opposite of back, like in a battle, the edge of something

monsoon—animal that eats snakes, something fast, really loud

4. After the students have offered a few guesses for each word, Ms. Levine shows her sentences for the words from step 2. She asks the class to redefine each word if necessary. Then she asks students whether they correctly guessed the meanings of each word. If not, she asks them to correct the definitions by using the context of the sentence they have just read. The class goes through each word in the same way, sharing its guesses, seeing the words in contextually rich sentences, and then redefining the words based on any new insights.

5. Ms. Levine assigns five volunteers to look up the words in the dictionary. Allison looks up the word *transpiration* and reads the definition out loud. "Transpiration—the process by which plants give off water vapor into the air." The four other volunteers do the same for *humidity, cumulus, front,* and *monsoon.* Ms. Levine then asks students to look at the revised definitions on the board and use the dictionary definitions to decide whether they are correct. If not, they have one more opportunity to write the correct definition on a quiz the next day. From the scores, Ms. Levine can assess the success of the strategy and students' knowledge of these important words.

Contextual Redefinition can be used in any grade for any subject area. After the lesson, point out to students that many times they can guess what a word means by using the context and come up with the same definition as the one in the dictionary, without having to use the dictionary. Students should be cautioned, however, that this strategy will not always work, since unknown words do not always appear in contextually rich sentences. The goal over time is for students to become more independent in their use of context as one possible way to figure out unknown words. Also, students need to be aware that as they read for meaning they have a number of strategies available to them (using the dictionary, using prefix and suffix meanings, and so on). With practice, they should be able to decide quickly whether to make a guess about an unknown word in context and continue reading to verify their guess, or to use another strategy.

Teachers have asked us whether students are likely to remember the guessed meaning rather than the real meaning, since guesses can often get very interesting and create more confusion than clarity. In our experience, if students do remember the guesses, they tend to link them to the real definition. For instance, it is not unusual for a teacher to hear a student say something like "I remember that I thought *transpiration* meant someone died, but I learned that it really is a way for plants to give off water vapor." The "weird" prediction tends to be a link to the real definition.

A major strength of Contextual Redefinition is that students are actively involved in predicting word meanings, which makes them naturally curious to see if they are correct, close to correct, or way off. This curiosity causes students to process word definitions more deeply into their long-term memory. Alternatively, when students must look up the definitions of isolated words in a dictionary, they lose interest and motivation, and they are much more likely to forget them since there is little depth of processing.

Semantic Feature Analysis

Semantic Feature Analysis (Pittelman et al., 1991) has been found to effectively increase content-area vocabulary knowledge and comprehension across grade levels. It requires students to categorize words and concepts. Categorization can be a powerful learning tool, since students must look deeply for similarities and differences between words. Students are far more likely to remember the meanings of these words than if they simply look them up in a dictionary. Semantic Feature Analysis can be used as a prereading strategy, with the goal of assessing background knowledge related to word meanings, or as a post-reading strategy, where the goal is to assess word learning, perhaps as an alternative to a quiz or test.

   In the following example, we describe the six steps to the lesson and show an example of each step in action. Mr. Ng is beginning a social studies lesson on landforms with his third-grade students.

1. Select a category. Choose a topic that will be the focus of a lesson. Ideally, the topic should be one with which students have some familiarity.

   Mr. Ng writes the word *landforms* on the board.

2. List category words. Prepare a list of vocabulary terms that link to the category identified in step 1.

   Mr. Ng decides that he wants to focus his lesson on the following: mountain, plain, desert, valley, and coast.

3. List features. Decide—along with students if desired—on features within the category you wish to analyze. These features should become obvious as the lesson is planned.

   In looking at the category words he has chosen and at the content he wants students to learn, Mr. Ng lists the following features of landforms: peaks, wet, dry, flat, steep sides.

4. Indicate feature possession. Construct a matrix of the category words from step 2 and the features from step 3. The category words are listed down the side of the page, and the feature words are listed across the top of the page. The students then decide which words contain, or relate to, which features, by entering a + in the intersecting cell if the word relates to the feature, or a – if the word does not relate to the feature.

   Mr. Ng creates the following matrix from the words and features identified in steps 2 and 3.

	peaks	wet	dry	flat	steep sides
mountain					
plain					
desert					
valley					
coast					

Note that the vocabulary words are listed vertically in the left column, and the features are listed across the top. Once the chart is constructed, the whole class analyzes each word by the feature. If the word contains that feature, the class tells Mr. Ng to put a + in the intersecting cell. If not, they tell him to put a – in the cell. For example, the class decides that mountains do (or could) contain peaks, so Mr. Ng puts a + in that cell. In the discussion, there are times when students decide, "It depends." For example, mountains might be dry or wet, and sometimes they can be both, depending on the weather. The class agrees to list both a + and a – when these situations occur. The students are also not quite sure if a valley has to have steep sides, so Mr. Ng puts a ? in the cell, to indicate that the answer is unknown at this point. When the students read the chapter and discuss landforms, they can look for the correct answer and revise that cell. Mr. Ng is careful not to tell students the information for unknown features. After discussing each word by each feature, the completed chart looks like this:

	peaks	wet	dry	flat	steep sides
mountain	+	+/–	+/–	–	+
plain	–	+/–	+/–	+	–
desert	–	–	+	+	–
valley	–	+/–	+/–	–	?
coast	–	+	–	+	–

5. Extend learning by adding words and features. Add new words or features to the matrix to expand the analysis and pinpoint additional areas to explore, especially ones that students may not have seen before. Fill in matrix cells with the appropriate symbols and ask students to analyze the features and then guess how the landform might look.

Mr. Ng adds the word *plateau* and indicates the correct features (no peaks, may be wet or dry, is flat, and has steep sides). He then invites the students to guess how a plateau might look. They correctly guess that a plateau is a landform that is flat, but has steep sides around it.

	peaks	wet	dry	flat	steep sides
mountain	+	+/–	+/–	–	+
plain	–	+/–	+/–	+	–
desert	–	–	+	+	–
valley	–	+/–	+/–	–	?
coast	–	+	–	+	–
plateau	–	+/–	+/–	+	+

6. Explore the matrix. Discuss interesting items from the matrix.

Mr. Ng decides that it would be exciting to explore several things inspired by the filled-in matrix. First, he asks the students which landform feature occurs least often. They decide on peaks. In the discussion that follows, the students agree that you only see peaks on mountains, which is why it does not appear frequently. He then asks them which features occur most often, and the class agrees on wet and dry. Students discuss why these features seem to be more common and decide that wet and dry weather can occur on almost any landform. It even rains in the desert occasionally!

THE VOCABULARY-ENRICHED CLASSROOM

Semantic Feature Analysis can be used as a prewriting strategy. For instance, Mr. Ng could ask his students to write several paragraphs comparing and contrasting what they know about different landforms, using all the vocabulary words from the matrix.

It is also an excellent prereading strategy. Students can fill in pluses and minuses for words with which they are familiar and put a question mark for those with which they are not. As they learn word meanings in the lesson, they can refer to the matrix and correct misinformation or replace the question marks. The completed matrix can be used to help study for a quiz or test. Semantic Feature Analysis can be used for postreading content assessment as well. Instead of giving a test, you can give students the matrix with the words and features filled in. From there, have students fill in the cells to demonstrate their understanding of the content words. This can be a good alternative to traditional assessments.

The symbols used in the matrix are flexible. For instance, if students are studying the planets and satellites, they could write in the number of known moons for each planet in the appropriate cell, rather than simply indicate whether or not that planet has satellites. Their matrix may look like this:

	hot	cold	number of known moons	habitable for humans
Mercury	+	–	0	–
Venus	+	–	0	–
Earth	+/–	+/–	1	+
Mars	–	+	2	–
Jupiter	–	+	about 60	–

Students could explore this matrix by discussing questions such as Do you notice a relationship between a planet's temperatures and its distance from the sun? What do you notice about the number of moons and a planet's distance from the sun? What do you think the word *habitable* may mean, since only one planet has this feature? What other features would you like to add to the matrix, based on what you know about planets?

You can also use Likert Scale numbers in the cells to indicate the degree to which a word possesses a certain feature. For instance, expanding on the example above, on a scale of

1 to 5 (1 is the coldest and 5 the hottest), how hot or cold is each planet compared with Earth?

You can insert pictures into the matrix cells. For example, different geometric shapes can be drawn into matrix cells, and the remaining columns can be used to list number of sides, number of angles, whether the angles must be equal, and so on.

Semantic Feature Analysis is an extremely flexible strategy that can be easily modified for all grades in almost any subject area. Teachers have used it with students with intellectual disabilities, preschoolers, and college professors.

You Try It

Students in grades 3–8 encounter new and challenging vocabulary in all kinds of texts. Teachers introduce words and concepts from textbooks and basal readers by having students preread the sentences in which these words appear before they read them independently. Contextual Redefinition is often used next as an effective prereading strategy for learning key vocabulary. Semantic Feature Analysis offers both pre- and post-reading opportunities, allowing students to process new word meanings in depth.

Often teachers introduce information with trade books or have students read from an array of children's and adolescent literature. The Vocabulary Self-Awareness Chart can support this kind of individual learning by providing a place for students to document words they want to learn or those identified by the teacher as necessary for comprehension of the material.

These vocabulary-learning strategies work with diverse learners, including those who need remediation. Although we would argue that all students can benefit from all of these strategies, they are especially helpful to learners whose comprehension needs are greatest, by making learning more active and personal. The Vocabulary Self-Awareness Chart and Semantic Feature Analysis also have the advantage of presenting information visually, so that students can see and explore relationships among concepts.

Finally, teachers can use the strategies described in this chapter with large and small groups. Also, by modeling them to large groups and allowing students to apply them in small groups and on their own, a "phased transfer" model of instruction (Wood, 2002), teachers can increase students' confidence and ownership of their content-specific word knowledge.

Summary

During a typical school year, students in grades 3–8 learn an enormous amount of new vocabulary—three thousand words a year, on average. If they are to learn— rather than simply memorize—important content-area words that are vital for success in school and beyond, they need the right tools. Vocabulary learning strategies such as Vocabulary Self-Awareness Chart, Contextual Redefinition, and Semantic Feature Analysis provide these tools. They offer teachers and students a manageable way to accomplish this goal, and have the potential to make word study more interesting and lasting. Moreover, teachers are more likely to continue to make learning more active when they see students independently increasing their word knowledge by applying the word-learning principles and vocabulary-building strategies described in this chapter. These gains inevitably lead to an increase in comprehension, which should be the ultimate goal in content-area teaching and learning.

Discussion Questions and Teaching Activities

1. Use the Contextual Redefinition strategy in a content area with your students over a two-week period. After repeatedly implementing the five steps, assess the degree to which your students learned the meanings of the target words.

2. Use the Semantic Feature Analysis strategy multiple times with your students until you are sure they can perform it independently. Then, have the entire class select a book about a topic that interests them, and ask students to apply the strategy to that book. With the class, discuss the range of book topics and how well the students were able to use this strategy independently. Before you ask them to repeat this process, think about what you learned from this initial experience.

CHAPTER FIVE

Helping Students Learn Unusual Words:
Homophones, Idioms, and Figurative Language

Jerry L. Johns, Northern Illinois University, and
Janet L. Pariza, Northeastern Illinois University

t's Friday, and Ms. Hernandez is giving a spelling test. She knows that many of her students will not do well on this particular test because the target words are homophones. Joey, like a few others, just doesn't get it. He first learned to spell by listening to the sounds of words. But in this week's words there are pairs (or is it pears?) of words that sound the same but are spelled differently. Homophones just don't make sense to him. Ms. Hernandez is frustrated when it comes to teaching homophones and other thorny words that she herself has to think about when writing. In fact, she has a reminder taped to her computer to help her avoid embarrassing mistakes with her own two problem words: *their* and *they're*.

Down the hall, Mr. Horner is attempting to explain figurative language to his fifth-grade students. Even some of his best readers are having trouble recognizing and understanding the rich, evocative language they encountered in the poem under discussion. Mr. Horner sometimes feels that he's in over his head. Is there a strategy he can use to increase his students' ability to recognize and understand figurative language, such as metaphors and similes?

Next door, in Ms. Taglia's ELL classroom, the students are grappling with idiomatic speech. Anna has just asked, "How can something have a different meaning than what

On the flip chart:

Idiom Four Square

Idiom	Intended Meaning
cutest little monkey	The newborn was so tiny and cute that Grandma compared him to a monkey

What It Says	What It Means

Third-grade teacher Rose Hernandez and her students enjoy learning 107 idioms through Idiom Four Square, which is described in this chapter.

the words say?" Even Ms. Taglia is dissatisfied with her explanation; she has really opened a can of worms with this one. There has to be a way to alert students to the presence of English idioms, especially in print, where the speaker's gestures don't convey meaning and the listener can't ask for clarification.

English is among the richest of languages. As Jespersen (1983), the father of modern linguistics, stated, writers of English are free to choose words from everyday language, native dialects, past and present authors, and other languages, both living and dead. "English dictionaries comprise a larger number of words than those of any other nation" (p. 16). The very facets of the language that create its richness create problems for native speakers and English-language learners (ELLs) alike. The language includes numerous homophones that complicate its already quirky spelling conventions. It also has enormous potential for poetic expressiveness, including idiomatic and figurative language. And it readily adopts words and phrases from other languages and just as readily coins new words and phrases. While creative writers relish such worldly treasures, the students and teachers of language are challenged and sometimes frustrated by the complexity of English.

In this chapter, we will focus on three types of unusual English words and word combinations that create challenges for students and teachers: homophones, idioms, and figurative language. Addressing these aspects of English in the classroom is important to students' overall vocabulary growth. Instruction that focuses on the many homophones in English furthers students' ability to interpret print precisely, to transfer spoken meaning effectively to print, and to understand and appreciate the polysemous nature of words. Instruction that focuses on idioms is important to all students, but especially to ELLs. Since idioms are numerous in English, understanding the possibility that a confusing phrase or a seemingly incongruous reference may be an idiom should allow the active reader to make a strategic shift to achieve comprehension. Instruction that focuses on figurative language furthers the reader's ability to make meaning from text and fosters an appreciation for the beauty of the written word. Instruction in all three of these aspects of English improves students' ability to construct meaning from a variety of texts and fosters the development of the kind of word consciousness that is an important component of word learning (Graves & Watts-Taffe, 2002). Three questions guide our discussion:

♦ What does research suggest about teaching in these challenging areas?

♦ What classroom strategies can teachers use to teach homophones, idioms, and figurative language?

♦ How can these strategies help students when they encounter homophones, idioms, and figurative language in a variety of texts?

What Research Suggests

Vocabulary development is one of the oldest and richest areas of investigation in education (Anderson & Freebody, 1981; Dale, 1965; Davis, 1943; Thorndike, 1917). In the last half of the twentieth century alone, numerous research studies attempted to determine the most effective methods for vocabulary instruction (Kame'enui, Dixon, & Carmine, 1987; McKeown, Beck, Omanson, & Perfetti, 1983; Nagy, 1988). In a meta-analysis of much of this research, Stahl (1986) concluded that generative methods of vocabulary instruction are more effective than additive methods. Generative methods are characterized by activities that require students to generate meaningful connections between prior knowledge and target words. For example, a student learning the word *hinder* may generate a visual association with a detour sign, something that hinders drivers. Additive methods are characterized by activities that involve rote memorization of simple word-specific definitions or synonyms for preselected words (Pariza, 2002). In the most recent *Handbook of Reading Research*, Blachowicz and Fisher (2000) also suggest generative methods for vocabulary study. Drawing from 20 years of vocabulary research, they recommend that, in addition to the learning principles cited in Chapter 1, vocabulary instruction be guided by four instructional principles: Students should (1) be active in developing their understanding of words and their own ways to learn them; (2) personalize word learning; (3) be immersed in words; and (4) build on multiple sources of information to learn words through repeated exposures (p. 504).

Generative methods are especially important for learning idioms and figurative language because students will encounter idioms and figurative language more frequently as they progress through their schooling. Idioms are often closely associated with a particular culture, group, or field, so encounters with new domains will continually present the learner with new idioms to interpret. Teachers can offer an introduction to how to learn these unusual words, but a definitive study of all possible idioms is not possible. The same is true for figurative language, since limitless combinations of English words can be made into figurative language and such combinations are constantly being added to our language. Although homophones can be learned through repetitive drill, research and practice have demonstrated that rote memorization of definitions is largely ineffective (J. A. Scott & Nagy, 1997; Stahl, 1986). In this chapter, we present strategies and classroom activities that you can use to actively involve students in generative learning of homophones, idioms, and figurative language.

Classroom Strategies for Teaching Homophones, Idioms, and Figurative Language

Homophones

Homonyms are words that are pronounced or spelled alike but have different meanings. Homographs are spelled alike but have different meanings and, sometimes, different pronunciations, such as *bass*, the kind of drum, and *bass*, the kind of fish. Homophones are words that are pronounced alike but spelled differently, such as *bear* and *bare*. The more than 200 homophone sets in the English language can be confusing, more so for the writer than for the reader. (See Figure 5.1.) For the reader, the context in which the homophone appears signals its meaning. For example, most readers would not confuse the homophones *they're* and *their* in the following sentence: "They're coming to our house for pizza and a movie tonight since we went to their house last time." However, many writers would confuse the same homophones when crafting such a sentence.

Since spelling is not the only source of confusion, the teacher must provide instruction that allows students to master both the spelling and the proper use of homophones. Activities such as those that follow will help, but we begin with a lesson to introduce students to homophones.

Homophone Sets

ail/ale	blue/blew	cheap/cheep
air/heir	board/bored	choose/chews
an/Ann	bold/bowled	climb/clime
ant/aunt	born/borne	close/clothes
ate/eight	boulder/bolder	cord/chord
bail/bale	bow/bough	core/corps
bait/bate	boy/buoy	course/coarse
bald/balled	brake/break	creek/creak
ball/bawl	bread/bred	cruise/crews
base/bass	bridal/bridle	dam/damn
bazaar/bizarre	browse/brows	days/daze
be/bee	but/butt	dear/deer
beach/beech	by/buy/bye	die/dye
bear/bare	carrot/carat/caret	died/dyed
beat/beet	cash/cache	do/dew/due
been/bin	cellar/seller	doe/dough
bell/belle	cent/sent/scent	done/dun
berry/bury	cereal/serial	earn/urn

Figure 5.1

Continued next page

eyelet/islet	medal/mettle/meddle	sight/site/cite
faint/feint	might/mite	so/sew/sow
fair/fare	missed/mist	soar/sore
faker/fakir	morn/mourn	socks/sox
feet/feat	morning/mourning	some/sum
find/fined	nay/neigh	son/sun
flair/flare	need/kneed/knead	soul/sole
flea/flee	new/knew/gnu	stair/stare
flew/flu/flue	night/knight	steak/stake
flower/flour	no/know	steel/steal
fold/foaled	not/knot	straight/strait
for/four/fore	oh/owe	style/stile
foul/fowl	one/won	sweet/suite
fourth/forth	or/ore	tacks/tax
fur/fir	our/hour	tail/tale
gate/gait	pail/pale	tea/tee
great/grate	pair/pear/pare	team/teem
guessed/guest	past/passed	tents/tense
guilt/gilt	paws/pause	there/they're/their
hair/hare	peace/piece	throne/thrown
hall/haul	pedal/petal/peddle	through/threw
hay/hey	peek/peak/pique	tic/tick
heard/herd	peel/peal	tied/tide
heel/heal	pier/peer	time/thyme
here/hear	plane/plain	to/two/too
hi/high	pole/poll	toe/tow
him/hymn	poor/pour	vale/veil
hoe/ho	prays/praise	vein/vane/vain
hole/whole	rain/reign/rein	vice/vise
horse/hoarse	rap/wrap	wade/weighed
I/eye/aye	real/reel	wait/weight
I'll/aisle/isle	red/read	waste/waist
in/inn	reed/read	wave/waive
it's/its	rest/wrest	way/weigh
jeans/genes	right/write/rite	we/wee
kernel/colonel	ring/wring	wear/where/ware
knave/nave	rode/road/rowed	we'd/weed
knit/nit	roll/role	week/weak
lead/led	root/route	we'll/wheel
leak/leek	rough/ruff	wet/whet
lie/lye	rye/wry	we've/weave
loan/lone	sail/sale	whale/wail/wale
made/maid	see/sea	wit/whit
mail/male	seem/seam	wrote/rote
main/mane/Maine	sees/seas/seize	you/ewe
mall/maul	sell/cell	your/you're
manner/manor	sheer/shear	
marry/merry/Mary	shoe/shoo	
maze/maize	shown/shone	
meat/meet	side/sighed	

Introducing Homophones

To understand homophones fully, they must be experienced in both oral and written contexts; therefore, introducing them to students provides an excellent opportunity to integrate all the language arts: speaking, listening, reading, writing, and thinking.

1. Select two or three homophone pairs that you wish to introduce to your students, such as *it's/its, to/too, see/sea, here/hear*, all of which have the added benefit of being high-frequency words. Or you may choose homophones that complement other current instruction. For example, if you are teaching long-vowel sounds, you may wish to use such pairs as *rode/road, sore/soar, tale/tail,* and *side/sighed.*

2. Create sentences that contain both words in each pair and write them on chart paper or sentence strips. Some examples follow:

   It's fun to watch a bird build its nest.

   I like to see the clear blue sea.

   Jimmy rode his bike down the road to Grandma's house.

   This book tells the tale of a bear with a very stubby tail.

3. Display the sentences, choose a volunteer to read the first one, and ask students to explain the difference between the underlined words. Guide students to focus on the fact that the words have different spellings and meanings but identical pronunciations.

4. Continue with the other sentences until students are able to articulate the essence of homophones—that the spelling, rather than the pronunciation, signals the appropriate meaning of the word to the reader.

5. Introduce students to the term *homophone*. This may also be a good place to introduce older students to etymology, the study of word origins and derivations. For example, you might share the etymologies of *tail/tale*. The word *tail* is derived from the Anglo-Saxon word *tægel*, the part of an animal that extends from the end opposite the head, but the word *tale* is derived from the Anglo-Saxon word *talu*, a complete accounting as in recounting events or tallying points. The current spellings of these words reflect their origins.

6. Ask students to list other homophones they know. Write all homophone pairs from the lesson on cards.

7. Assess students' knowledge of homophones by writing a sentence that contains a homophone pairing and ask students to write the meaning of both words. For instance, using the sentence "I like to see the clear blue sea," you may ask students, "In this sentence, what does the first *see* mean? What does the second *sea* mean?"

8. Display cards of homophone pairs in a homophone section of your word wall. Begin with the pairs you presented in a lesson and the ones that students contributed, and add others as you and your students encounter them in subsequent lessons and independent reading.

Once you've introduced students to homophones, expand their knowledge of homophone pairs and provide adequate practice to ensure that they use the appropriate spelling for the word they want. Such practice can be accomplished in many ways, but we suggest the following activity. It gives your students an opportunity for generative processing as well as for increased engagement and enjoyment in word learning.

Homophone Win, Lose, or Draw

This adaptation of Bear, Invernizzi, Templeton, and Johnston's (2004) word game requires students to generate visual images for common homophones while reviewing their spelling and usage. As stated in Chapters 1 and 3, the use of visualization is an important learning modality in vocabulary instruction.

1. Identify eight to ten homophone pairs that you want your students to master, such as those that they misspell frequently.

2. Construct a deck of homophone cards out of index cards by writing a homophone pair on each card, with both words printed on the front of the card.

3. Create two drawing stations on opposite sides of the room, with chart paper, a dry-erase board, or a chalkboard, and a variety of colored markers or chalk.

4. Divide the class into two teams. Allow each team to sit in a semicircle around its drawing station and to choose one student to serve as the artist for the first round.

5. Pull one card from the deck and show it simultaneously to the two artists. Whisper to each artist which words on this card they are to draw. From there, the artists move to their respective stations and draw one word in the pair, and their teams try to guess the correct homophone, charades fashion. When an artist receives a correct response he or she calls upon a teammate to spell both words in the pair and to correctly use each in a sentence.

6. Award a point to the first team to provide the correct information, and have the first artists turn the drawing stations over to other team members for the next round. Play continues in the same fashion until all the words in the deck have been drawn or until all team members have had a turn at being artist or the time allotted to the activity has passed.

Resources for Homophone Instruction

The Prince Left His Prints by A. Rondeau (Abdo).

The Knight Waits at Night by A. Rondeau (Abdo).

Harry Is Not Hairy by P. Scheunemann (Abdo).

Eight Ate: A Feast of Homonym Riddles by M. Terban (Clarion Books).

Check for other titles by these authors.

Idioms

An idiom is a phrase that has a meaning different from the literal meaning of its words. Rather, the expression represents a single concept that is understood by the group that uses it in everyday communication. Knowing an idiom's origins is important because it provides students with the information they need to make educated guesses about its meaning. For example, in the context of theater or show business, the idiom "laid an egg" describes a very bad or embarrassing performance. If students are taught that in Shakespeare's time, audience members who did not like a performance threw eggs at the actors, the meaning of the idiom becomes clear. However, in a book about raising

Classroom Tips

Heather Rennie, a fifth-grade teacher at Westview School in Wood Dale, Illinois, has been including Homophone Win, Lose, or Draw as a regular part of word study for the past two years. She has some advice for teachers who are employing the game for the first time:

♦ Introduce the words prior to playing the game. Homophone Win, Lose, or Draw is for practice, not initial instruction.

♦ Model the activity for the students and make certain they grasp meanings of the homophone pair. The first time she used the game with her students, Ms. Rennie chose the pair *made/maid* and drew a picture of a girl holding a broom to illustrate *maid*, while the whole class guessed the homophone pair she was illustrating.

♦ Prevent the tendency to imitate. When student artists selected the pair *made/maid*, they also drew pictures of a girl with a broom. To avoid this kind of imitation, remove the already used pairs from the deck. After several intervening rounds, return the cards to the deck.

♦ Don't do this activity too frequently. Once every couple of weeks is enough for reviewing spelling and usage of homophones.

♦ Set up fair playing conditions. Ms. Rennie positions herself exactly halfway between the two drawing stations so students won't complain that one team's artist has an advantage by being closer to the station when the word is revealed.

♦ Use the game itself to reinforce classroom management. Students love this game so much that they request to play it during class holiday parties, but their engagement and enjoyment sometimes lead to loud voices and rowdy behavior. If necessary, deduct a point from an unruly team or end the game if both teams lose control.

♦ Set a time limit for the game and let the students know it prior to play.

♦ Plan for subsequent activities. Ms. Rennie does word study just before lunch, so her students have time to release the energy generated by the game before returning to the classroom. If such scheduling is not possible for you, follow Homophone Win, Lose, or Draw with a calming activity, such as reading aloud to the students.

chickens, the expression "laid an egg" would mean what the words literally say. Just as with homophones, it is the context that signals the meaning.

All languages have idioms with fascinating histories; English has thousands of such idioms (D. J. Johnson, B. V. H. Johnson, & Schlichting, 2004; Terban, 1996). One characteristic of idioms is that they are fixed expressions; neither the words nor the order in which they appear can be changed without changing the meaning. Idioms are typically informal and are not often found in textbooks. Whether they are encountered in speech or writing, idioms can confuse all students, especially ELLs, unless instruction on their origins is provided. Such instruction can invite rich and interesting language study.

Introducing Idioms

Your students have probably heard and used idioms in their own conversations and writing, even if you teach in the primary grades. Between the ages of 7 and 11, children acquire idiom understanding more rapidly than at other times in their language development; however, they may not yet be capable of producing idioms in their own speech and writing (Levorato & Cacciari, 1995). Again, we begin with an introductory activity.

1. Prior to the lesson, collect and record examples of idioms from students' oral language as well as idioms your students are likely to hear or read, for example, "frog in the throat," "raining cats and dogs," "crying her/his eyes out," or "busy as a bee."

2. Choose an idiom from your list and write a brief script that provides clues to its meaning. For example, the following script could be used to illustrate the idioms "lay an egg" and "break a leg."

Daughter:	(*with crown on head*) How does my costume look?
Mom:	Great. You make a wonderful princess.
Daughter:	I think I'm too nervous to remember my lines.
Mom:	Oh, dear, I think you'll do just fine.
Daughter:	What if the horn doesn't sound when I'm supposed to go on stage?
Mom:	Relax, dear, everything will be just fine.
Daughter:	But what if I lay an egg?
Mom:	Now quit worrying and listen for your entrance cue.

(Horn sounds and Daughter turns to move away from Mom as if to go on stage.)

Mom: Break a leg, dear!

3. Enlist the help of students to rehearse the script and act it out for the class.

4. Following the performance, ask students a question that suggests a literal interpretation of the idiom. For example, "How could the daughter lay an egg?" or "Does Mom really want her daughter to break her leg?"

5. Ask students to explain the meanings of the idioms and, more important, how they know that the words shouldn't be interpreted literally.

6. Introduce students to the term *idiom*. This may be a good time to introduce older students to the related concepts *literal*, *connotative*, and *denotative*. Peggy Parrish's Amelia Bedelia series is an excellent resource since the books' humor arises from literal interpretations of idiomatic language.

As students' understanding of idioms increases, they will become more conscious of idioms in the language they hear and read. Giving students time in class to discuss idioms they encounter will facilitate students' awareness and comprehension of them. Instruction in idioms should be three-pronged: First, it should generate awareness that idioms are common in English, particularly in spoken English. Second, it should familiarize students with the intended meanings of common idioms. Third, it should reinforce the ability to investigate the contexts in which unfamiliar words and phrases appear for clues to unlocking their meanings. The following strategy will help you accomplish all three.

Idiom Four Square

This adaptation of Four Square (Johns & Berglund 2002; Lenski, Wham, & Johns, 2003) builds students' ability to identify, define, and use idioms by having them create visual representations of the literal and intended meanings of idioms.

1. Draw a square with four quadrants on the board or on chart paper. Label the quadrants from left to right, top to bottom: "Idiom," "In Other Words," "What It Says," and "What It Means." (See Figure 5.2.)

Idiom Four Square

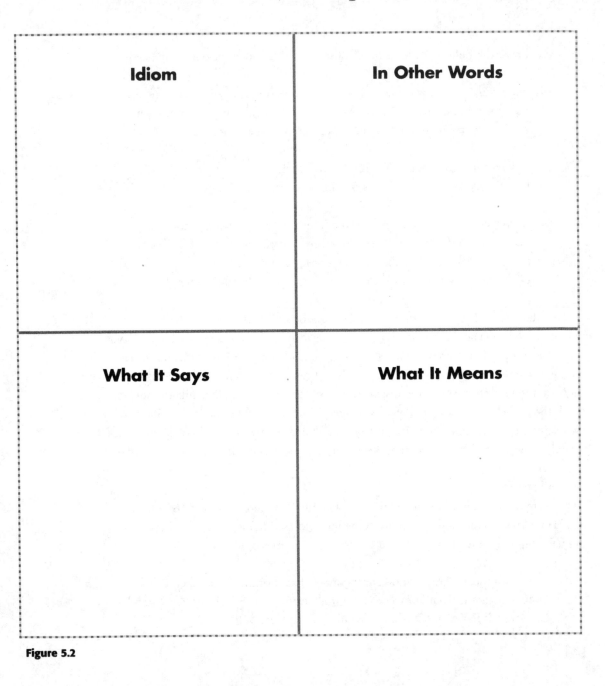

Idiom	In Other Words
What It Says	**What It Means**

Figure 5.2

2. Model the strategy using an idiom selected from a text or conversation. For this lesson, we will use an idiom from an excerpt from *Junie B. Jones and a Little Monkey Business* (Park, 1993), in which Junie B.'s misunderstanding of an idiomatic expression creates trouble and humor.

3. Set up the excerpt containing the idiom by explaining the situation to students. *Junie B.'s mother is in the hospital where she has just had a baby. Junie B. is staying with her grandpa, when her grandma Mille comes home to tell them about the new baby.* Then read the excerpt aloud:

> And she said that Mother had a baby!
>
> And it was the boy kind!
>
> Then me and her and my grandpa all did a big giant hug!
>
> And Grandma Mille picked me up. And she swinged me in the air.
>
> "You're just going to love him, Junie B.!" she said. "Your new brother is the cutest little monkey I've ever seen!"

4. Write "cutest little monkey" in the "Idiom" quadrant. Then ask students to share their ideas about the idiom's meaning. Be certain that students remember that Junie B.'s grandmother is speaking about Junie B.'s new baby brother. Making inferences of any kind, but especially about idioms, requires readers to use the clues presented in the text.

5. When all the students have had a chance to share their ideas, move to the "In Other Words" quadrant and write what the idiom means. For this example, you might write, "The newborn was so tiny and cute that Grandma compared him to a monkey." Students who have had experiences with newborns may be able to expound on this comparison by noting that newborns are curled, have long fingers, and often have dark hair, all traits of a little monkey.

6. In the "What It Says" quadrant, draw a picture of the idiom's literal meaning. For the Junie B. example, you would draw a picture of a little monkey.

7. Move to the "What It Means" quadrant. Ask students what picture you should draw to represent the idiom's intended meaning. Here you would draw a picture of a newborn baby. Sharing the rest of the story will help students become aware of how idioms can lead to misunderstandings.

8. Use Idiom Four Square several times with the whole class until students become familiar with it. Then share the reproducible master with students. As they gain familiarity with the strategy, guide students to complete Idiom Four Square in pairs or individually whenever students bring to class idioms they've encountered in reading or listening.

Classroom Tips

Edye Kaplan-Schwarz, an ELL specialist at North Shore School District in Highland Park, Illinois, and Donna Kaatz who teaches students with learning disabilities in Niles Township District in Morton Grove, Illinois, have successfully faced the challenge of teaching idioms to their students. They offer the following suggestions on using Idiom Four Square:

♦ Explain Idiom Four Square thoroughly and provide multiple examples of visual representations for selected idioms. These experienced teachers reiterate what Stahl (1986) and Nagy (1988) report about effective vocabulary instruction. Students need to understand both what the idiom means and how it is used. Extended explanations satisfy both requirements.

♦ Ask ELL students to share common idioms from their native languages. These can be translated into English, explained, and drawn using Idiom Four Square. Such sharing encourages greater understanding and acceptance of other cultures and provides opportunity for language enrichment. We suggest that you do this only occasionally, though, because they are often very difficult to translate.

♦ Devote extra time to the drawings when working with students with learning disabilities. Pictures often help make the abstract more concrete and easier to remember.

♦ Designate a portion of your word wall for displaying Idiom Four Square examples or collect several examples from your students and compile them in a class book. Students will take pride in seeing their work made public, and reviewing it will reinforce their knowledge of idioms.

Resources for Idiom Instruction

The King Who Rained by F. Gwynne. (Simon & Schuster).

There's a Frog in My Throat: 440 Animal Sayings a Little Bird Told Me by L. Leedy and P. Street. (Holiday House).

Junie B. Jones and a Little Monkey Business by B. Park. (Random House).

Amelia Bedelia by P. Parrish. (HarperCollins).

Scholastic Dictionary of Idioms: More Than 600 Phrases, Sayings, & Expressions by M. Terban. (Scholastic Reference).

Punching the Clock: Funny Action Idioms by M. Terban. (Clarion Books).

Check for other titles by these authors and search the word "idioms" online.

Figurative Language

Figurative language comprises many different kinds of expressive language, including commonly recognizable figures of speech and the common literary techniques of metaphor and alliteration. Writers use figurative language for many reasons: to make the abstract concrete, to evoke sensory impressions, to create a particular effect, and to add passion, power, and punch to their language. Students often encounter figurative language in their reading. Here, we will concentrate on two common forms of figurative language: simile and metaphor. A simile compares people, places, things, or ideas using the comparison words *like* or *as*; a metaphor compares two people, places, things, or ideas without using comparison words.

Introducing Figurative Language

Cognitive linguistics tells us that figurative language does not belong solely to the poets but is both fundamental and pervasive in everyday language (Ponterotto, 1994). As such, your students have most likely encountered and even used similes and metaphors. We begin with an introductory lesson.

1. Ask students to describe a recent event or situation that had exceptional qualities. For this example, we will use a heavy snowfall. High temperatures, heavy rainfall, or extended periods of drought may be more appropriate for your region of the country. You might say, "Last week we had our first heavy snowfall and school was canceled because seven inches fell during the night. By morning, the roads were closed by the drifting snow."

2. Ask students to construct a list of descriptive words that apply to the event and record the words on the board or on chart paper. For a heavy snowfall, students may come up with *wet, heavy, cold, white, drifting, exciting, dangerous, slippery, fun to play in.*

3. Using the words on the list, create a simile by comparing snow to something that is not usually associated with snow. Give students a few examples to get them started.

The snow was as wet as the baby's soaked diaper.

The snow was heavy, like the winter blanket on my bed.

Encourage students to have fun creating similes with the words on the list.

4. Select one or two comparisons and tell students that they are called similes. Define *simile* as an expression that describes a person, place, thing, or idea by comparing it to something else, using *like* or *as*. Help students remember the meaning of the word *simile* by pointing out that its spelling is similar to the word *similar*, but be certain students understand that truly effective similes make a connection between two things that are *not* obviously similar.

It is worth noting that many similes have become common in our everyday language, such as "hungry as a bear," "slow as molasses," "quiet as a mouse," "working like a horse," and "as easy as pie." Explain to students that these similes have lost their effectiveness through overuse. From there, introduce students to the term *cliché*. It is also worth noting that whole classes of similes exist, among them those that compare life to sports, especially baseball ("he's batting a thousand," "making the big leagues"); love to war or madness ("battle of the sexes," "insanely jealous"); good to up ("high as a kite," "things are looking up"); bad to down ("down in the dumps," "took a downturn"); and life to a gambling game ("play the cards you're dealt," "don't bet on it"). These classes of comparisons have generated many common similes and metaphors (Ponterotto, 1994).

5. Once students have a basic understanding of simile, introduce them to metaphor. Explain that a metaphor is like a simile but that it doesn't use *like* or *as*. Write pairs of examples like the following, and underline the similes and metaphors:

> The snow was like a wet diaper. The snow was a wet diaper.
>
> The snow was <u>as heavy as</u> a winter blanket. A <u>heavy blanket of snow</u> covered the ground.

6. Have students change the similes they created earlier into metaphors. Or allow them to write a few of their own.

7. Post the new terms *simile* and *metaphor* along with several examples of each in a prominent location on the word wall.

Once you have introduced students to similes and metaphors, you may wish to extend instruction in figurative language to improve reading comprehension. Since metaphor and simile are both forms of comparison, the task for the reader is to understand the relationship between the two unlike elements being compared. The following lesson helps students gain practice in understanding these two forms of figurative language.

Discover the Author's Connection

It is a good idea to teach students to make connections to the text they are reading. Making text-to-self, text-to-text, and text-to-world connections improves comprehension. In Discover the Author's Connection, a during-reading discussion strategy, we ask students to build upon the practice of making connections to interpret figurative language. In this strategy students will unpack the similes and metaphors they encounter in order to understand the connection the author made between the two elements being compared.

1. Select a short text that contains figurative language; poetry works well for this lesson. Predetermine places in the text where you can stop and question students in order to help them understand a simile or metaphor that's been used. For our explanation, we will use an excerpt from a poem by Mary O'Neill, from her book *Hailstones and Halibut Bones: Adventures in Color* (1989).

2. Introduce students to the author as someone who is trying to communicate ideas to readers through writing. To introduce Mary O'Neill you may say the following.

> Mary O'Neill always wanted to be a professional writer. When she was a girl growing up in Ohio, she wrote plays for her younger brothers and sisters. When she grew up, she wrote advertisements and short stories. For many years during her life, she wrote down her ideas and feelings about colors and kept them in her desk drawer. These were her private feelings. She never intended to share those ideas with others, but one day, her editor convinced Mary to use her ideas about color for a new book of poems. Mary hoped her readers would understand her feelings and ideas about colors when they read her poems.
>
> Poetry can be difficult to understand, especially when it contains similes and metaphors. We are going to learn a strategy that will help us work with the author's words to understand the ideas even when the text seems difficult or confusing. This strategy will help you read poetry, since similes and metaphors are more common in poetry than in your social studies textbook.

3. Begin with a complete reading of the selection. Then reread to the end of the first predetermined stop. We have chosen to focus on four lines from the poem "What Is Gold?" (p. 9).

> Gold is the sunshine
>
> Light and thin
>
> Warm as a muffin
>
> On your skin.

4. Ask students questions that will help them discover the connections the author has made in the similes and metaphors in the text chosen. Your discussion may go something like this:

Teacher: Are there any similes or metaphors in these lines?

Student 1:   There's the word *as*. That's the word in a simile, right?

Teacher: Yes, *like* and *as* are words used in similes. So what two things is the author comparing in the simile?

Student 2:   A muffin.

Teacher: And what else? You need two things to make a simile.

Student 3:   Warm.

Student 1:   What's warm?

Student 2:   The sunshine. Yeah, "sunshine light and thin warm as a muffin."

Teacher: Very good. So what two things is the author connecting in the simile?

Student 4:   The sunshine and a muffin.

Teacher: And what exactly about the sunshine is she comparing to a muffin?

Student 3:   That it's warm.

Teacher: Okay, so we have the warmth of the sun being compared to a muffin. What connection do you think Mary O'Neill is making between these two things?

(Students do not respond.)

Teacher: How do you feel about a warm muffin?

Student 1:   Good. I love them, especially with butter.

Student 2:   Yeah, but you can't eat the sun.

Teacher: Remember a simile compares two unlike persons, places, things, or events. It's the reader's task to discover the connection the author made between the two elements. How do you think Mary O'Neill feels about warm muffins?

Student 3:	I think she likes them.
Teacher:	And how do you think she feels about warm sunshine on her skin?
Student 3:	I think she likes it, too.
Teacher:	Why do you think that?
Student 2:	Because she says it's like a muffin, and we all like muffins.
Student 1:	Maybe she likes the feeling of the sunshine as much as she likes muffins.
Student 3:	Yeah, the feelings are the same. She likes them both.

5. Continue to read the text, stopping at other predetermined places to ask similar questions about similes and metaphors until the students are able to figure out successfully the author's connection.

6. As students practice with Discover the Author's Connection, have them create lists of questions to help them understand metaphors and similes, or you can prepare a class list of questions. Display the questions on chart paper or put them on bookmarks for students to use whenever they encounter figurative language. A list should include the following fundamental questions:

What is the simile or metaphor in this writing?

What two things is the author comparing in this simile or metaphor?

What connection does the author make between these two things?

How does the author's connection help me to understand this text?

How does the author's connection enhance the reading experience?

Classroom Tips

Glenda Peck, a former art teacher and now a fourth-grade teacher at Alice Gustafson Elementary School in Batavia, Illinois, welcomes the opportunity to introduce her students to figurative language and always enjoys reading their attempts at it in their own writing. She offers the following suggestions.

♦   Begin with simple metaphors or similes that can be easily understood by your students. They must have adequate background knowledge of both elements in the comparison to be able to understand the author's connection. Mrs. Peck uses the color poems of Mary O'Neill (1989) because of their accessibility.

♦   Model Discover the Author's Connection several times before asking students to work independently. Mrs. Peck finds that her students have become comfortable making their own connections to text but are challenged when asked to interpret the author's connection. Some students may require additional support for this strategy during guided reading; others may benefit from collaborative peer groups.

♦   Encourage students to create visual representations of the figurative language they encounter in prose or poetry. Drawing images inspired by the author's words strengthens their ability to visualize, helps them comprehend figurative language, and transforms abstract ideas into concrete ones.

♦   Allow students to create and illustrate their own color poems. To reinforce the strategy, have students share their own simile and metaphor connections with peer readers.

♦   To further students' ability to understand and appreciate simile and metaphor, find a book rich in figurative language that can be used as a class Read Aloud or that can be adopted for novel study. Mrs. Peck uses Michael Dorris's *Morning Girl* (1999), a richly descriptive novel that tells the story of a family of native people in the time before Columbus discovers their island home. The book fits well with her social studies curriculum while reinforcing her comprehension instruction.

Resources for Figurative Language Instruction

Dictionary of Colorful Phrases by G. Carothers and J. Lacey. (Sterling).

Morning Girl by M. Dorris. (Hyperion).

Using Picture Storybooks to Teach Literary Devices by S. Hall. (Oryx Press).

Hailstones and Halibut Bones: Adventures in Color by M. O'Neill. (Doubleday Books).

It Figures!: Fun Figures of Speech by M. Terban. (Clarion Books).

Check for other titles by these authors and search the phrase "figurative language" online.

You Try It

During any teacher-directed reading activity, whether with the whole class or a small group, you can take advantage of the teachable moment when students encounter homophones, idioms, or figurative language. Such mini-lessons do not necessarily have to interrupt the activity. When a homophone is encountered, for example, call attention to it and note its spelling and usage. Ask students to come up with the spelling and usage of its counterpart. Students who continue to be confused by homophones in their own writing can create a personal homophone dictionary in which they record their own mnemonics that they can use to associate each word in the pair with its meaning. They can also use it to record new homophone pairs they identify during Homophone Win, Lose, or Draw and other class activities. By using these dictionaries while writing, students should eventually be able to overcome the improper use of common homophones.

After students have gained an increased awareness of idioms and figurative language through explicit instruction and practice, continue to monitor the texts students are reading for examples of both language forms. As students become more adept at using context to define idioms and using Discover the Author's Connection to interpret figurative language, gradually remove support for more competent readers while maintaining it for those who are still struggling. However, when students encounter unusual idioms or more sophisticated figurative language, reteaching and guided practice with the strategies may be necessary, especially for ELLs and struggling readers.

Summary

In keeping with the research-supported learning principles described in Chapter 1, as well as with the instructional suggestions of Blachowicz and Fisher (2000), all vocabulary lessons should be generative and should increase the potential for independent word learning. The introductory lessons and strategies described in this chapter are designed with these goals in mind.

Furthermore, we believe these lessons and strategies have great potential for increasing word consciousness, an essential element in sustained vocabulary growth and reading development. Also, homophones, idioms, and figurative language are often components in wordplay such as puns. Studying them can contribute humor to the classroom while increasing attention to and awareness of words. Readers who are more aware of the language they encounter in oral and written forms are more likely to excel at learning new words. Since increased vocabulary knowledge correlates with reading development and positive attitudes toward reading, any instruction that fosters such growth and allows students to share in the richness of the English language is of great value.

Discussion Questions and Teaching Activities

1. Homophones, idioms, and figurative language are often difficult for students to learn. Do you believe this is true? If so, why? Which strategies presented by the authors will help to make your instructional efforts more effective?

2. Introduce and practice the Discover the Author's Connection strategy. Then give students a trade book that is unfamiliar to them and ask them to interpret independently the figurative language used by the author.

CHAPTER SIX

Effective Vocabulary Instruction
for Struggling Readers

Diane Lapp, James Flood, and **Sharon Flood,**
all of San Diego State University

"What makes reading difficult for you?" fifth-grade teacher Ms. Jackson asks Anthony, who very quickly responds, "The *words*." When she presses him to explain what makes reading easier for some people than others, he says, "They know the words and can read fast." While reading involves more than just knowing words, there is a solid research base that supports the insights of this young struggling reader. A strong vocabulary promotes, and is a predictor of, reading fluency, comprehension, and achievement (NRP, 2000). The opposite is also true; readers who experience problems with fluency and comprehension often have a weak vocabulary (Anderson & Henne, 1993; Baumann, Kame'enui, & Ash, 2003; Beck et al.,1982; Beck et al., 2002; Daneman, 1991; Davis, 1943, 1968; Graves, 1986; Nagy and Anderson, 1984; NRP, 2000). Additionally, the struggling reader often exhibits a superficial knowledge of words but not an understanding of their multiple meanings (Shand, 1993).

Third-grade teacher Mary Daniels guides students through the Example/Non-Example strategy. Yesterday, she used this strategy to teach the meaning of *opportunity*. The chart she created is posted on the blackboard.

Researchers have also noted a disturbing catch-22: The fewer words one knows, the more difficulty one has with the task of reading. The more difficult the task, the less often it is performed. The cycle never ends—the less one reads, the fewer vocabulary words one learns (Nagy, 1988; Nagy & Anderson, 1984; Maria, 1990). As a result, less able readers lack the proficiency to engage in free-time reading to make significant vocabulary gains (Beck et al., 2002).

Providing effective vocabulary instruction for struggling readers is the focus for this chapter. The first part identifies the characteristics of the reader who is struggling toward success. We also address issues related to when and how vocabulary should be learned, and how a lack of vocabulary knowledge affects every student's, but especially the struggling reader's, potential for language, reading, writing, and learning success. The second part of the chapter identifies three instructional strategies that support vocabulary and literacy learning for struggling readers.

We define a struggling reader as a student who lacks the skills to comprehend grade-level texts. While there may be a combination of physical, psychological, neuro-logical, socioeconomic, linguistic, cultural, and educational factors that interfere with a student's reading progress, we emphasize educational and instructional issues in our discussion of vocabulary knowledge and its impact on reading comprehension. Students cannot achieve success as readers if teachers merely identify a poorly developed skill and then give opportunities for practicing it outside the context of exciting books and oral language experiences (Palinscar & Klenk, 1992). Therefore, in this chapter, we support teachers as they attempt to make vocabulary learning a part of everything that is occurring in the classroom rather than relegating it to an isolated time of the day.

What Factors Significantly Affect Vocabulary Learning?

Beck, McKeown, and McCaslin (1983) noted that a large and rich vocabulary is characteristic of a well-educated individual. Most of us would agree, but we are often perplexed about how to get every student to this point. So, on a one-to-ten scale, with ten being the most effective, how do you rate your knowledge about how you teach vocabulary to readers who are struggling toward success? The fact that you are reading this chapter suggests that you probably have a good base of understanding; probably also you realize that students' vocabulary knowledge is strongly related to their school achievement and reading performance.

Along with the quality of the instruction they receive, students' socioeconomic status (SES) plays an important role in their vocabulary development (Beck et al., 2002; Duke, 2000; Smith, 1941). Students from higher SES backgrounds across the grade levels may know from two to four times as many words as those from low SES backgrounds (Corson, 1989; Smith 1941; White, Graves, & Slater, 1990). This may be attributed to both schooling and the language environment at home.

From infancy, we begin building concepts about the world through our ever-expanding experiences, such as going to the beach, the zoo, traveling, living on a farm, living in a city, attending preschool, engaging in reading and writing activities at home, visiting the library for school-related activities or pleasure. Whatever our experiences, they contribute to our knowledge about the world. Engaging in everyday conversations, reading, and being read to help students in grades 3–7 significantly increase their vocabularies (Jenkins & Dixon, 1983; Nagy, Anderson, & Hermann, 1987). The participants in conversations about books (parents and other adults in the community) and the books that children are listening to and reading certainly influence the types of language being shared, modeled, and learned.

As our knowledge of the world grows, so do the number of concepts that we understand and the language that represents these concepts. This knowledge provides the basis for understanding words we encounter when reading. A great deal of vocabulary is learned from wide reading and talking about what is read (Nagy, 1988; Nagy and Anderson, 1984) or from what is called a natural-acquisition-of-words approach. Children who are involved in that approach and receive explicit vocabulary instruction at school experience an additional 6 to 30 percent increase in vocabulary (NRP, 2000; Stahl & Fairbanks, 1986).

Differences in reading proficiencies expand as students move beyond the primary grades and as the text-based vocabulary they encounter becomes more technical, more abstract, and harder to comprehend (Chall, Jacobs, & Baldwin, 1990). Most of the words that appear in primary-grade books are usually part of children's speaking and listening vocabularies. This, however, changes significantly as children are required to do more content-area reading from texts that contain difficult-to-read words that are not a part of their oral vocabularies.

As educators, we have little ability to alter a student's SES, but we do have the potential to ensure that every student is engaged in instruction that advances his or her knowledge. This instruction must be precise if we are to close the gap between students' vocabularies. We must make it a priority to give vocabulary instruction that embraces both wide reading and direct explanation of the meanings of words through thought-provoking, interactive, engaging lessons. The strategies offered in this chapter help you to provide effective vocabulary instruction for struggling readers.

What Does It Mean to Know a Word?

The first question that we need to ask is, What does it really mean to know the meaning of a word? Dale, O'Rourke, and Bamman (1971) cautioned that words are neither known nor unknown, but that instead there are degrees of knowing a word. They identify four stages:

1. having never seen or heard the word;

2. having heard the word, but not knowing what it means;

3. recognizing the word in context; and

4. knowing and using the word.

Beck and her colleagues make an important distinction between shallow and deeper word knowledge. Shallow word knowledge refers to memorizing definitions of words without a deeper understanding of the concepts they represent. Students with deep word knowledge understand these concepts and can use words flexibly in a variety of contexts (2002). They also understand the connections between new and known uses of the information (Stahl & Fairbanks, 1986). They can acquire this depth of understanding if they are actively engaged in the repeated, gradual learning of vocabulary (Baumann et al, 2003; Blachowicz & P. Fisher, 2000). Truly knowing the word *product* means that, in addition to understanding that it is "the result of" or a "number resulting from multiplication," or "something that has been produced," you can easily use it in speaking, reading, and writing. This expanded or deeper understanding of a word is the product of real-word life experiences, classroom instruction, reading, and conversation.

According to Nagy and Anderson (1984), as students in grades 3–9 read, they encounter approximately 88,500 different word families (groups of words consisting of a root with all of its compounds and derivatives—for example, *vest, invest, investments, divest, divestiture*). However, not all of these word families have high utility for readers. In fact, Nagy and Anderson estimate that approximately half of these families are used so rarely that a reader may encounter them only once in a lifetime. Given the variety of word families used in classrooms and the number of them used in instructional materials, it's not surprising that many teachers wonder which words to choose for explicit instruction.

The good news is that vocabulary scholars have studied this issue for decades (Dale et al., 1971; Stahl & Fairbanks, 1986; Graves, 1986; Beck et al., 2002) and have come up with some excellent guidelines for helping teachers choose word families, guidelines that we share in this chapter.

What Is Meaningful Vocabulary Instruction?

Meaningful vocabulary instruction is complex because it involves teaching students specific word meanings and also word-learning techniques that will help them become independent learners. Becoming an independent learner is a must, since words are merely labels for concepts, and each concept is more than the simple word definition. One hundred or 1,000 words may be required to describe a concept (Beck et al., 2002). Therefore, successful vocabulary instruction ensures that children are able to continually expand their language on their own. Here are some ways to do that.

Selecting the Words

One of the questions we are most frequently asked by teachers is, "How do I select words to use for instruction?" The words you should teach and the sequence in which you should introduce them depend on the texts you expect students to read. Why? Because the more words students understand, the stronger their overall comprehension of the text will be (Nagy & Scott, 2004). To help you pinpoint the appropriate words, let's look at the work of Dale and his colleagues (1971), Graves (2000), and Beck and her colleagues (2002). They suggest that teachers concentrate their instruction on "almost-known" words in stages 2 and 3 to help students move them into stage 4, knowing and using the word. Graves advises making a distinction between teaching new concepts and teaching new labels for familiar concepts. To do so, he offers the following categories as a manageable way to sort words:

- high-frequency words (*although*, *usually*)

- domain-specific technical vocabulary (*equation*)

- low-frequency words (*metacognitive*)

- high-utility words (*gasoline*)

As stated in Chapter 1, the important words to teach are the ones that are critical to comprehending the text. Realizing that you can successfully teach approximately eight to ten words a week (Scott, Jamieson-Noel, & Asselin, 2003), you'll want to give priority to those words that students are likely to encounter frequently and in many contexts. If the word has both high utility and will be encountered often, it should be taught.

Beck and her colleagues (2002) suggest that it's useful to consider the three different tiers of words found in a mature, literate individual's vocabulary. The first tier consists of basic words such as *school, hot, red, mother, cat,* and *hospital.* These words are in the spoken vocabularies of most students but may not be in their reading vocabulary when they first enter school. Most educators would agree that little, if any, time needs to be spent teaching the meanings of these words. However, in order to become fluent readers, students need to possess these words in their sight-word repertoire.

The second tier consists of high-utility words such as *convenient, general, moral,* and *compromise.* Students may encounter these words in a variety of contexts, so you will want to provide explicit instruction in their meaning and usage (Beck, McKeown, & Omanson, 1987; Brassell & Flood, 2004; Flood, Lapp, & S. Flood, 2005; Lapp, Flood, Brock, & Fisher, in press).

The third vocabulary tier consists of words that tend to be used in specific domains, such as *hemp, fibula, nucleotides,* and *marsupial.* These words are best taught when they are necessary for passage comprehension, as in discussing *fibula* in a lesson on the skeletal system. On the other hand, a specialized word such as *mauve* may be mentioned incidentally in a story as part of the snapshot describing the many colors observed in a restaurant's decor. If the meaning of the word is not critical to understanding the passage, you do not need to provide direct instruction.

Figure 6.1 illustrates the basic (Tier 1), high-utility (Tier 2), and technical (Tier 3) words that may be found in a unit on volcanoes. Examples for teaching the high-utility (Tier 2) words are provided because these are the "almost-known" words that, with instruction, children will know and use. We also explain how we decided which words are Tier 2 and which are Tier 3 words. We also draw on the work of Graves, Juel, and Graves (1998), who suggest that words can be taught by

♦ learning a new meaning for a known word,

♦ learning the meaning of a new word representing a known concept,

♦ learning the meaning of a new word representing an unknown concept, and

♦ clarifying and enriching the meaning of a known word.

Basic Words (Tier 1 Words)	High-Utility Words (Tier 2 Words)	Technical Words (Tier 3 Words)
forget	geologist	tectonic plates
smoke	pressure	magma
fall	expand	mantle
lost	erupt	lava
soda bottle	prediction	

Figure 6.1: Topic of study: Why Mount St. Helens Blew Its Top

You may be asking yourself how we decided which were the Tier 2 (high-utility) words in this unit of study. It's a crucial question as we make decisions about which words should be taught from a unit of study. The answer is easy. First, preview the text and select all of the words that are important (critical to understanding the text), useful (words that will appear in many other contexts), and difficult (unknown to the students). Although many published programs include lists of vocabulary that have been identified as Tier 2 words, think about your students to determine the degree to which these words are known by them. To do this, you may want to use the criteria recommended by Graves, Slater, and White (1996) who suggest two critical steps in selecting Tier 2 words:

1. Determine whether the word is important by asking these questions:

♦ Is an understanding of the word necessary for students to comprehend the passage in which it is found?

♦ Can students determine the meaning of the word themselves through structural and/or contextual clues?

♦ Can learning the word help reinforce a skill that students will need later? (For example, understanding the word *unicycle* would help students who had not mastered the prefix *uni-*.)

- Is this word useful? (That is, is it a Tier 2 word that the students will likely encounter often?) It's important to clarify the word's usefulness and importance. To do so, consider the frequency of its use. One method is to use the two-year test. Ask yourself, How much will students need the word in the next few years? And in what ways do they need to know the word? If they won't need this word in the next few years, then postpone it.

If the answers to the first two questions are yes and no respectively, then it is probably not necessary to spend time teaching context-clue strategies as described in Chapters 1 and 2. However, if you answer yes to the last two questions, then consider using the effective strategies described later in the chapter to make the word a part of the students' productive vocabulary. Answering these questions will help you determine whether the word should be a part of their expressive (speaking and writing) or receptive (reading and listening) vocabularies. Remember, when selecting which words to teach, consider the importance and usefulness of each word.

2. Determine the degree to which the words are unknown by the students. This can be accomplished by

- asking students which words they know in a selection of words appearing in a text about to be studied;

- giving pretests to determine which words in a selection the students do not know;

- assessing students' knowledge and performance through informal classroom discussions, writing, and productions;

- using *The Living Word Vocabulary* (Dale & O'Rourke, 1986). This book reports the frequency of occurrence of approximately 30,000 words. It presents the words, their meaning, and the grade level at which at least two-thirds of the students knew the word. With this information, you can make general predictions about which words your students will be likely to know or not know. Also the *American Heritage Word Frequency Book* (Carroll, Davies, & Richman, 1971) lists the frequency of approximately 86,000 words found in materials for school-age children. Once you have decided which words to teach, you can decide how and when to teach them.

Teaching Tier 2 Words

After identifying key words to teach, you need to develop instruction that engages and motivates students. That will enable them to develop a deep understanding of and a genuine ability to use the targeted vocabulary. For example, for the Mount St. Helens unit, we identified the Tier 2 words *geologist, pressure, expand, erupt,* and *prediction.* To provide a context for learning these five words, we have identified three instructional strategies that empower students as independent, self-regulating word learners. While this is important for every student, struggling readers need to be engaged by nonthreatening strategies that support their independence, awareness, and joy for language. These three strategies provide this opportunity.

The strategies of Text Impressions, Contextual Redefiniton, and Example and Non-Example help the teacher give explicit instruction that scaffolds each student's growth toward success and independence. They provide the structure to immerse students in engaging learning and the various types of support and practice they need over time to gain a deep understanding of Tier 2 words. As their knowledge base grows, all readers (especially struggling readers) become strategic readers with word knowledge they need to comprehend what they are reading. They also learn how to acquire the meaning of unfamiliar words. These students gain knowledge, self-confidence, and the motivation to function independently as readers.

Text Impressions

Text Impressions, also sometimes called Story Impressions (McGinley & Denner, 1987) or Semantic Impressions (Richek, 2005), invites students to review a list of words, compose a paragraph using these words, and engage in discussion on a topic they are about to study. Here's how it works:

Prepare to Teach
1. Select 10 to 20 words and phrases from a targeted text that are essential to understanding the key elements of the topic, using the criteria developed earlier.

2. List the words and phrases vertically with arrows indicating the sequence in which they appear in the text. A selected phrase should not contain more than three content words. An example of words taken from the text about Mount St. Helens may look like the list shown in Figure 6.2.

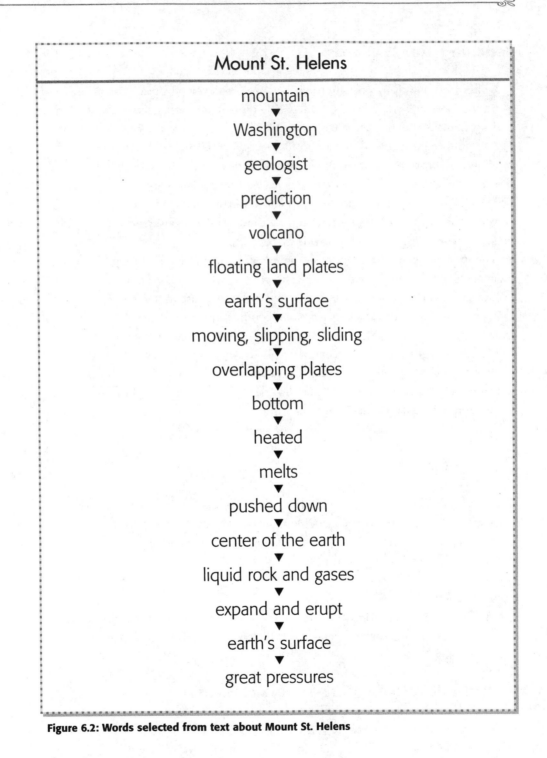

Mount St. Helens

mountain
▼
Washington
▼
geologist
▼
prediction
▼
volcano
▼
floating land plates
▼
earth's surface
▼
moving, slipping, sliding
▼
overlapping plates
▼
bottom
▼
heated
▼
melts
▼
pushed down
▼
center of the earth
▼
liquid rock and gases
▼
expand and erupt
▼
earth's surface
▼
great pressures

Figure 6.2: Words selected from text about Mount St. Helens

Teach

3. Read through the words and phrases with students and explain that they will be using them to write their impressions of the text they are about to read. Have them pronounce each word and phrase, and engage them in an exploratory conversation about it. (Is it a descriptive word or phrase? Is it a noun—the name of a person, place, or thing? A verb—an action word? Does it give you a clue as to what the text might be about?) This is a good opportunity to invite partner talk as a way to allow students time to really think about the words before sharing them as a whole class. In the study of Mount St. Helens we have identified Tier 2 words as *geologist, pressure, expand, erupt,* and *prediction.*

4. Invite students to make general predictions about the topic by using these words. Once they've done this as a class, let them work together as partners or in small groups to write a collaborative paragraph connecting the words and phrases. If you are teaching young children, you may need to conduct this entire activity with the whole class, with you as the scribe.

5. Once paragraphs have been written, invite students to share them and explain the thinking behind them. We find that the first time we introduce Text Impressions, students understand it better if we model the process on a familiar topic (for example, behavior of cats or dogs, making a sandwich).

6. Ask students to read the text and add a sticky note to each page where a Tier 2 word appears. When they've finished reading, they should revisit their paragraphs to summarize and make revisions based on the new information. They may also wish to add illustrations.

7. Engage students in a final conversation about their writings, newly learned information, the definitions of the Tier 2 words, oral language and writing development, internalized vocabulary learning, and comprehension of nonnarrative text. For example, you may ask questions like "How did using Tier 2 words increase the quality of your writing?" and "How many edits involved Tier 2 words?"

Because of the contextual presentation of words shared though Text Impressions, students' individual needs are met as they learn a new meaning for a known word, learn the meaning of a new word representing a known concept, learn the meaning of a new word representing an unknown concept, and clarify and enrich the meaning of a known word (Graves et al., 1998).

Contextual Redefinition

Contextual Redefinition (Bean, 1981; Brassell & Flood, 2004; J. W. Cunningham et al., 1981; Readence et al., 1998; Tierney, Readence, & Dishner, 1995) is an instructional strategy that can be used to help children (1) understand the importance of using context and structural analysis to determine the meaning of unfamiliar words; (2) use the context to make educated guesses about the meanings of unfamiliar words; (3) engage in the discovery of new words; and (4) converse about the ways in which they derive the meaning of a word. (For more on Contextual Redefinition, see page 64.) Here's how it works:

Prepare to Teach

1. Select Tier 2 words from an appropriate grade-level text passage.

2. Find a sentence from the text for each word (or create your own) and write it on the board, an overhead transparency, or sentence strip. These sentences should contain enough context clues to enable students to figure out the words' meanings. For example, if the target word is *geologist*, you may write "A scientist who studies volcanoes."

Teach

3. Using a chart like the one in Figure 6.3, share the selected words with the students and ask them to say each word, identify how well they know the word, predict a meaning, and explain their prediction. They can work with a partner or as a whole class. We have found that by turning to a partner and discussing what they are learning, students engage later in richer conversations with the whole class. Encourage them to use dictionaries if they need definition clues.

WORDS	0=Don't know 1=Have heard 2=Know & use	Predicted Meaning Before Reading	Meaning After Reading	Context Clues
geologist	0	a scientist		
expand				
pressure				
erupt				
prediction				

(Brassell & Flood, 2004, p. 17) Reprinted with the permission of Academic Professional Development.
Figure 6.3: A Contextual Redefinition chart

4. Using the prepared sentences, ask students to look at each word in its appropriate context and compare it with its definition. Invite them to make revisions if necessary. Also, encourage them to use a dictionary, so they gain familiarity using it and begin to think of it as a resource. Ask them which clues in the sentence helped them to figure out the meaning.

WORDS	0=Don't know 1=Have heard 2=Know & use	Predicted Meaning Before Reading	Meaning After Reading	Context Clues
geologist	0	a scientist	a scientist who studies volcanoes	Because of their study of land formations, geologists can predict when a volcano eruption might occur.
expand				
pressure				
erupt				
prediction				

(Brassell & Flood, 2004, p.17) Reprinted with the permission of Academic Professional Development.

Figure 6.4: A Contextual Redefinition chart with added sentences

5. Apply sticky notes to the pages where the words appear. Read the targeted text as students follow along. When they have finished reading and discussing the text, revisit the new words and use the context to complete the chart shown in Figure 6.3. Invite students to revise or confirm their predictions and to explain how they used the context clues to figure out the words. Ask them which clues finally gave them the meaning. (See Figure 6.4.)

When children are taught to use contextual information to define Tier 2 words, they engage in powerful, in-depth learning—sharing ideas about possible definitions and then using clues from their reading to verify or redefine the selected words. Struggling readers become less fearful of print as they "realize that it is okay to take a stab at unfamiliar words and figure out an approximate meaning from the context" (Calkins, 2001, p.168). By encouraging students to try to figure out the meaning of a word from its context, you teach them to self-regulate their reading. It's important, though, to warn students that there may not be enough clues given to enable the reader to get a full definition of the word. Tell students that when this happens they should decide whether they understand the sentence or passage well enough to keep reading without totally understanding the word. If the answer is yes, they should put a sticky note on the page, continue reading, and return later with a dictionary to confirm or redefine their prediction of the word meaning.

When revisiting an unknown word, students should think about whether their understanding of the sentence became stronger once they understood the word. They should also be required to keep a vocabulary notebook in which to write these words, their definitions, and tips that help them to remember the meaning. They should return often to their notebooks for review and support when writing. Reading comprehension improves significantly when students have multiple exposures to a word in a variety of contexts (Stahl & Kapinus, 2001). Using the word in multiple ways enables the student to discern its meaning quickly and fluently when they come across the word in their reading.

Example and Non-Example

This strategy helps students analyze and practice essential characteristics of Tier 2 words while eliminating nonessential characteristics (Frayer, Frederick, & Klausmeier, 1969; Tierney, et al., 1995; Brassell & Flood, 2004). Here's how it works:

Prepare To Teach

1. Select five to eight Tier 2 words from the targeted text.

2. Write each word, a definition, and an example or situation on a separate index card for partner groups or on a transparency or chart for a larger group of students. Then write a related question or questions for students to answer.

> **Word:** pressure
>
> **Definition:** the force exerted by one thing against another
>
> **Example:** A pan of boiling water is on the stove. The lid on the pan is popping up and down. Is there pressure in the pan? Why or why not?

3. Write additional examples and non-examples of each word (and questions about these words) beneath the first example. These examples can be created by partners or by the whole group.

> **Word:** pressure
>
> **Definition:** the force exerted by one thing against another
>
> **Example:** A pan of boiling water is on the stove. The lid on the pan is popping up and down. Is there pressure in the pan? Why or why not?
>
> **Non-example:** A boy is pulling a wagon down the street. Is this an example of pressure?

Teach

4. Give students a blank vocabulary sheet similar to the one shown in Figure 6.5 and have them work with a partner or as a whole class to categorize the information shown on each card, transparency, or chart. They will be completing columns 1, 2, and 3 (definition, example, non-example) on their vocabulary sheet. Provide as much space as needed on the vocabulary sheet for the study of each targeted word. Display a target word (e.g., *geologist*) and its definition. Read it with students. Then present the examples and non-examples of the word: *Some scientists have studied the layers of rock in the Grand Canyon to see when they were formed. Are these scientists geologists? Why?*

Word: geologist

Definition:	Example:	Non-Example:	Text-Context:
A scientist who studies the structure of the earth's crust, its layers, and rock formations is a geologist.	Some scientists have studied the layers of rock in the Grand Canyon to see when they were formed.	Some scientists study plants that grow on the earth's surface.	Geologists who repeated surveys of Mount St. Helens during April and May showed that the bulge was growing northward at an average rate of about five feet per day.

Word: erupt

Definition:	Example:	Non-Example:	Text-Context:

Word: expand

Definition:	Example:	Non-Example:	Text-Context:

Figure 6.5: Vocabulary sheet of examples and non-examples of Tier 2 words

5. When all examples and non-examples have been completed, encourage a class discussion of what information prompted their decisions. At the end of the discussion, compare the students' charts with your own.

6. Read the targeted text together and use sticky notes to mark the Tier 2 terms.

7. After discussing the text, revisit the examples and non-examples to clear up any confusion. Also use the text to complete the Text-Context column of the chart in Figure 6.5. Model for students how they can use a dictionary and a thesaurus to extend their knowledge of the word and its definition in other contexts. Teach them how to survey the context of the example for clues that offer a definition, synonym, or comparison (Searfoss & Readence, 1989). This empowers them to acquire word meanings when a teacher is not by their side.

8. Once they are comfortable with a word, have them work with their partner using the text context, dictionary, and thesaurus to write their own examples and non-examples. Students should write each word and its example in their writing notebook. These can be shared with the whole class as a game called Can We Stump You? We play this game by inviting partners to share their examples and then giving points to the other partner teams who correctly identify the examples and non-examples. The winning team or teams get to select a book they would like to hear as a Read Aloud.

As students discuss each word, its definition, and examples and non-examples, they begin to identify and practice using the significant features of each word. By the time they encounter the word in their later reading, it is familiar and does not impede their comprehension. By working with the word in context, students gain a deeper understanding of the subtleties of its definition. They learn how to use their expanding knowledge base, which grows from reading and talking about words, to acquire new words. This familiarity with words and with how to unlock the meaning of new ones grows stronger with time because the struggling reader is no longer intimidated by an unknown word. Struggling readers become empowered by their ability to master word meanings, an ability common to proficient readers (Lipson & Wixson, 2003). (See Chapter 7 for more information on Example and Non-Example.)

Summary

Researchers have demonstrated that vocabulary, or word knowledge, is linked inextricably to reading comprehension in many complex ways (Davis, 1943, 1968; Nagy, 1988; Singer, 1965). While the meanings of many words can be learned through reading, speaking, and listening, it is essential to provide struggling readers with effective, explicit vocabulary instruction. Text Impressions, Contextual Redefiniton, and Example and Non-Example are among many strategies that can be used to provide that instruction (P. M. Cunningham & Hall, 1994c; Brassell & Flood, 2004; Buis, 2005). As students assume independence for the next steps in a successful learning journey, teachers can conclude that their instruction has been effective.

Discussion Questions and Teaching Activities

1. Analyze the vocabulary lessons you have taught so far this year or in the past year. What percentage of the words that you taught were Tier 1 words as described by the authors? What percentage were Tier 2? Tier 3? What does this tell you about the words that you have taught?

2. The authors present three strategies—Text Impressions, Contextual Redefinition, and Example and Non-Example—that can be used with struggling readers and that support their independence in using language and build their awareness and joy of language. Teach one lesson on each of these strategies and determine which of them best served your instructional objective(s). Why did it? Which strategy did the students seem to enjoy most? Why?

CHAPTER SEVEN

Effective Vocabulary Instruction for English–Language Learners

Michael F. Graves, University of Minnesota, and
Jill Fitzgerald, the University of North Carolina at Chapel Hill

Mr. Marquez third-grade classroom is made up of eight African-American children, seven Anglo children, five Vietnamese children who are learning English, two Latino students who are learning English as a second language, and one Native American Indian child. One of the Vietnamese children, Tu Kien, can read in English at grade level. Kien Tu and Bigh Van can read in English at second-grade level. Tran and Lee, who recently arrived in the United States, can read on grade level in Vietnamese but are just beginning to learn to read in English. The Latino students were born in the United States and can read in English on grade level.

The students and Mr. Marquez are studying different cultures in social studies. At the moment, they are in the midst of an integrated unit on Vietnamese society. Mr. Marquez's main goals for today's lesson are for the students to learn about some Vietnamese celebrations and to appreciate their meanings. He has chosen a selection on paper blossoms from the text *Vietnam: A Portrait of the Country Through Its Festivals and*

Students in Juan Marquez's class are learning the meanings of the prefixes *un-, re-, in-/im-/ir-/il-,* and *non-* which make up 62 percent of the prefixed words in the students' core reading program.

Traditions (Grolier Educational, 2002). Mr. Marquez has decided to do a guided reading with the students. The text could be easily read by students who can read on the third- or fourth-grade level in English. One main idea in the selection is that during the Tet festival, spring blossoms fill the streets and houses because the people believe that flowers welcome good spirits. One of Mr. Marquez's vocabulary goals is for the students to know concepts for the words *blossom* and *tissue*—at least the ones exemplified in the context of the Tet festival—as well as the English-language labels for the concepts. Most of the students probably know at least some aspects of the concepts, but they may not grasp the finer distinction of *blossom* as a verb, "to blossom," that is, "to unfold in a gracious, lovely, beautiful, way." Similarly, the meaning of *tissue* as "thinly layered matter," such as the tissue in a blossom petal, will most likely be new for most of his students.

In the morning, while the rest of the class is in literature circle discussions, Mr. Marquez takes the five Vietnamese children aside and explains that later in the afternoon, he would like them to teach their classmates about the significance of blossoms in the Tet festival and show them how to make paper blossoms that they will display in the room. He gives a copy of the 30-page, richly illustrated book to the children and asks Tu Kien to read it to the others while they follow along. He asks Kien Tu and Bigh Van to explain in Vietnamese what they learn to Tran and Lee and emphasizes that they should use the pictures as much as possible as they explain. When the students finish reading and explaining, he sits with them and writes the words *blossom* and *tissue* on a white board, noting that these are two important words that they will need when they teach the class later.

To help the students refine their understandings of the two words, Mr. Marquez uses a Paired Question technique. He shows the boys two questions at a time, one that can be answered yes and one that can be answered no. He begins with easy question pairs and moves to more difficult ones:

Mr. Marquez: Do flowers have a blossom?

Children: *(mainly Tu Kien, Kien Tu, and Bigh Van reply)*: Yes!

Mr. Marquez: Do dogs have a blossom?

Children: Noooo!

Mr. Marquez: Can a tissue tear?

Children: Yes.

Mr. Marquez: Can a tissue cry?

Children: No.

(Mr. Marquez asks harder questions.)

Mr. Marquez: Can a person blossom?

Children: No!

(Ms. Wright now explains the word's meaning when used as a verb.)

Mr. Marquez: Can a book blossom?

Children: No!

Mr. Marquez: Can a tissue be made of paper?

Children: Yes.

Mr. Marquez: Is there tissue in a blossom?

Children: No!

(Mr. Marquez explains the meaning of tissue as it relates to the word blossom.)

Finally, Mr. Marquez reviews the vocabulary-building strategy of using context to infer word meanings. He shows the students the sentences "The flower was beautiful. Its blossom was pink and white." Then, he gives the students pink, white, and green crayons and asks them to draw something to represent the sentences. Tu Kien translates for Tran and Lee. The students draw flowers that correctly represent the two sentences. Mr. Marquez then performs a Think Aloud as he reads and points to the two sentences and explains that if the students did not know the meaning of the word *blossom*, they could have figured it out by reading the rest of the two sentences: only one part of the flower is likely to be pink and white.

Four Components of a Comprehensive Vocabulary Program for English-Language Learners and Why They Are Important

Mr. Marquez engaged his English-language learners in four different types of vocabulary activities. When he asked Tu Kien to read aloud to the others and Kien Tu and Bigh Van to discuss the selection's meaning, he provided rich and varied language experiences similar to those described by Block and Mangieri in Chapter 1. When he used the Paired Question technique, he taught individual words. When he talked about using context to infer word meanings, he was reviewing a word-learning strategy. Finally, throughout the lesson, he was developing the students' word consciousness. These four types of activities—providing rich and varied language experiences, teaching individual words, teaching word-learning strategies, and fostering word consciousness—constitute what we believe is a comprehensive and powerful program of vocabulary instruction for native English speakers (M. F. Graves, in press) and English-language learners. We explore each of these activities in depth in this chapter.

The vocabulary-learning task is huge. The books and other reading materials used by schoolchildren include more than 180,000 different words. A typical child enters school with a very small reading vocabulary. Once she's in school, however, her vocabulary is likely to soar at a rate of three thousand to four thousand words a year, reaching twenty-five thousand words by eighth grade and about fifty thousand words by the end of high school (M. F. Graves, in press; Nagy & Hermann, 1987).

As such, a comprehensive and powerful vocabulary program is important for all students, particularly for English-language learners (American Educational Research Association [AERA], 2004; Nation, 2001; Schmitt, 2000) for a number of reasons:

- English-language learners face the same huge learning task that native speakers do, but because they begin learning English later in their lives, their vocabulary learning needs to be accelerated.

- Vocabulary knowledge is strongly linked to both oral and reading comprehension, for all students, including English-language learners (Fitzgerald & Graves, 2004; Shanahan, in press).

- Vocabulary is one of the most crucial correlates of school success (Hart & Risley, 2003).

- School texts that English-language learners must read include a good deal of sophisticated vocabulary (Graves & Slater, in press).

- The reading test performance of English-language learners is dependent upon wide-ranging vocabulary knowledge (García, 1991).

- Acquiring a deep understanding of word meanings can be especially difficult for English-language learners (Verhallen & Schoonen, 1993).

- In languages that, like Spanish, have large numbers of English cognates (words that are similar in appearance and meaning, such as *special* and *especial*), it is important for students to learn to recognize English cognates and thereby add to their English vocabulary (García, 1998), something that not all students do (García & Nagy, 1993).

Teaching Vocabulary to English-Language Learners

In this section, we describe and present examples of each component of the four-part program.

Providing Rich and Varied Language Experiences

By "language experiences" we mean listening, speaking, reading, and writing. In the preschool years, children need to listen and speak as much as possible. They need to engage in real discussions—give-and-take conversations in which home caregivers and, later, classroom teachers give them the opportunity to think about and discuss topics of interest in an open, positive, and supportive climate. Anything we can do to promote real discussions in school and out of it is worthwhile.

Reading to children is also worthwhile. As teachers, we should frequently read to children, model our enthusiasm for reading, and do everything we can to get parents and other caregivers involved in reading to, and with, their children. Children learn most of their vocabulary from reading (Sternberg, 1983). Therefore, if we substantially increase the amount of reading they do, we can markedly increase their vocabularies. Moreover, wide reading fosters automaticity, provides knowledge about different topics and literary forms, and puts students on the road to becoming lifelong readers.

Finally, as we now know but somehow did not know a few years ago, writing is a powerful ally and aid to reading. From the very beginning, students need to engage frequently in paired reading and writing activities, some of which focus on learning word meanings.

In addition to doing a lot of listening, speaking, reading, and writing, primary-grade students with relatively small vocabularies—including many English-language learners—will profit from "interactive oral reading." In interactive oral reading, both the student or students and the reading partner—usually an adult—transact with one another and the text while reading aloud. If children are going to learn new words, words that are not already in their listening vocabularies, they need oral language activities of this sort.

The following description of effective interactive oral reading draws heavily on the work of Jeanne De Temple and Catherine Snow (2003) as well as on our own synthesis of the literature. Effective interactive oral reading

1. **is just that: interactive.** That is, both the reader (usually the teacher) and the students play active roles. The reader (usually the teacher) frequently pauses, prompts children to respond, and follows up those responses with answers and perhaps more prompts. For instance, the reader might pause and say, "What do you think about that?" or "Why do you suppose that happened?" or "What do you think will happen next?" Students respond to the prompts or questions, elaborate on some of their responses, and perhaps ask questions of their own. For example, the children might say, "My Mom does not do that" or "He was a bad dog" or "Now he eats it." Additionally, the interactions are frequently supportive and instructive. In other words, the reader scaffolds students' efforts to understand the words and the text.

2. **usually involves multiple readings of the book.** This enables the students and the reader to revisit the topic and words several times, and it allows students to begin actively using some of the words they have heard and perhaps have had explained in previous readings.

3. **directly focuses children's attention on a relatively small number of words.** Programs often focus on 10 to 20 words a week. In some cases, the word work comes during the first reading, in some cases during subsequent readings, and in some cases after the book has been read.

4. **requires readers to read fluently, with appropriate intonation and expression.** Readers need to engage students with an animated and lively reading style. Such renditions provide students with additional clues to making meaning, intonation, and the natural rhythm, melody, and rhyme of the English language.

5. **requires carefully selected books.** The books need to be interesting and enjoyable for students and should stretch their thinking a bit. Of course, the books also need to include some challenging words that are worth study and have the potential to enhance students' vocabularies.

Teaching Individual Words

Different words present students with very different learning challenges, depending on factors such as how much students already know about the word, whether a student's native language contains a cognate of the word, whether a student's native language contains a word representing the same concept, how well you want students to learn the word, and whether learning the word requires students to learn a new and difficult concept (Graves, in press). Each of these word-learning challenges requires a different sort of instruction, which may sound daunting. But there are a variety of approaches that can and should be used. Here, we give an example of a very powerful technique for one of the most important challenges—learning words that represent new and difficult concepts. Techniques appropriate for other word-learning tasks can be found in Beck et al., (2002), Graves (in press), and Stahl & Nagy (in press).

English-language learners need to learn new concepts and the labels for those concepts. We have found a set of six steps developed by Dorothy Frayer and her colleagues (Frayer, et al., 1969) to be effective:

- define a new concept;

- distinguish between the new concept and similar, but different ones;

- give examples of the concept;

- give non-examples of the concept;

- ask students to distinguish between examples and non-examples; and

- have students give examples and non-examples while providing them with positive and constructive feedback. (See Chapter 6 for more information on examples and non-examples.)

To illustrate this approach, we describe part of a very brief guided-reading lesson Ms. García is teaching in her third-grade classroom. In the class, there are twelve African-American children, eight Anglo students, and three Latino students who arrived at the school in the spring of first grade. The three Latino children, María, Rosa, and Marco, are reading in English at about a mid-first-grade level. The class is beginning to learn about Latin American culture. Today Ms. García wants the students to understand what Latin America is and where it is located. She has written a brief text that explains that Latin America refers to several countries, which she names. She will use the text to help the students understand what Latin America is and to identify the countries on the globe. Yesterday, she brought a globe to class and placed it on her desk and was surprised when some of the children asked, "What's that?" Today, she begins her brief guided-reading lesson by introducing the topic and then teaching the students the concept of *globe*. We will now illustrate how she teaches the concept within this lesson.

1. Define the new concept.

Ms. García starts by giving the children a definition of *globe* and describing some of its attributes. She shows a poster with the following three sentences and reads them: "A *globe* represents a planet. This globe represents our planet, earth. A globe is a sphere, meaning shaped like a ball." As she says the words *sphere* and *ball*, she motions with her hands to make the shapes. "It shows countries and where they are." Next, she points to the globe she has brought to school. She says, "This is a globe of the earth. It is shaped like a ball, and it's round. See the lines showing the countries?" Now Ms. García references a cognate in Spanish—*globo*. Although her Latino students cannot read in Spanish, she thinks they might be familiar with the word in aural language. She writes *globe* and *globo* on the white board, points to each, and says each aloud. She makes sure that Maria, Rosa, and Marco are looking and listening. Ms. García says, "These are the same words. One is English, and one is Spanish. Notice that they look a lot alike."

2. Distinguish the new concept from similar but different concepts.

Learning the boundaries for concepts is important to clear understanding. For instance, a woman recently told one of us that as she and her family were driving through the country one day her daughter began pointing to the cows and saying, "Cow. Cow. Cow." The mother was excited and proud to see that her prior teaching about cows and what they looked like was taking hold. As they drove on, the daughter noticed some horses in the field, pointed, and said, "Cow! Cow! Cow!" The mother was deflated. This is a good example of partial concept learning. The daughter had learned critical attributes of what a cow is—it has four legs, a long tail, stands in the field, and so on. At the same time, she had not learned what it was *not*—that there are characteristics that other animals share, but that exclude them from the category *cow*.

Being aware of this, Ms. García wisely helps the children to understand some ways in which the concept *globe* overlaps with other concepts, but also how *globe* is distinguished from them. She shows a world map and says, "This is a map. It shows the earth too, but in a different way. How is it different?" Rosa says, "It's flat," and Ms. García says, "Yes, a globe is round. A map is flat." She then shows the students a contour map, says the words, and writes them on the board. She says, "A contour map also shows the earth, but in a different way. How is it different from a globe?" Maria says, "It's bumpy." Ms. García says, "Yes. A globe is round. A map is flat. A contour map is flat and bumpy." (This lesson uses the Example and Non-Example technique described in Chapter 6.)

3. **Give examples and non-examples.**

Ms. García points to the globe and says, "The most common globe is a globe of the earth. Globes come in other sizes and colors though." She then shows a miniature globe of the earth, a cobalt blue globe ornament and says, "This is a globe too. But it's not a globe of the earth. It's one I have in my garden because I think it's pretty."

Ms. García then shows a map of Arkansas and says, "This is not a globe." She shows a map of her neighborhood and says, "This is not a globe."

4. **Present examples and non-examples and ask students to distinguish them.**

Ms. García shows an aerial photo of New York State (non-example), a red sphere representing Mars (example), a walking map of Charleston (non-example), a ball-shaped model of the moon (example). She points to each and asks the children to tell whether each is an example of a globe. As the children respond, she tells them if they are right or not.

5. **Have students come up with their own examples and non-examples.**

Finally, Ms. García asks the students if they can think of some other examples of a globe. Some students say, "An orange." "A soccer ball." "A basketball." "A penny." "All of those," Ms. Garcia says, "are globes except the penny. Can anyone tell why a penny is not a globe?" Marco says, "Because it's flat." "Right," says Ms. García. "Now, what are things that might be similar, but aren't globes?" Students say, "Maps." Ms. García then concludes this part of her lesson by summarizing the definition of *globe*.

Teaching concepts using the Frayer steps can take some time, and it can also involve some preparation on the part of the teacher. However, for important concepts, the results are well worth the effort, and, in many cases, English-language learners will only learn the new concepts deeply if considerable time is spent. The Frayer method provides a viable and effective lesson structure for such concept learning, one that is time-tested with native-language speakers, and also one that is likely to be particularly beneficial for English-language learners precisely because it is so structured.

Teaching Word-Learning Strategies

Learning individual words is important for English-language learners, because of the large number of words they must learn in order to match the vocabularies of their English- speaking classmates. Learning strategies for figuring out words on their own is even more important. Three word-learning strategies are particularly valuable: using context to infer the meanings of unknown words, using word parts to deduce the meanings of unknown words, and learning to use the dictionary. In this section, we focus on using one type of word part—the prefix—to unlock the meanings of words.

Instruction in prefixes is particularly worthwhile for English-language learners for several reasons. First, there are a relatively small number of prefixes—making them easy to learn—but they are used in a large number of words. About 70 years ago, Stauffer (1942) found that nearly one-fourth of the twenty thousand words in Thorndike's (1932) list were prefixed words, and that the 15 most frequently occurring prefixes occurred in more than four thousand words. More recently, White, Sowell, and Yanagihara (1989) noted that the three most frequent prefixes (*un-*, *re-*, and *in-*) account for 50 percent of prefixed words. Second, prefixes tend to be consistently spelled and consistently positioned at the beginning of words, making them easy to spot. Third, prefixes usually have a clear lexical meaning.

Our approach to teaching prefixes (Graves, 2000) includes four steps: (1) introduce, clarify, motivate, and provide overview; (2) provide explicit instruction on three prefixes; (3) teach the Prefix Removal and Replacement Strategy for figuring out word meanings; and (4) review the strategy. We illustrate the steps in an English-as-a-second-language pullout class in which the teacher, Mr. Mach, is working with five students whose oral English levels are rated as "very low-intermediate" for their age and grade on a commonly administered assessment. Three are Latino students in fourth grade, Gerardo, Abriana, and Juan, who read on a second-grade level in English. One is a Hmong student, who uses his English name, Ken; he reads on a third-grade level in English. Another is a Tarascan Indian student from Mexico, Marco, who is in fifth grade and reads on a second-grade level in English.

1. Introduce, clarify, motivate, and provide overview.

On the first day, Mr. Mach introduces the concept of prefixes and the strategy of using them to unlock the meanings of unknown words and motivates the students by stressing the value of prefixes. Mr. Mach displays a poster with the title "Prefixes—One Key to Learning Word Meaning" at the top. He points to the title and says, "If you learn about this thing called prefixes, you will be able to figure out meanings of words in English—when you hear them and read them. This will also help you when you write in English."

He then asks the students what they already know about prefixes. Ken says, "Nothing." Mr. Mach uncovers the next lines on the poster and points to each as he reads and elaborates upon it:

Prefix: a group of letters at the front of word
un = not

♦ Never alone. Always with a word.
*un*happy

♦ Changes the word meaning.
happy/*un*happy

♦ If it is a prefix, when you take it away, you usually still have a real word.
*un*happy: happy – *un*. *Happy* is a real word.
So *un-* is a prefix.
*un*cle: cle – *un*. *Cle* is not a real word.
So *un* is not a prefix.

Mr. Mach asks the students if they know any other prefixes, and all say "No." He then writes three prefixes and their meanings on a white board— *un-* (not), *re-* (again), and *in-* (not). He notes that these are the three prefixes they will learn together over the next few days. He asks the students to write the three prefixes in a list on a piece of paper and tells them they have a homework assignment—they should find one word for each prefix, write the three words on the paper, and bring the list back tomorrow.

2. Provide explicit instruction on three prefixes.

On the second day, Mr. Mach begins by reviewing the poster. Next, he asks the students to show him their homework. Abriana, Juan, and Ken show him their completed papers, but Gerardo and Marco have nothing to show. Mr. Mach writes the students' selections on a whiteboard under the appropriate prefix heading, purposefully putting "correct" choices at the top:

un-	*re-*	*in-*
*un*done	*re*do	*in*correct
*un*tied	*re*start	*in*complete
*un*said	*re*nder	*in*fant

Mr. Mach: (*points to* undone, *and says it.*) Is *un* a prefix here, Ken?

Ken: Yes.

Mr. Mach: How do you know?

Ken: I can cover up the *un* and what's left is *done*, and that's a real word.

Mr. Mach: Good. What does *undone* mean?

Ken: Not done.

(*Mr. Mach repeats these steps for* untied, *asking Julia to answer.*)

(*For* unsaid, *Mr. Mach begins in the same way, asking Juan, "Is* un *a prefix here?"*)

Juan: Well, yes.

Mr. Mach: Why then?

Juan: Because *said* is a real word when you take away the *un*.

Mr. Mach continues with the remaining words in the same fashion, erasing the incorrect words at the end.

Next, Mr. Mach tells the students that now they will be learning more about using these three prefixes to unlock meanings of words. First, he shows this poster:

The Prefix re-

1. The teacher asked Julio to rewrite his spelling test because his writing was so messy the she could not read it.
   rewrite—to write again.

2. Lee had to restate her joke. Her grandfather did not hear it.
   restate—to say again.

3. If commence means begin, then recommence means _____.

Mr. Mach leads the students from the meaning of the familiar prefixed word to the meaning of the prefix:

Mr. Mach: (*after reading the first sentence*) If Abriana were asked to rewrite a test, what must she do?

Ken: She has to take it over. She has to take it again.

Mr. Mach: Yes. What is the meaning of *re-*, Marco?

Marco: Again. A second time. Over again.

Mr. Mach repeats this process for the second sentence on the poster and ends by asking Abriana to fill in the blank for the third sentence as he reads it. Abriana does so correctly.

After this, Mr. Mach hands each of the students a check sheet, reads the directions, and asks them to complete the sheet on their own. When the students are done, he gives immediate feedback. He repeats the process for the other two prefixes.

3. Teach the Prefix Removal and Replacement Strategy to figure out word meanings.

On the third day, Mr. Mach begins the session by showing a poster titled "The Prefix Removal and Replacement Strategy." On the poster is a list:

- Remove the prefix.

- Ask yourself:
  Is there a real word left?
  What does the prefix mean? Add that meaning to the meaning of the rest of the word.
  So what does the prefixed word mean?

- Try the prefixed word in a sentence.

Mr. Mach then models using the Prefix Removal and Replacement Strategy with the word *uncover*, reading the poster line by line and showing how he uses the steps to figure out the meaning of the word. He then asks Ken to do the steps with the word *recook*, and Marco to do the steps with the word *renumber*. Finally, he repeats the procedures he used on the second day to teach three additional prefixes—*dis-*, *en-*, and *non-*.

4. Review the strategy.

On the fourth day, Mr. Mach points to the poster and reviews the strategy. Then, he provides guided practice by having students each use the strategy one at a time with a new set of words for the prefixes *dis-*, *en-*, and *non-*.

As the final activity, Mr. Mach gives the students a quiz that requires them to state the steps of the prefix strategy and give the meanings of the six prefixes that were taught. He corrects the quiz immediately and gives the students feedback before they return to their classes.

Fostering Word Consciousness

Word consciousness refers to awareness of words, interest in words, and knowledge about words and the way they work (Anderson & Nagy, 1992; Graves & Watts-Taffe, 2002; Nagy & Scott, 2004). Students who are word conscious are aware of the words around them—ones they read and hear, write and speak. They have an appreciation of the power of words, an understanding of why certain words are used instead of others, and a sense of the words that could be used in place of those they've selected to write or say. They are also cognizant of first encounters with new words and interested in learning these words and using them skillfully and precisely.

Like the first three parts of the comprehensive vocabulary program we advocate, word consciousness is important for all students but particularly for English-language learners. Because they have more English words to learn than their English-speaking classmates and because most of their word learning is taking place incidentally as they are reading and listening, word consciousness is crucial to English learners' success in expanding the breadth and depth of their word knowledge over the course of their lifetimes.

Word consciousness should be fostered in all students, from preschoolers to high schoolers and beyond. Approaches to fostering it include modeling, recognizing, and encouraging adept diction; promoting wordplay; providing rich and expressive instruction; involving students in original investigations involving words; and teaching students a variety of useful facts about words (Graves, in press; Graves & Watts-Taffe, 2002). To illustrate how these approaches can be taught, we present the following description of a classroom, as observed by Peter Dewitz (personal communication, October 16, 2004).

Henry Koch, a sixth-grade English teacher at a large suburban middle school, has been teaching for 25 years. In that time, he has seen his classroom change from one in which English was the only language spoken to one in which half the students speak English as their native language and the other half speak a variety of languages including Spanish, Vietnamese, Somali, Thai, and Arabic. Knowing that idioms represent a major learning challenge for the vast majority of English-language learners, Mr. Koch has planned a six-week original investigation to deal with them. Here's how it works:

1. Define idiom.

Mr. Koch begins the activity by telling students that idioms are "common English phrases whose meanings cannot be understood from the combined meaning of their individual words." (See more about teaching idioms in Chapter 5.)

2. Provide examples of idioms.

He then gives some examples of idioms, explains how each idiom works, and gives a sentence or short paragraph that illustrates the use of each of them. "Have many irons in the fire" doesn't usually refer to fire or to irons. Instead it refers to a situation in which a person has a number of options or a number of things going on at once. The idiom suggests this meaning because if someone literally has many irons in the fire, he or she has a number of irons hot and ready to use. "Val wasn't that unhappy when she didn't get the first job she applied for because she had many irons in the fire."

3. Explain why idioms are important but challenging to learn.

After giving these explanations and examples, Mr. Koch tells the students that there are thousands of idioms in English, that they are tricky to understand, and that they pose a real challenge for people learning English. So the class is going to investigate, share, discuss, and try to better understand idioms over the next six weeks.

4. Engage students in a vocabulary-building activity.

Mr Koch teams each English-language learner with a native English speaker. Since the class consists of about half English-language learners and about half native speakers, this works. If some teams have three members, that's okay. Each day, three teams are responsible for bringing in their own idiom, explaining it to the class, and posting it on the Idiom Board. Teams post them on $5\frac{1}{2}$-by-8-inch cards on a large bulletin board that occupies much of one classroom wall. The card includes the idiom, its meaning, and a sentence or short paragraph illustrating its meaning. Since there are about 15 teams, each is responsible for contributing one or two a week over the six weeks; the Idiom Board should contain about 90 entries by the end of the investigation.

The idioms can be ones that the English-language learner on the team knows, ones that the native speaker on the team knows, or ones that a friend or relative of either member of the team knows. Mr. Koch encourages students from taking idioms from the Internet or a dictionary such as the *Longman American Idioms Dictionary* (Pearson Education, 1999).

In addition to making an oral presentation about their idioms, teams earn 5 points for posting it on a card. The card include spaces for other teams to record experiences they have had with that idiom. A sample card for the idiom "pump iron" is shown in Figure 7.1.

"Pump iron" Do heavy lifting to build up your muscles. Juan had been pumping iron for two years, and although he was short he now looked like a body builder.		
Team AD/KD Used it.	Team DD/TK Heard it.	Team BB/MG Found it on Internet.
Team MV/RL Found it on Internet.	Team LL/PA Used it.	

Figure 7.1: Bulletin-board card for idiom activity

As can be seen, five other teams have had experiences with the idiom: two teams had used it, one team had heard it, and two had found it on the Internet.

Teams earn 1 point for each entry they make on a card and are on their honor to record only experiences that actually happen. However, each day right after the new idioms are introduced, other teams can challenge those who have posted experiences. If challenged, the posting team has to describe where they heard or used the idiom, indicate where they found it on the Internet, or explain any other type of experience they have had with it. If they can explain, they earn 2 points. If they cannot explain, the challenging team earns 2 points.

5. Review concepts and strategies.

At the end of the sixth week, Mr. Koch tallies the points, recognizes the team or teams with the most points, stresses the importance of idioms, and encourages his English-language learners to be on the lookout for them. He also suggests that when his English-language learners come across a phrase they believe is an idiom, they can confirm it by talking with one of their native-speaking classmates or by checking one of the several copies of the *Longman American Idioms Dictionary* that are kept in the classroom.

This class investigation has three main purposes. First, it teaches English-language learners a substantial number of idioms. Second, it alerts all students, but particularly English-language learners, to be on the look-out for idioms they need to master. Finally, it teaches all students something about how the English language works.

Classroom Tips

Many common English words have multiple meanings. For example, *table* can mean a piece of furniture or a graphic representation of data. *Custom* can mean an old habit or something that is made to order. Learning multiple meanings is a challenge for all students, but it is a particular challenge for English-language learners. Word consciousness games can help make students aware of the fact that many words have multiple meanings. The work of Richard Lederer (1988) can be an invaluable guide in developing such games. It is also important to teach ELLs several lessons consisting of multiple-meaning words.

You Try It

The vocabulary program we describe here and the accompanying techniques—the Frayer method, teaching prefixes, and doing a word-of-the-day activity—are applicable in a variety of settings and situations. The program can be used in combination with a basal program, for remediation, with the whole class, with small groups, with trade books, with classes that contain exclusively English-language learners, and with classes that contain English-language learners and native English speakers. But, of course, the nature of the instruction differs from one situation to another.

Here are some examples. If you are using a basal program, it will undoubtedly include some instruction that focuses on individual words. However, little if any of that instruction is going to be nearly as deep or powerful as the Frayer method. So be sure to teach some words using that method. When using trade books, you are on your own when it comes to selecting vocabulary words to teach and devising methods to teach them. Therefore, we suggest targeting the vocabulary most crucial for understanding the text and using a variety of methods such as those described in Beck et al. (2002), Graves (in press), and Stahl and Nagy (in press).

All of the techniques can be used with either whole classes or small groups, depending upon who will profit from the instruction—all of your students or only some of them.

Finally, if you are working with students reading below grade level, whether they are exclusively English-language learners or both English-language learners and native speakers, having a robust and comprehensive program is important. Building such a program usually means using whatever vocabulary instruction is included in the basic program you are using and adding them to that. Be sure that you spend some time on providing rich and varied language experiences, some time teaching individual words, some time teaching word-learning strategies, and some time fostering word consciousness.

Summary

Building and using a rich, robust vocabulary is important in school and out of school. The number of words that students typically learn by the time they graduate from high school is huge, approximately fifty thousand words (Graves, in press; Nagy & Hermann, 1987). This is a particularly substantial task for English-language learners. A vocabulary program such as the one outlined here—one that provides students with rich and varied language experiences, teaches individual words, teaches word-learning strategies, and fosters word consciousness—provides English-language learners with the assistance, skills, and motivation they need in order to develop powerful English vocabularies. We recommend that teachers at all grade levels and in all subject areas work together to implement such a program.

Discussion Questions and Teaching Activities

1. In this chapter, Ms. García teaches her students the concept of *globe*. Using the same steps that she does, design a lesson in which you introduce and then teach a concept that is unfamiliar to your students. Rate the value of this lesson to your students.

2. The authors describe why word consciousness is crucial to English-language learners and present several strategies for teaching it. Try two or more of these strategies in your classroom. Which one proved to be most effective with your students? Why was it so successful?

CHAPTER EIGHT

Effective Vocabulary Instruction
for Gifted Students

David Lund, Southern Utah University

Ms. Anders, a third-grade teacher in a suburban school in the Southeast, understands the needs of all of her students. Her class is typical of the area. Students are bussed to the school from downtown in order to meet the ethnic ratio regulations of the state—a minimum of 45 percent of the students in any given school must be classified as minorities. And just as in any other suburban classroom, students' abilities and skills vary. Some struggle with skills expected of kindergartners, while others are gifted, showing skills above their grade level.

Ms. Anders understands the close relationship between spelling and vocabulary. She believes that integrating spelling and vocabulary across the curriculum helps students attain the deep understanding necessary for using a word in everyday situations.

Because of these beliefs, she has developed an individualized integration strategy to accomplish her spelling and vocabulary instructional objectives. She gives spelling words to students in sets of ten. After taking the pretest for the set, students replace correctly spelled words with words of their choice for the remainder of the week's spelling and vocabulary instruction activities. Ms. Anders encourages students to add words of personal interest and words that are thematically related to the original spelling and vocabulary words. These words come from a variety of sources—a special topic in which students are interested; challenging words that are not necessarily part of the curriculum; words that are just interesting to learn (such as *origin* and *structure*); and dictionaries, thesauruses, and other interesting books in which students are encouraged to search. Students who are classified as gifted tend to spell more of the original words correctly and thus add more of their own words to their lists.

Locating definitions online is a great way to build vocabulary using technology. Students at Oakmont Elementary do this each week. They especially enjoy finding word meanings on the Web site www.dictionary.com.

In subsequent assignments, students use the words in journal writing, quick writes on various topics, and other creative projects. Finally, on the last day of the series of lessons, students take a self-created dictation test based on a paragraph they created in which they used ten spelling words. After a full year of such instruction, the gifted students in this class are consistently exhibiting an ability to write at a fifth- to seventh-grade level, with correspondingly difficult vocabulary. For example, one gifted second grader added the names of all 50 states and their capitals, as well as the names of all U. S. presidents through William Jefferson Clinton, to his vocabulary. The strategy is designed to appeal to children with a specific academic ability—in this case in language arts—and with better-than-average intellectual skills, and provides them with appropriate academic work.

This anecdote illustrates one teacher's attempt to provide instruction appropriate for gifted learners in her classroom. In this chapter, I will describe characteristics of gifted learners and research-based strategies that promote appropriate vocabulary instruction for them.

Characteristics of Gifted Word Learners

What does it meant to be counted as a gifted student? According to the 1978 Gifted and Talented Children's Act (PL 95-561, Section 902):

> The term gifted and talented children means children and, whenever applicable, youth who are identified at the pre-school, elementary, or secondary level as possessing demonstrated or potential abilities that give evidence of high performance capabilities in areas such as intellectual, creative, specific academic, or leadership ability, or in the performing and visual arts, and who by reason thereof, require services or activities not ordinarily provided by the school.

This is just one of many similar definitions (see also, Hallahan & Kauffman, 2003; or Lewis & Doorlag, 2003) used to help identify gifted and talented students. Many of these definitions list areas of giftedness, including but not necessarily limited to general intellectual ability, specific academic aptitude, creative or productive thinking, leadership ability, special ability in the visual and performing arts, enhanced psychomotor ability, and physical activity. Students may be gifted in any number of these areas. The majority of these definitions also break giftedness into three distinct sets of characteristics, and gifted children may possess any number of them: general behavioral, including common sense, willpower, perseverance, a desire to excel, self-confidence, prudence and forethought; learning prowess, such as superior intelligence or a desire to know; and creative capacity or the ability to create original work. These gifted students may also exhibit better-than-average social, emotional, physical, or intellectual skills.

In recent years, Howard Gardner's theory of multiple intelligences has seemed to provide a framework with which the many characteristics of giftedness can be understood in a clear and succinct way. As noted above, Gardner (1999) points out that it is highly unlikely that any single child will exhibit all of these characteristics. It has been said that we are all gifted or slow depending on the task at hand. Figure 8.1 shows the possible relationships of Gardner's eight intelligences (see the entry on Gardner's multiple intelligences in the *Encyclopedia of Informal Education* by Mark Smith, 2002) to the various aspects of the definition of giftedness used in this chapter.

Gardner's Intelligence—Talents; Possible Careers	General Characteristics of Gifted Learners	Areas Related to Vocabulary Skills
1. Linguistic intelligence—sensitive to language in all forms, easily learns language; may become writer, politician, actor, lawyer	Superior intellect, better-than-average intellectual skill	General intellectual ability, specific academic aptitude, performing arts; enhanced background vocabulary, ease of learning and using new vocabulary
2. Logical-mathematical intelligence—easily and logically analyzes problems, thinks deductively, analyzes patterns, understands scientific method; may become scientist, mathematician	Better-than-average intellectual skill	Specific academic aptitude; enhanced ability to learn math and science vocabulary (including symbols)
3. Musical intelligence—performs, composes, and appreciates music, recognizes pitch, tone, and rhythm; may become composer, performer, or both	Originality	Visual and performing arts, creative or productive thinking; enhanced ability to read, understand, and use (in performance and composition) musical symbols and vocabulary

Gardner's Intelligence—Talents; Possible Careers	General Characteristics of Gifted Learners	Areas Related to Vocabulary Skills
4. Bodily-kinesthetic intelligence—uses body to solve problems and perform physical acts, mentally coordinates physical movement; may become athlete, dancer, stunt person, etc.	Better-than-average physical skill	Physical activity, psychomotor ability; enhanced ability to use, and knowledge of, vocabulary of movement and vocabulary related to mental control of movement
5. Spatial intelligence—recognizes patterns and how they fit within designs; may become architect, artist, designer	Originality, better-than-average intellectual skill	Creative or productive thinking, visual arts; enhanced understanding of and ability to use productive and creative vocabulary and the vocabulary of the visual arts
6. Interpersonal intelligence—understand people and their motivations, can work with almost anyone; may become educator, leader, salesperson, counselor	Originality, common sense, prudence and forethought, better-than-average social and emotional skill	Leadership ability, productive thinking; better-than-average knowledge of and ability to use persuasive vocabulary
7. Intrapersonal intelligence—understanding of self and feelings, uses self-knowledge to plan personal life; may become psychologist, personal planner	A desire to know, better-than-average emotional skill, willpower, common sense, perseverance, self-confidence	Creative or productive thinking; enhanced ability to understand and use creative and productive, as well as metacognitive, vocabularies
8. Naturalist intelligence—notices, groups, and utilizes environmental features; may become naturalist, ranger, anthropologist	Superior general intelligence, better-than-average intellectual skill	Leadership ability, Specific academic ability; enhanced ability to understand and use vocabulary associated with the environment and to use it to persuade others in the direction of environmental issues

Figure 8.1: Possible relationships between Howard Gardner's multiple intelligences and aspects of giftedness

Things to Consider When Teaching Vocabulary to Gifted Learners

Gifted children are often ignored or penalized because of their enhanced abilities. This challenge for gifted students was recognized in 1954 by Margaret Mead and continues to be a problem today. She wrote:

> In American education, we have tended to . . . disallow special gifts. By this refusal to recognize special gifts, we have wasted and dissipated, driven into apathy or schizophrenia, uncounted numbers of gifted children. If they learn easily, they are penalized for having nothing to do; if they excel in some outstanding way, they are penalized as being conspicuously better than the peer group. (pp. 211–212)

It is clear that to meet the needs of all of the students in the classroom, the teacher must look to additional and/or differentiated instruction, including vocabulary instruction, for the gifted students in the class.

There are other factors in today's society that have a significant effect on the instruction of gifted children. Students today are in many ways the same as they have been for decades or even centuries; however, each new generation of students brings with it new cultural and societal characteristics that set them apart from the generations that have come before them. The current generation of students, specifically those born after 1978, as explained in Chapter 10, is often referred to as "Generation Y." According to Suzanne Soule (2001), this group of young people, at more than 70 million, is the largest and most ethnically diverse generation in the history of the United States, and it is certain that many of them fall into categories of giftedness. They exhibit their rightful share of unique characteristics and face some very different challenges. In terms of vocabulary, as related to Kate Manuel's (2002) three major identifying characteristics of the Generation Y student, they have grown up in an age replete with the new technologies described by Semali (2001), giving them a positive outlook toward, and a unique perspective and knowledge of, the vocabulary associated with the new technology. Gifted students' knowledge of this vocabulary and their ability to use it may be enhanced, particularly because they desire to be completely in charge of their own "digital universe" (Manuel, 2002, p. 203).

Furthermore, gifted Generation Y students exhibit a very low threshold of boredom and a high degree of unwillingness to memorize the material that is to be learned in the classroom (Manuel, 2002). They are usually more ready to accept more-engaging and generative types of vocabulary instruction, as described in Chapter 1. And gifted students may exhibit an enhanced ability to generate novel uses of vocabulary. They will be more motivated to acquire and use new vocabulary in more realistic and engaging situations. Gifted students may have an enhanced ability to create and maintain highly social learning situations. Each of these characteristics has definite implications for the classroom teacher and for vocabulary instruction (NRP, 2001). Providing vocabulary instruction to the gifted Generation Y student may appear to be a daunting task.

A final consideration for teachers engaged in vocabulary instruction for gifted students is related to the work of the National Reading Panel (2001). Its work has provided a list of techniques and strategies for vocabulary instruction that research has shown to be effective. These techniques can be divided into the following groups:

- Computer/Multimedia Instruction

- Dictionary/Glossary

- Key Word Method

- Association Method

- Repeated/Multiple Exposure

- Context Methods

- Preinstruction of Vocabulary Words

- Roots/Affixes Analysis, Restructuring the Task (for example, altering the text)

- Wide Reading

- Elaborate/Rich Instruction

- Interactive Vocabulary Techniques

- Decoding Techniques

- Text Revision

- Active Engagement

There may be other techniques that are useful as well. For example, the use of graphics or imagery would intuitively seem to be very useful in vocabulary instruction. It does not appear on the list only because there is no scientific study supporting its effectiveness.

Techniques and Strategies for Teaching Vocabulary to Gifted Learners

There are specific instructional accommodations recommended by Manuel (2002) for teaching gifted students and a number of strategies and techniques for vocabulary instruction that meet these needs. The accommodations include:

- ◆ Cater to the interests of gifted students.

- ◆ Provide for their needs.

- ◆ Give work appropriate to ability.

- ◆ Avoid unnecessary drill and practice.

- ◆ Respect students as individuals.

- ◆ Provide opportunity for interaction.

- ◆ Provide opportunity for risk taking.

- ◆ Encourage the use of high-level thinking skills.

- ◆ Provide speech-stimulating activities.

The strategies and techniques for vocabulary instruction that follow are presented in the form of anecdotes or brief descriptions and are organized around the framework of Gardner's multiple intelligences. Each concludes with the gifted characteristic(s) and accommodation(s) for which it has been adapted as well as the NRP instructional category or categories into which it most closely fits. Many of the strategies and techniques will contain specific adaptations designed to appeal to today's Generation Y student.

Linguistic Intelligence

Students who are linguistically gifted need to be involved in activities that allow them to use their skills as an effective tool for acquiring vocabulary, such as these:

Playing Hink Pink (one-syllable rhymes of two words—for example, *sad dad*) or Hinky Pinky (two-syllable rhymes of two words—for example, *yellow fellow*). Have students create their own Hink Pinks or Hinky Pinkys, then create the clues that go with them (a clue for *sad dad* would be "an unhappy father," and for *yellow fellow* a possible clue could be "a jaundiced man"), and trade them with classmates to figure out. Students showing special ability in linguistic intelligence may be asked to extend this activity to three-syllable rhymes and accompanying clues. This activity promotes the development of descriptive language. (Gifted characteristics: superior intelligence, originality, better-than-average intellectual skill. Gifted accommodations: provide work appropriate to ability, provide abstract exercises, provide opportunity for interaction, and provide speech-stimulating activities. NRP category: Association Method.)

Creating bi- or trilingual (or more if there are more than two first languages other than English represented in the class) dictionaries for classroom use. This activity helps all participants become more aware of the cultural vocabulary of each student in the classroom. Students create the dictionary by listing the English vocabulary words to be learned in the class in the first column and then placing translations in the next column or columns. For example *cat* may be a first-grade vocabulary word. Figure 8.2 shows an example of the dictionary, using *cat*.

English	Spanish	German	Picture
cat	(el) gato	(die) katze	

Figure 8.2: Trilingual picture dictionary

The translations can be found by going to any one of a number of Internet-based translation sites, such as <u>Free Translation</u> at http://www.freetranslation.com or <u>Alta Vista Babel Fish Translation</u> at http://world.altavista.com. The gifted students could then use these dictionaries to tutor the English-language learners in a flashcard-type activity by pointing to the picture, and having the ELL repeat the word in each language. (Gifted characteristics: better-than-average intellectual and social skills. Gifted accommodations: cater to interests, provide opportunity for interaction, provide speech-stimulating activities. NRP categories: Association Method and Computer/Multimedia Instruction.)

Looking up and using new words. Locating definitions for weekly vocabulary words in Internet-based dictionaries, glossaries, or thesauruses, writing new sentences with the words, and having linguistically talented students create word games with them. This activity promotes word recognition and literal comprehension. Dictionary.com (http://dictionary.reference.com) provides free access to a dictionary and a thesaurus. At Fun-with-words.com (http://www.fun-with-words.com) patterns for such word games can be found. (Gifted characteristics: better-than-average intellectual skill, originality. Gifted accommodations: cater to interests, provide opportunity for interaction, provide speech-stimulating activities, avoid unnecessary drill and practice, give work appropriate to ability, encourage the use of high-level thinking skills. NRP categories: Computer Multimedia Instruction, Dictionary/Glossary.)

Searching for etymologies on the Internet. This activity promotes the value of looking deeply into the word, well beyond memorizing the definition and using the word in a decontextualized sentence. This appeals to the gifted student's desire to know. Students create a chart with four columns. Figure 8.3 shows an example of this strategy, using the vocabulary word *malaria*.

Word	Etymology (where the word comes from)	Meaning	Interesting fact or story
malaria	Mediaeval Latin	mal = bad and aria = air; so "bad air"	When the Romans ventured into the swamps around Rome, they often became ill. Since the air smelled bad, the Romans named the illness malaria, being unaware that it was actually caused by protozoa injected into humans during the bite of a mosquito.

Figure 8.3: An example of searching for a word's etymology on the Internet

Fun-with-words.com contains interesting information on word origins as well as fun and sometimes quirky facts about many English words. (Gifted characteristics: better-than-average intellectual skill, desire to know. Gifted accommodations: cater to interests, give work appropriate to ability, provide speech-stimulating activities. NRP categories: Root/Affixes Analysis, Active Engagement, Dictionary/Glossary.)

Finding and sharing the Word of the Day. This could be assigned as an enrichment activity to linguistically gifted students. The word could come from a variety of sources, helping students expand their usable vocabulary. For example, gifted students may find an exceptionally interesting word in their reading, or they may go to one of a number of Internet sites that list a word of the day. The student in charge of that day's Word of the Day activity would be responsible for locating the day's word and sharing it with the class, which would include defining the word and explaining in detail how the word is used in an appropriate context. Examples of possible words for this activity include *epidermis, pugnacious, Cyrillic.* (Gifted characteristics: better-than-average intellectual skill, desire to know, self-confidence, desire to excel. Gifted accommodations: cater to interests, give work appropriate to ability, provide speech-stimulating activities, provide opportunity for risk taking. NRP categories: Concept Method, Dictionary/Glossary.)

Using students' knowledge of affixes to form as many different words from a single root word as possible. Figure 8.4 shows how this may look, using the word *work.*

Word— definition	"New" words with affixes	Meaning	Real or not real, based on dictionary
Work— to perform a task	prefixes		
	rework	to perform a task again	real
	inwork	to perform inside of something	not real
	unwork	to not perform a task	not real
	suffixes		
	workable	a task that is able to be done	real
	workness	a task to be performed	not real
	worker	a person that performs a task	real

Figure 8.4: Student affix chart for *work*

Once as many words as possible have been formed, students write a definition for each word. Then they use a regular or Internet dictionary to verify that all of the words they have created are real words and eliminate those that are not. As a final step, students could write a short essay or story using as many of the words as possible. (Gifted characteristics: better-than-average intellectual skill, desire to know, self-confidence, desire to excel. Gifted accommodations: cater to interests, give work appropriate to ability, provide opportunity for risk taking. NRP categories: Concept Method, Keyword Method, Roots/Affixes Analysis.)

Adapting Gail Tompkins's Word Clusters Strategy for linguistically talented students (Tompkins & Blanchfield, 2004, pp. 156–160). Have students choose from their assigned vocabulary words one word that has at least three meanings. They then write a paragraph, poem, or short story using the word at least three times, each with a different meaning. For example, in a second-grade class the assigned vocabulary word is *mountain*. Its three meanings are: (1) a very high hill; (2) of or having to do with mountains; and (3) a very large stack of anything. The poem may read as follows:

I climbed a mountain, very high,

To breathe the mountain air.

I found the snow piled high and deep,

In mountains everywhere.

(Gifted characteristics: Superior intelligence, originality, better-than-average intellectual skill. Gifted accommodations: provide work appropriate to ability, provide abstract exercises. NRP categories: Dictionary/Glossary and Interactive Vocabulary Techniques.)

Writing a fiction story that uses the vocabulary words from a content unit. For example, for students in a third-grade class learning about fractions, the vocabulary words would include *numerator, denominator, fraction,* etc. Once the story is written, have students choose an online publisher and get their story published. A list of sites is located at the end of the chapter. (Gifted characteristics: superior intelligence, originality, better-than-average intellectual skill. Gifted accommodations: provide work appropriate to ability, encourage the use of high-level thinking skills. NRP category: Text Revision.)

Logical-Mathematical Intelligence

Students who are gifted in logic-mathematics are often skilled problem solvers and understand the scientific method. In addition, they are often adept at recognizing patterns in nature and mathematics. Vocabulary instructional techniques for these students include the following:

Engaging in a word-transformation exercise. Choose two different vocabulary words of the same length such as *gate* and *pots*. Students change one letter at a time, creating new words, until the second vocabulary word has been formed: *gate, rate, rats, rots, pots*. To add an element of difficulty for the gifted student, and to assist the struggling student in making these transformations, definitions for all words must be given:

- gate—an entrance in a fence
- rate—cost per hour
- rats—plural of rat
- rots—becomes decayed
- pots—pans

(Gifted characteristics: common sense, better-than-average intellectual skill. Gifted accommodations: provide work appropriate to ability, encourage the use of high-level thinking skills. NRP category: Dictionary/Glossary, Interactive Vocabulary Techniques.)

Directing students to Fun-with-words.com at http://www.fun-with-words.com, which has a variety of word games that employ logical concepts, similar to the activity listed above. (Gifted characteristics: better-than-average intellectual skill, willpower, perseverance. Gifted accommodations: cater to interests, avoid unnecessary drill and practice, give work appropriate to ability, encourage the use of high-level thinking skills. NRP categories: Computer/Multimedia Instruction, Active Engagement.)

Creating newspaper cryptoquotes. For example, have second-grade students studying the United States write a three-sentence paragraph using the vocabulary words from the unit. The words *George Washington*, *president*, *elected*, *general*, and *army* could yield the following paragraph:

> George Washington was a general in the army. He was elected the first president of the United States. The people liked him.

They then create a secret code by substituting letters for each other in some pattern (for example, by offsetting the alphabet by three letters so *a* becomes *d*, *b* becomes *e*, *c* becomes *f*, and so on), and rewrite the paragraph with the new code. Finally, they exchange the coded paragraphs with one another for decoding.

The cryptoquote created would be:

> Jhrujh Zdvklqjwrq zdv d jhqhudo lq wkh dupb.
> Kh zdv hohfwhg wkh iluvw suhvlghqw ri wkh
> Xqlwhg Vwdwhv. Wkh shrsoh olnhg klp.

(Gifted characteristics: better-than-average intellectual skill, willpower, perseverance. Gifted accommodations: cater to interests, avoid unnecessary drill and practice, give work appropriate to ability, encourage the use of high-level thinking skills. NRP category: Restructuring the Task.)

Musical Intelligence

These students show exceptional skill in composing or performing music. Techniques to enhance the vocabulary experience of these students include the following:

Writing a four-line poem. Students use the vocabulary words and a specific rhyming pattern (for example, *aa bb*), then set the poem to music. For example, a poem from a sixth-grade class studying Egypt, with *pyramid, sphinx,* and *pharaoh* as vocabulary words, may read:

> The sphinx in Egypt is so old;
>
> It's made of stone, not wood or gold.
>
> The pyramids stand near, so tall;
>
> The pharaohs built them one and all.

(Gifted characteristics: better-than-average intellectual skill, desire to excel, originality. Gifted accommodations: cater to interests, provide opportunity for risk taking, give work appropriate to ability, encourage the use of high-level thinking skills. NRP categories: Interactive Vocabulary Techniques, Repeated/Multiple Exposure, Active Engagement.)

Creating "musical innovations." Students rewrite the lyrics to familiar songs using vocabulary words from a content-area subject and then perform the songs. For example, in the third-grade science class the subject is worms. Using the familiar children's song, "Twinkle, Twinkle, Little Star," students may compose an innovation like the following:

Wiggle, wiggle, little worm,

How I love to watch you squirm.

As you eat the dirt and mud,

I see only lots of crud!

Wiggle, wiggle, little worm,

How I love to watch you squirm!

(Gifted characteristics: better-than-average intellectual skill, desire to excel, originality. Gifted accommodations: cater to interests, provide opportunity for risk taking, give work appropriate to ability, use high-level thinking skills. NRP categories: Restructuring the Task, Interactive Vocabulary Techniques, Repeated/Multiple Exposure, Elaborate/Rich Instruction, Active Engagement.)

Bodily-Kinesthetic Intelligence

Students who have exceptional ability to understand and control their bodies by using their minds may find the following vocabulary activities engaging:

Carrying out the activity Dance the Words. In this activity, single students, or groups of two or three, create a dance inspired by the meaning of a word. It is followed by another dance, in which students spell the word by forming each letter with a short pause in between. Other groups of students race against one another to guess the word. (Gifted characteristics: better-than-average intellectual skill, desire to excel, originality. Gifted accommodations: cater to interests, provide opportunity for risk taking, give work appropriate to ability, encourage the use of high-level thinking skills. NRP categories: Interactive Vocabulary Techniques, Decoding Instruction, and Active Engagement.)

Adapting a variation of Tompkins's activity Where in the World (Tompkins and Blanchfield, 2004, pp. 126–129). Teams of students are given ten world words such as *taco, lasagna, bratwurst, babushka, gaucho, Mardi Gras, crumpet, czar, kiwi*, and *Suez Canal* (a good list can be found on page 128 of Tompkins's book). Each word is on a large card. The students are required to look up the words in a tag-team fashion, one at a time, find the meaning and the country of origin of the word (it may be useful to have them use the Internet for this part of the contest), write both on the back of the card, and then run to a large world map at the front of the room and place or pin the card on the country of origin. (Gifted characteristics: better-than-average intellectual skill, a desire to know, superior intelligence. Gifted accommodations: cater to interests, provide opportunity for interaction, avoid unnecessary drill and practice, give work appropriate to ability. NRP categories: Computer/Multimedia Instruction, Dictionary/Glossary, Roots/Affixes Analysis, Association Method.)

Spatial Intelligence

Students with unusual abilities to recognize patterns in wide spaces and more confined areas and utilize the patterns to create graphic representations possess spatial intelligence. For example, they might readily discern the relationships between primary and complementary colors and how they might be used in a painting, or they might notice the patterns created by the growth of trees in a forest and develop plans for an apartment complex based on those patterns. They could be motivated by participation in many vocabulary activities, including those described in the following anecdote and the subsequent strategies.

In a fifth-grade classroom in a southwestern Utah suburb, the teacher is introducing vocabulary that students will encounter while reading a biography of Martin Luther King, Jr. Most of the students, even gifted students, struggle with the specific vocabulary of civil rights. Several of her gifted students exhibit a propensity toward graphic images. They also possess specific gifts or talents in one, two, or all three of Gardner's linguistic, spatial, and interpersonal intelligences. She has a plan to enhance her vocabulary lesson for all of her students and, at the same time, take advantage of the special intelligence of the graphic-savvy students in her classroom. The National Reading Panel lists visual representations as one of the possibilities for Computer/Multimedia Instruction (2001, pp. 4–33 to 4–35). The teacher, mindful of the NRP research, has given her students a list of the vocabulary words from the chapter and has assigned them to find animated and/or nonanimated graphic representations of each word on the Internet and create a dictionary in PowerPoint. Each page in the presentation contains the word, its definition, a sentence in which the word is used, and the graphic representation. In this case, the students work in groups, with a gifted student in each group. One of the words to be encountered in the story is *segregation*. The PowerPoint page for this word has the sentence "*Segregation* means to divide races, so the colored people have their own school, and the white people have their own school." The graphic illustration at the bottom of the page shows two schools, each with a sign above the school—"Colored Only" over one and "White Only" over the other. The groups share their dictionaries with the rest of the class, and then the students proceed to read the chapter. The gifted students have used their specific talents in spatial intelligence to assist in the vocabulary instruction. (Gifted characteristics: better-than-average intellectual skill, originality. Gifted accommodations: cater to interests, provide opportunity for interaction, provide speech-stimulating activities, avoid unnecessary drill and practice, give work appropriate to ability. NRP categories: Computer/Multimedia Instruction, and Preinstruction of Vocabulary Words.)

In addition, strong spatial abilities may be motivated to participate in the following vocabulary activities:

Finding strange expressions. Assign each spatially or linguistically gifted student in the class the task of locating at least ten idiomatic or strange expressions in their reading, such as "She had a frog in her throat" or "He has ants in his pants." For each one, students use the Internet and/or a graphic-design program to create two visual representations of the expression—one should convey the accepted figurative meaning of the expression, and the other should depict the literal meaning. Then students write a short paragraph or story using the expression both of the ways depicted by their graphic illustrations. Finally, students share their paragraphs and graphic illustrations with one another. For example, a *car pool* may be depicted as a group of people sharing transportation by automobile or as a swimming pool for cars. Figure 8.5 depicts the visual part of the car pool example. This activity is an adaptation of Cecil's (2004) Strange

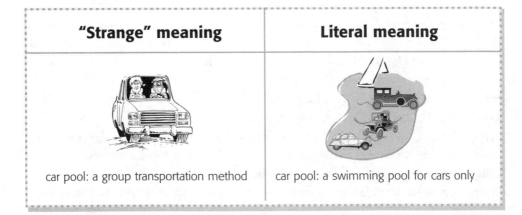

"Strange" meaning	Literal meaning
car pool: a group transportation method	car pool: a swimming pool for cars only

Expressions activity.

(Gifted characteristics: superior intelligence, originality, Better-than-average intellectual skill, a desire to know. Gifted accommodations: cater to interests, provide work appropriate to ability, provide abstract exercises, provide opportunity for interaction, and provide speech-stimulating activities. NRP category: Restructuring the Task, Interactive Vocabulary Techniques, Elaborate/Rich Instruction, Computer/Multimedia Instruction.)

Carrying out the activity Design a Room. In this activity, students choose the five most important vocabulary words from a single science or social studies chapter and design a room in which each word is depicted by a mural on one of the four walls and the ceiling, with the most important one found on the ceiling. Divide the class into five teams with a spatially talented team leader. Each team is in charge of one mural. On a large piece of posterboard, each team creates a prototype of its word mural. Other vocabulary words could also be graphically integrated into the murals, where appropriate. For example, the five words chosen for a U. S. history unit on the Revolutionary War may be *revolution, independence, fight, taxation,* and *oppression*. The class has chosen *independence* as the most important word. The murals may include the following: the signing of the Declaration of Independence for *independence,* to be painted on the ceiling, the Boston Tea Party to represent *taxation* on one wall, the Battle of Bunker Hill painted on another wall to represent *fight,* Paul Revere's ride to represent *revolution* on the third wall, and on the final wall the redcoats marching through the streets of Boston to represent *oppression*. (Gifted characteristics: originality, better-than-average intellectual skill, a desire to know. Gifted accommodations: cater to interests, provide work appropriate to ability, provide abstract exercises, provide opportunity for interaction. NRP categories: Association Method, Elaborate/Rich Instruction, Interactive Vocabulary Techniques.)

Adapting the cubing activity from Readence et al. (2004, pp. 222–223). Spatially talented students describe a word on the six sides of a cube, with a different aspect of the word on each side—define it, compare it, associate it, analyze it, find its etymology, and use it appropriately. Rather than writing on the cube, the student graphically represents the ideas on the cube. For example, for the math vocabulary word *octagon,* a student may draw or place the following pictures on the cube: a picture of an octagon with an "8" in the center to define it, a picture of a hexagon with a red circle crossed by a diagonal line and a "6" in the center to compare it, a picture of a stop sign to associate it, a picture of Europe with Greece highlighted to represent its etymology, and a picture of an octagon with its sides numbered to use it appropriately. (Gifted characteristics: originality, better-than-average intellectual skill, a desire to excel. Gifted accommodations: cater to interests, provide work appropriate to ability, provide abstract exercises, encourage the use of high-level thinking skills. NRP categories: Association Method, Concept Method, Elaborate/Rich Instruction, Interactive Vocabulary Techniques.)

Interpersonal Intelligence

Students who possess a great ability to work with others, who can motivate them to take action, and understand them are often successful in group activities. An anecdotal example of such students comes from a suburban, Rocky Mountain secondary school, in the 1969–70 school year. The school's language arts teachers believed that average should mean just that. Hence, students who met the rigorous minimum reading requirements received a grade of C. The required reading list had to be supplemented by reading and reporting on two additional books per nine-week term to earn an above-average B and by four additional books to earn the outstanding A grade. The teachers were progressive and the list of possible titles was reasonably extensive. Further, they were also willing to entertain other suggestions from the students on how to earn the above-average and out-standing grades. A group of five students, all gifted in interpersonal intelligence, but also in a variety of other intelligences, approached the language arts team and asked if they might write a book to earn the A's. Specifically, they said that they did not particularly care for the required list of literature or for the optional list either. These five students found science fiction and fantasy books the most interesting, so they came up with their own reading list and final project.

After several days of deliberation, the language arts team approved their proposal—to write a fantasy and science fiction parody of *The Pearl* by John Steinbeck (1945). During the course of the school year, most of this small group read all of the books written by J. R. R. Tolkein, Robert Heinlein, and Frank Herbert, as well as books written by Ursula K. LeGuin, Terry Brooks, Isaac Asimov, and C. S. Lewis, among others. They called their book *The Precious*. Upon completion, the more-than-200-page manuscript contained a number of illustrations drawn by group members and textual elements of fantasy and science fiction in a story that was very much in the style of the Harvard Lampoon. The teachers had imposed a single, specific stipulation on the group, designed to enhance their learning of vocabulary. They were to pay particular attention to the descriptive vocabulary in the text and as far as possible, use no descriptive noun, verb, adjective, or adverb more than once in the manuscript. Thus, *big* appeared only once. In other places, it was replaced by *huge, gigantic, monstrous*, and so on. A thesaurus was on hand at each writing session, and each word used was marked in the thesaurus, to avoid repetition. To the best of the group's ability, no word was used twice until every other synonym was exhausted. Imagine how much more sophisticated this project might have been with the availability of the new tools to which Generation Y students are accustomed. (Gifted characteristics: originality, better-than-average intellectual and social skills, a desire to excel, superior intelligence, a desire to know, perseverance, self-confidence. Gifted accommodations: cater to interests, provide work appropriate to ability, provide abstract exercises, encourage the use of high-level thinking skills, respect them as individuals, provide opportunity for risk taking. NRP categories: Wide Reading, Elaborate/Rich Instruction, Dictionary/ Glossary, Restructuring of the Task, Concept Method, Association Method, Interactive Vocabulary Techniques.)

Other vocabulary activities for these gifted students include the following:

Using a group variation of Eileen Boland's Key Word Collection strategy (Tompkins & Blanchfield, 2004, pp. 66–68). In this strategy, a group of students is assigned a portion of text or a trade book from the current unit. An interpersonally gifted student is designated the team leader. The group reads the text in literature-circle format, writing down new and different words they encounter. They fill in a three-column Key Concept Chart by writing the word in the first column and writing the possible definitions in the second column. Then they reread the passage where the word was found, marking the correct definition from the list of possibilities. Finally, they fill in the third column with the etymology of the word. An example follows.

Words	Possible Definitions	Etymology
tramp (p. 4)	1. ~~walk heavily~~ 2. ~~sound of a heavy step~~ 3. hobo	Verb made from Middle Low German word trampen, to walk heavily, a person who walks heavily, 1388
mezzanine (p. 5)	A low story between two higher stories of a building	Italian mezzanino, meaning middle, 1711

Figure 8.6: A sample Key Concept Chart, based on *The Family Under the Bridge*, Chapter 1, pp. 1–8, by Natalie Savage Carlson (1958, 1990)

The team leader is in charge of sharing what was learned with the rest of the class. Definitions and etymologies might come from the Web sites such as <u>Fun-with-words.com</u> at http://www.fun-with-words.com, the <u>Online Etymology Dictionary</u> at http://www.etymonline.com, or <u>Dictionary.com</u> at http://www.dictionary.reference.com. (Gifted characteristics: better-than-average intellectual and social skills, a desire to excel, a desire to know. Gifted accommodations: cater to interests, provide work appropriate to ability, provide abstract exercises, encourage the use of high-level thinking skills, respect students as individuals, provide opportunity for risk taking, provide speech-stimulating activity. NRP categories: Elaborate/Rich Instruction, Dictionary/Glossary, Association Method, Context Methods.)

Dramatizing the words by adapting Janice Peltzer's Building Vocabulary Comprehension through Dramatization strategy in Tompkins and Blanchfield (2004). Divide the class into groups of three or four students, again with one of the interpersonally gifted students in each group, to keep the group on task. Each group is given one word and instructed to write and rehearse a two-minute drama that will depict the meaning of the word. All words are written on the board or a poster with the correct definition and two possible but incorrect definitions. The plays are performed, with the word displayed as the title. The other students must choose the correct definition from the list, based on the performance. (Gifted characteristics: better-than-average intellectual, physical, and social skills, a desire to excel. Gifted accommodations: cater to interests, provide work appropriate to ability, provide abstract exercises, encourage the use of high-level thinking skills, provide opportunity for risk taking, provide speech-stimulating activity. NRP categories: Interactive Vocabulary Techniques, Dictionary/Glossary, Elaborate/Rich Instruction.)

Intrapersonal Intelligence

These introspective students are highly skilled at understanding personal needs and planning to meet them. They may be motivated by the following activities:

Creating a key-concept poster for a current vocabulary word (Tompkins & Blanchfield, 2004). In this strategy, intrapersonally talented students choose the three or four most important words from the text they are reading. For example, in a fourth-grade class studying the 50 states, a student may choose *climate, population density,* and *culture* from the introductory chapter in the text. Next, a draft of a visual representation for each word is created. In conference with an assigned team of other students, the gifted student chooses which one of their three or four drafts the group will turn into a poster. Next, they compose a paragraph explaining the chosen draft illustration. They will then conference with the teacher to edit the work. Finally, the group uses a graphic design program to create a computer-generated poster with the chosen word at the top, the illustration of the word in the middle, and the paragraph explaining the illustration at the bottom. (Gifted characteristics: better-than-average intellectual skill, a desire to excel. Gifted accommodations: cater to interests, provide work appropriate to ability, provide abstract exercises, encourage the use of high-level thinking skills, provide opportunity for risk taking. NRP category: Concept Method.)

Play Beef Up the Paragraph, an adaptation of the Beef It Up strategy (Cecil, 2004 pp.151–152). Individual students are assigned to "beef up" a paragraph from the text they are reading by adding words that show feelings, enhancing existing details, and exchanging existing words for more exciting words. Once new paragraphs are edited, students can share them with peers in the class, and show how the beefed-up paragraph is different from the original text. For example, in a fourth-grade science class, the students are studying matter. They come across the following paragraph in their text:

> "Matter can be found in three forms. Some matter, like water, can be found as a gas, a liquid, or a solid. Some matter, like gold, is usually found in solid form, but if heated can be melted into a liquid."

The beefed-up paragraph might read as follows:

> Matter is very interesting, having three distinct forms. For example, water can be found as a gas, like the water vapor in a cloud; or it can be in solid form, like the ice cubes in your soda on a hot, summer day; finally, it can be a liquid, just the right temperature for taking a relaxing bath.

(Gifted characteristics: better-than-average intellectual skill, a desire to excel. Gifted accommodations: cater to interests, provide work appropriate to ability, provide abstract exercises, encourage the use of high-level thinking skills, provide opportunity for risk taking. NRP category: Restructuring the Task.)

Naturalist Intelligence

These gifted students have a heightened capacity to understand environmental and cultural factors. Specific kinds of vocabulary instruction that will appeal to them could include the following:

Creating a Web-based, graphic representation of a current science topic such as the solar system. Vocabulary words such as *Venus, Mars, orbit,* and *asteroids* would be used as labels. The vocabulary words could be hot-linked so that definitions and descriptions of the processes would appear in pop-up windows. Figure 8.7 illustrates a possible Web page, with one pop-up window open.

Figure 8.7: Example of Web-based page on the solar system with labels and one pop-up window. Picture used courtesy of Thinkquest team 25097; retrieved from http://library.thinkqu est.org/25097/graph ics/g_main.htm

(Gifted characteristics: better-than-average intellectual skill, desire to excel. Gifted accommodations: cater to interests, avoid unnecessary drill and practice, give work appropriate to ability, encourage the use of high-level thinking skills. NRP categories: Dictionary/Glossary, Computer/Multimedia Instruction.)

Creating a National Parks Data Chart. In this activity, students with naturalist intelligence complete a chart that lists the U. S. National Parks along the left column. Subsequent columns list characteristics of the parks; for example, climate, geographical features, location. (See Figure 8.8 for an example.)

Name	Location	Climate	Geographical features	Animals found in the park
Yellowstone National Park	northeast corner of Wyoming	four seasons, cold winters, mild summers, not much rain	geysers, boiling mud pots, mineral pools, mountains, rivers with spectacular waterfalls, a large lake	bears, bison, elk, deer, wolves, coyotes, many birds (eagles, hawks, etc.), squirrels and chipmunks
Everglades National Park	center of the Florida peninsula	tropical	mostly swampland	alligators, manatees, water moccasins

Figure 8.8: National Parks Data Chart

This activity helps students develop their vocabulary of natural phenomena. Students can then share what they have learned with the class, using their posters. (Gifted characteristics: better-than-average intellectual skill, desire to excel. Gifted accommodations: cater to interests, give work appropriate to ability, encourage the use of high-level thinking skills, provide speech-stimulating activities. NRP category: Association Method.)

Summary

Vocabulary instruction for gifted students is much the same as it is for any other student. It makes sense for classroom vocabulary instruction to take advantage of the characteristics of this group of students whenever and wherever possible. Current research indicates that generally students are not gifted in all areas, but rather that many students are gifted in one or more. Howard Gardner's theory of multiple intelligences provides a valuable framework that teachers can use as they try to identify specific methods of vocabulary instruction that will appeal to the wide variety of students in their classroom. Effectively enhancing or adapting the whole-class instruction will keep gifted students motivated to succeed and learn.

Discussion Questions and Teaching Activities

1. Generation Y students like to be actively engaged in the learning process. Examine the lessons that you have taught in the past three weeks. To what degree have your students been active? What changes are you contemplating in order to raise the incidence of such learning in your classroom?

2. Take a careful look at *each* student in your classroom. Ascertain whether the individual is gifted in the following intelligence areas: linguistic, logical-mathematical, musical, bodily-kinesthetic, spatial, interpersonal, intrapersonal, and naturalist. (Remember, a student may be gifted in one area but not another, so be sure to look at each area independently.) What does this information tell you about your class as a whole? What actions will you take so that students who are gifted in an area will continue to develop their abilities? How do you plan to use these gifted students as resources to help other students gain greater vocabularies?

Publishing Venues for Students

Web Sites That Publish Student Work

Cyberkids at http://www.cyberkids.com
An online magazine featuring writing and art by kids. It is sponsored by Mountain Lake Software.

The Diary Project at http://www.well.com
An invitation to young people globally to send in diary entries that they can share with each other on the Internet.

ISN KidNews at http://www.umassd.edu
International Student Newswire is a news service for students and teachers around the world. Anyone may use stories from the service, and anyone may submit stories.

Kidopedia at http://kidopedia
An encyclopedia written by children from schools around the world. Read the articles that are available so far, and find out how you can participate.

KidPub at http://www.kidpub.org/kidpub
KidPub is a place for children to publish stories on the World Wide Web and to read stories published by other children. This is a free service sponsored by En-Garde Technical Communication.

MidLink Magazine at http://longwood.cs.ucf.edu/~MidLink
An electronic magazine created for and by children ages 8 to 18.

NewsWave Canada at http://www.occdsb.on.ca/~sel/newswave
An online newsmagazine written by kids for kids, with participation from schools around the world.

Put My Story on the World Wide Web, Writing contests from the Youth Division, and the Internet Public Library all at http://ipl.sils.umich.edu.

Stage Hand Puppets activity page at http://fox.nstn.ca
Puppetry activities mostly for kids, plus an opportunity for kids to submit their own puppet scripts and puppet designs.

Periodicals That Publish Student Work

Chickadee, The Young Naturalist Foundation. 59 Front St., E Toronto, ON MSE 1B3 Canada. (Age range 4 to 8. The environment. Accepts letters for Something to Chirp About, a monthly feature.)

Child Life, P.O. Box 576B, Indianapolis, IN 46206. (Age range 7 to 9. Health, safety, and nutrition. Accepts poetry, stories up to 500 words, jokes and riddles. All Yours features letters to the editor.)

Children's Digest, P.O. Box 576B, Indianapolis, IN 46206. (Age range 8 to 10. Health, safety, and nutrition. Accepts poetry, jokes, riddles, stories up to 700 words. In What Do You Think? children respond to questions asked in earlier issues.)

Children's Playmate, P.O. Box 576B, Indianapolis, IN 46206. (Age range 5 to 7. Accepts artwork and poetry.)

Cricket, P.O. Box 100, La Salle, IL 61301. (Age range 6 to 12. Literary. Accepts children's contributions for Letterbox and Cricket League. Cricket League contests are held monthly in two or three categories—drawing, poetry, and short story. Rules for the contests are explained in each issue.)

Ebony Jr! 820 S. Michigan Ave., Chicago, IL 60605. (Children. Accepts original poems, short stories, essays, jokes riddles, cartoons and artwork.)

The Electric Company. 200 Watt St., P.O. Box 2924, Boulder, CO 80322. (Age range 6 to 9. General interest. Unsolicited material accepted, including jokes for Tickle Yourself. Specific guidelines for other contributions, such as poetry, short stories and essays appear in each issue.)

Highlights for Children, 803 Church St., Honesdale, PA 18431. (Age range 2 to 12. General interest. Accepts original poetry, short stories, jokes, riddles, brief personal narratives, letters to the editor, and Creatures Nobody Has Ever Seen. All contributions are acknowledged with an extremely kind letter.)

Humpty Dumpty, P.O. Box 567B, Indianapolis, IN 46206. (Age range 4 to 6. Health, safety, and nutrition. Accepts children's artwork.)

Jack and Jill. P.O. Box 567B, Indianapolis, IN 46206. (Age range 6 to 8. Health, safety, and nutrition. Accepts artwork, poetry, jokes, and riddles, letters to the editor, and short stories up to 500 words.)

The McGuffey Writer, 400A McGuffey Hall, Miami University, Oxford, OH 45056. (Age range preschool to 18. Children's writing. Accepts poetry, cartoons and art as well as short stories and essays. Word limit is two typewritten pages. Longer works are often excerpted.)

Pennywhistle Press, Box 500-P, Washington, D. C. 20044. (Age range 4 to 12. General-interest weekly. Accepts drawings, jokes, riddles, and letters to Mailbag. Contests are held periodically.)

Stone Soup, Children's Art Foundation, P.O. Box 83, Santa Cruz, CA 95063. (Age range 6 to 13. Literary. Accepts poetry, short stories, drawings and book reviews. Longer works that describe personal experiences are encouraged. Children interested in doing book reviews should address their correspondence to Jerry Mandel. Stone Soup will provide the book to be reviewed.)

Turtle, P.O. Box 567B, Indianapolis, IN 46206. (Age range 2 to 5. Accepts children's artwork.)

Vocabulary Assessment:
A Key to Planning Vocabulary Instruction

Rita M. Bean, University of Pittsburgh, and
Allison Swan, West Virginia University

"I was tenth, and when Mrs. Page called out my word, I spelled: 'Capital M-I-S-S, capital A-L-A-I-N-E-U-S' and added, 'the woman on green spaghetti boxes whose hair is the color of uncooked pasta and it turns into spaghetti at the ends.'"

With that response, Sage, the main character in Debra Frasier's *Miss Alaineus* (2000), loses her class vocabulary bee. Instead of looking up *miscellaneous*, a word she's only heard (not read), she creates a definition based on her experience with the word at the grocery store. In our experience, Sage's shortcut approach to arriving at word meanings is common among students who are frequently expected to "look the word up and write the definition." Although Sage's classmates tease her about her response initially, the story has a happy ending. However, as we all know, not all vocabulary stories end happily.

Gayle Biemeret uses dramatic enactments to assess her students' knowledge of the week's new vocabulary words. These enactments enable students to place the words in a context in which knowledge of their meanings becomes more automatic.

CHAPTER 9: VOCABULARY ASSESSMENT

165

Even the youngest of children come to school with four overlapping vocabularies: listening and reading (receptive) and speaking and writing (expressive). The National Reading Panel (2000) states that there is no single approach to teaching these vocabularies; teachers should use a combination of direct and indirect approaches, as described in Chapters 1–8. Nagy and Anderson (1984) estimate that the average student learns about three thousand words per year, a number that is impossible to teach through direct instruction. Beck et al. (2002) suggest that four hundred words a year can be taught through direct instruction. These numbers apply to the average student, so what does this all mean for the struggling reader and the student whose first language is not English? More important, how can teachers get an accurate picture of all four of their students' vocabularies in order to plan appropriate instruction for them, especially for those students who need additional support?

Given the established connection between vocabulary and comprehension, there is no doubt that vocabulary instruction is a vital component of literacy development. As a consequence, groups such as the National Assessment of Educational Progress (NAEP) are planning to institute a subtest in 2009 to measure students' vocabulary achievement.

There are many research-based approaches for teaching vocabulary, as illustrated in other chapters in this text. However, that is not the case for assessing vocabulary. Indeed, according to Biemiller (2004), the difficulty of assessing vocabulary may be one reason why vocabulary instruction gets so little attention in the primary grades.

Often vocabulary assessment is equated with being able to define a word. Yet, one may not truly know a word by knowing its definition. Asking students to memorize a definition, especially for testing purposes, doesn't help us to measure their depth of understanding. However, asking them if they recognize a word, can access its meaning, and pronounce it quickly does so. This is very different from asking students to remember a verbal definition (Nagy and Scott, 2000). Considering this fact, how can we measure vocabulary knowledge in ways that will help us plan effective instruction?

In this chapter, we explore vocabulary assessment as it relates to everyday classroom settings and to situations in which teachers or reading specialists want to get additional information about students' performance, especially students who may need additional experiences or support to enhance their vocabulary. We organize our discussion around three questions:

- What do teachers need to know about vocabulary development and assessment?

- What are some general principles of assessing vocabulary?

- What formal and informal measures can be used to assess students' vocabulary?

What Do Teachers Need to Know About Vocabulary Development and Assessment?

Vocabulary knowledge is complex. Teachers often identify vocabulary knowledge as a key to reading success. Yet when teachers are asked how to measure vocabulary, they often have to stop and ask themselves, "How do I know what my students know and don't know about vocabulary?" One reason for this is that it is difficult to measure a students' vocabulary knowledge, primarily because the notion of knowing a word is complex. Nagy and Scott (2004) discuss five aspects of complexity: incrementality, polysemy, multidimensionality, interrelatedness, and heterogeneity (p. 270). Each of these aspects has implications for instruction and for measuring or assessing what students know about words:

Incrementality Learning a word takes place over time. As explained in Chapter 6, Dale, O'Rourke, and Bamman (1971) identified four stages of knowing a word: I never saw it; I heard it but don't know what it means; I recognize it in context as having something to do with . . . ; and, I know it well. As students see, hear, read, and write specific words, they move through these stages and become more cognizant of the meanings of words and their nuances.

Polysemy The fact that words have multiple meanings and that context provides important clues to the specific meaning of a particular word (e.g., "The river bank was slippery because of heavy rains") is also important when thinking about word knowledge. Nagy and Scott (2004) point out that the more frequently a word is used, the more likely it is to have multiple meanings. By starting instruction with common words such as *table, beautiful,* and *active,* teachers can build on students' prior knowledge of those words to point to their multiple meanings.

Multidimensionality Again, as explained in Chapter 6, because vocabulary learning follows four stages, from not knowing the word at all to complete knowledge (Dale et al., 1971), students may know the definition for a word but may not be able to use it appropriately in a sentence. They may know the word in its oral or spoken form, but not in its written form. For example, Amy, one of our students, quickly read this headline in the food section of her local newspaper: "Hard-cooked eggs segue from basket to table with ease," but was uncertain about the meaning of *segue.* After consulting her dictionary, she was surprised to find out that what she thought was pronounced "seg-oo" was really pronounced "seg-way"! Certainly Amy had recognized the word one way— through her spoken language—but she did not recognize the word in print.

Another way of thinking about multidimensionality is by looking at the work of Graves (2000), who discusses three different kinds of word-learning tasks: learning new words for familiar concepts, encountering words that are unknown or represent unfamiliar concepts, and learning new meanings for familiar words. When students learn that the word *diminutive* means miniature or small, they are learning a new word for a familiar concept. When they learn about photosynthesis in science they are learning a new word and a new concept. And as students continue to have exposure to words such as *cell*, *bank*, and *stage*, they learn new meanings for them.

Interrelatedness This aspect of complexity relates to the importance of linking the word to be learned with familiar words and concepts. What part of speech is the word (noun, adjective, verb, and so forth)? Are there other words with which this word is associated (*football: punt, tackle, linebacker, scrimmage*)? Too often, words are taught and tested as though they are isolated units of knowledge (Nagy & Scott, 2004).

Heterogeneity The kind of word to be learned is important in defining what it means to know that word. There is a difference between learning the meaning of high-frequency function words such as *the*, *that*, and *if* and learning the meaning of a word like *circumference*. Nagy & Scott (2004) highlight the fact that "word knowledge is applied knowledge: A person who knows a word can recognize it, and use it, in novel contexts, and uses knowledge of the word, in combination with other types of knowledge, to construct a meaning for a text" (p. 273). This notion has important implications for assessing word knowledge, suggesting that providing a definition of a word does not assure that that student truly knows it.

Identifying Words Students Should Know

Although lists of frequently used words are available, deciding which words students should know at specific grade levels is probably best determined by the demands of the curriculum and the classroom. As Block and Mangieri explain in Chapter 1, vocabulary instruction must emphasize high-frequency words, or words that occur frequently in print. Furthermore, there should be an emphasis on the multiple meaning of words. We suggest that teachers assess all word-meaning clues and vocabulary-building strategies described in Chapter 1, using these evaluative categories: (1) students' knowledge of lists of high-utility words; (2) students' knowledge of words they encounter in conversations or in a specific subject area; (3) students' knowledge of the meanings of word parts and structures; and (4) students' knowledge of root words and word etymology. We describe how each of these categories helps to determine students' success.

Students' Knowledge of Lists of High-Utility Words

One approach to determine which words to teach is to develop a commonly agreed-upon list, possibly by grade level or subject area. To accomplish this objective, schools or school districts should develop word lists to be learned by students for each grade level. Such lists may include words important to reading comprehension in general or words derived from each grade's curriculum.

Universally accepted, curriculum-based words upon which tests can be developed are also found in *The Living Word Vocabulary* (Dale & O'Rourke, 1986). Further, words from your basal or anthology can be selected for assessment purposes, although generally words below the fourth-grade level in basals are already in students' oral vocabulary. As stated above, for each topic, students will need to learn specific words (*democracy, constitution, Congress, freedom*)—words that are well suited for a commonly agreed-upon list.

Students' Knowledge of Words They Encounter in Conversations or in a Specific Subject Area

Reading aloud to students is an excellent way to increase their vocabulary, especially that of struggling readers (S. A. Stahl & Shiel, 1992). You can identify words for additional exposure and practice from the books you choose. For example, in the book *Click, Clack, Moo: Cows That Type* (2000), author Doreen Cronin indicates that the farmer is "furious" with the cows' behavior. After reading the book, you can reread the sentence in which that word appears and discuss what the author means by it. You can then provide examples of when you have been furious and also ask students for examples.

Words can also come from the students themselves—specifically, from the books that students are reading independently or from classroom conversations. As students meet unfamiliar words in their reading and talking, you can discuss their meaning and expand students' knowledge of them. Students' interests and needs should guide your choice of words to be learned.

Great Sources for Unique Words

Books by Marvin Terban
(http://www.houghtonmifflinbooks.com)

Columns by Marilyn Vos Savant
(http://www.marilynvossavant.com)

Comic strips by Bob Thaves (http://www.frankandernest.com)

Students' Knowledge of the Meanings of Word Parts and Structures

Students can be assessed according to what they know about how a word's structure contributes to its meaning, as so aptly described in Chapters 1 and 3. Studying word structure, also known as morphological or structural analysis, in its simplest form, includes direct instruction of root words, suffixes, and prefixes. As students move through the earlier grades, morphological analysis takes the place of phonemic awareness as a vital linguistic skill (Carlisle, 2003). Teaching morphological analysis is an effective strategy for increasing vocabulary knowledge, especially in grades 4 and up (Nagy, Diakidoy & Anderson, 1993). Being aware of the morphological units in words can have a significant impact on reading ability and is important in vocabulary growth. In fact, 60 percent of the new words a student encounters in reading in grades 4 and up can be figured out by analyzing their parts (Nagy & Anderson, 1984). Combining instruction in morphological analysis with instruction in using context can also have a positive effect on students' vocabulary growth (Baumann, Edwards, Boland, Olejnik, & Kame'enui 2003).

Students' Knowledge of Root Words and Word Etymology

Biemiller and Slonium (2001) estimate the average reader will acquire nine thousand root words by the end of elementary school—eight hundred to nine hundred root words per year. Direct instruction and indirect exposure to root words will help students increase their understanding of them. Nifty Thrifty Fifty is a list of polysyllabic words containing prefixes, suffixes, and root words found in *Month-by-Month Phonics for Upper Grades* (P. M. Cunningham & Hall, 1998). The words from this list can be used for instructional and assessment purposes. When teachers want to identify specific words for tests, they can also ask students to study the etymology of the words. Such study can get students interested in and motivated to learn words that are not on the test.

In sum, given the complexity of knowing a word, special attention must be given to the selection of words for vocabulary tests. These words must be part of the instruction students receive in the basic vocabulary-building strategies described in Chapter 1. The meaning of the word will most likely be clear to students if they have truly learned the strategy you've taught. For example, if you have taught the morphological analysis strategy using the family of words that begin with the prefix *pre-*, a test question could be, "What can be learned from studying movie previews?" This question cannot be answered without the use of morphological analysis and also inferential thinking, which is an essential component in all vocabulary assessments, as described in Chapter 1.

What Are Some General Principles of Assessing Vocabulary?

In this section, we discuss goals and purposes that are important to making decisions about assessing vocabulary, the value of authentic assessment of students' depth of understanding of words, and the relationship between vocabulary and comprehension as it relates to vocabulary tests.

Goals and Purposes Matter

The reason for giving the assessment is key to determining the type of assessment that should be used. For example, if a school district is interested in knowing whether vocabulary instruction has been effective in the school as a whole, it may choose to administer a norm-referenced standardized assessment such as the Gates MacGinitie Reading Test (MacGinitie, MacGinitie, Maria, & Dreyer, 2000). This is a group-administered, multiple-choice assessment of reading vocabulary. Such a test enables a school to compare its students at a specific grade level with a nationwide sample of other students at the same grade level. We discuss standardized assessment measures in greater depth later in the chapter.

On the other hand, if a teacher is interested in knowing whether students have learned the vocabulary in a specific content area, she can create a criterion-referenced test that assesses students' knowledge of specific words and their ability to apply vocabulary-building strategies.

Likewise, if a reading specialist is interested in knowing more about struggling readers' vocabulary knowledge, she may have students orally define words that she says to them. She may also ask students questions about words in a passage they have read. This approach can be very helpful when a student misreads a word; the reading specialist can say the word and perform a Think Aloud about that word's meaning-based clue and a strategy that can be used to learn the word and others like it. Then she can ask the student to talk about its meaning. From the reply, she can determine whether the problem is related to decoding deficiencies or to vocabulary-building knowledge.

Authentic Measures Matter

Teachers can also get a sense of students' vocabulary knowledge through the use of authentic measures such as informal conversations with students, checklists or rubrics, informal observations, and students' own self-assessment of their understanding of words. For example, engaging in discussions with students in reading and writing conferences is an excellent way to evaluate students' vocabulary growth. Recently, Rita had a conversation with her young grandson, a preschooler, about a robin's eggshell that they had picked up from the grass. They talked about how fragile the shell was, how easily it could break, and he compared it to special water glasses that his mother had forbidden him to use! Certainly, this child is beginning to get an understanding of the meaning of *fragile*. Subjective rubrics for scoring writing samples is another form of authentic assessment. They require teachers to be kid-watchers (Goodman, 1978) and sensitive observers (Clay, 1998).

Metacognitive tasks—such as keeping self-evaluation checklists—that encourage students to think about their own understanding of words are also great for assessing students' vocabulary growth. Unfortunately, given the amount of time they take to administer and the large number of words that students should know at every grade, many teachers cannot find time to write such metacognitive tests for all words. Later in this chapter, we explain how to carry out several of these authentic vocabulary assessments.

Depth of Understanding Matters

Assessments tasks cover a range of difficulty. There are easy tasks, such as asking students to recognize or select the right response (for example, which of the following words has about the same meaning as *large: enormous, small, pretty, delicate*). Recall tasks, such as asking a student to generate a definition or identify synonyms of known words, are more challenging. The most thorough and valid assessments transcend these levels of understanding by requiring students to infer how and when a word could be used in their lives. S. A. Stahl (1985) identified that each task level requires a different depth of processing. For example, students should be evaluated according to how well they

- ◆ make an association between a new word and the appropriate use of that word in their conversations and writing.

- ◆ understand a word in a sentence by doing something to show that they know the definition—for example, finding an antonym, classifying the word.

- ◆ generate a novel use of the word—for example, write an original sentence or provide a written or oral restatement of the definition.

The Comprehension Connection Matters

As mentioned earlier, there is a close and reciprocal relationship between vocabulary and comprehension. Lack of vocabulary usually has a negative impact on comprehension, and poor comprehension limits the ability to acquire new vocabulary words. For instance, consider the meanings of the word *cell*.

> **cell** (sel) *n.* a small room in a prison, convent or monastery; any small hollow place; the basic unit of living matter, of which plants and animals are made; electric cell; a small group that acts as a political, social or religious unit for a larger sometimes revolutionary organization. (From the *Thorndike Barnhart Advanced Dictionary* [1993].)

If a student had only one definition of *cell*—say, "a basic unit of living matter"— how would it affect his comprehension? A discussion in social studies on terrorist sleeper cells would be very confusing, right? Understanding the connection between vocabulary and comprehension helps you assess students because you can more clearly identify whether comprehension problems are being caused by weak vocabulary skills or something else.

What Formal and Informal Measures Can Be Used to Assess Students' Vocabulary?

In this section, we extend our discussion of formal and informal vocabulary assessment, stressing that informal measures may be more useful to classroom teachers, reading specialists, and other educators in planning instruction. That said, we also identify and discuss the strengths and limitations of various formal measures that may be helpful to administrators who need to get a broad understanding of a school's vocabulary program. We also describe informal tests that may be used to obtain more in-depth information about students with language or vocabulary difficulties.

Our stance on assessment is closely aligned with P. Johnson and Costello's (2005). They assert that measurement needs to be grounded in an understanding of literacy and society, stressing that literacy is more than a set of skills and strategies. They strongly urge us to use assessment as a means of learning more about students and what they understand as they are engaged in authentic reading and writing activities, and they make some important recommendations for how such evaluations can occur. These recommendations serve as a basis for the assessment principles we describe later in this chapter:

- The teacher is the primary agent of assessment. As such, assessment can occur moment by moment during the act of teaching.

- Students' self-assessments can raise their awareness of literacy and of themselves as literate people.

- Informal assessments can help teachers plan effective instructional activities.

P. Johnson and Costello refer to the purposes and types of literacy assessment as either summative (backward looking) or formative (forward looking). Summative assessment usually summarizes or judges performance. It may not be helpful in improving the quality of literacy learning for students because it identifies skills, strategies, and processes that have already become automatic for individual learners. On the other hand, formative assessment, in which teachers and students participate in assessment while new skills, strategies, and processes are being taught, provides information about how quickly and how well students are learning them. In this section, we first identify formal tests that measure vocabulary. We then discuss informal procedures.

Formal

Most formal assessments of vocabulary are norm-referenced, group-administered survey tests that provide information about how students in a grade, school, or district compare with others across the state or country. They may also be individually administered by a reading specialist, speech therapist, special educator, or guidance counselor to obtain diagnostic information about an individual student.

Although survey tests can be helpful in obtaining comparative information, they have several limitations:

First, many of these tests do not measure knowledge of a word in depth (Beck et al., 2002; McCormick, 1995). Only partial knowledge is required for a student to, for example, match a word to a definition or to decide which word would best fill the blank in a sentence. Survey tests do not measure students' knowledge of the many different meanings of a word. A student may know that the word *run* means "to move quickly" but may not know it also means "to occur tirelessly."

Second, if a survey test requires students to read a passage and choose words to fill the blanks, the teacher has no way of knowing whether incorrect answers are due to problems with vocabulary, decoding, comprehension, or a combination of the three.

Third, because many standardized tests are timed, students who read slowly are at a disadvantage. These students may not be able to finish the test (McCormick, 1995), even though they may be aware of many of the unattempted words' meanings.

Fourth, the words on these tests most likely represent only a small sample of the many words that students know.

Fifth, these tests do not provide the type of diagnostic information that will help teachers make decisions about how to implement an effective vocabulary program for individual students in their classrooms.

Sixth, some formal tests, like the CELF (Semel, Wiig, & Secord, 2003), require specialized training for administering and interpreting results and are time-consuming to administer.

When choosing a test, it is critical to obtain information about its technical aspects such as reliability, validity, and appropriateness for a specific group of students. Some standardized tests may not be appropriate for students whose backgrounds, culture, and language are different from the group on which the test's norm was established.

Southwest Educational Development Laboratory has created a detailed database of a variety of primary-grade literacy assessments. It can be found at http://www.sedl.org/reading/rad/. Information about specific tests is also available in professional texts such as *Early Reading Assessment* (Rathvon, 2004), *Assessment and Instruction of Reading and Writing Difficulties: An Interactive Approach* (Lipson & Wixson, 2003), and *Reading Problems: Assessment and Teaching Strategies* (Richek, Caldwell, Jennings, & Lerner, 2002).

In Figure 9.1, we list some of the standardized tests that may be useful. We identify each test, its source and Web site, the grade levels for which it is available, and some information about the test and administering it (for example, Does the test require students to read or does it measure auditory vocabulary? Does the test require individual administration or can it be administered to a group of students?). Some of the tests measure only vocabulary (such as the Peabody Picture Vocabulary Test) while others are more comprehensive assessments of literacy development (such as the Clinical Evaluation of Language Fundamentals).

Test	Publisher	Age/Grade	Format Auditory/ Reading	Details (Individual or Group; Time)
Boehm-3 Boehm Test of Basic Concepts (3rd edition, 2001; Spanish version available)	Harcourt http://www. hbtpc.com	Grades K–2	Auditory	Group; 30–45 mins.
CELF Clinical Evaluation of Language Fundamentals (4th edition, 2003)	Harcourt http://www. hbtpc.com	Ages 6–21	Auditory	Individual; 30–45 mins.
CREVT-2 Comprehensive Receptive and Expressive Vocabulary Test (2nd Edition, 2002)	Pro-Ed Associates http://www. proedinc. com	Ages 4.0 to 9.11	Auditory	Individual; 20–30 mins.
DARTTS Diagnostic Assessments of Reading with Trial Teaching Strategies (1992)	Riverside Publishing Company http://www. riverpub.com	Grades 1–12	Auditory	Individual; 20–30 mins.
EVT Expressive Vocabulary Test (1997)	American Guidance Service http://www. agsnet.com	Ages $2^1/_2$–90+	Auditory	Individual; 15 mins.
GMRT Gates-MacGinitie Reading Tests (4th edition, 2000)	Riverside Publishing Company http://www. riverpub.com	Grades K–2; 2–12	Auditory/ Reading	Group/ individual; 55–105 mins.

Figure 9.1: Measures for Assessing Meaning Vocabulary

Test	Publisher	Age/Grade	Format Auditory/ Reading	Details (Individual or Group; Time)
Nelson-Denny Reading Test (1993)	Riverside Publishing Company http://www.riverpub.com	High school; college	Reading	Group; 45 mins.
PPVT Peabody Picture Vocabulary Test (3rd edition, 1997; Spanish & bilingual versions available)	American Guidance Service http://www.agsnet.com	Ages 2 1/2–90+	Auditory	Individual; 10–15 mins.
SDRT Stanford Diagnostic Reading Test (4th edition, 2001)	Harcourt http://www.hbtpc.com	Grades 1.5–3.5 3.5–13.0	Auditory/ Reading	Group; 100 mins.
TOLD Test of Language Development (3rd edition, 1997)	Pro-Ed Associates http://www.proedinc.com	Ages 4.0 to 8.11 (primary); 8.0 to 12.11 (intermediate)	Auditory	Individual; 30–60 mins.
TORC-3 Test of Reading Comprehension (3rd edition, 1995)	Pro-Ed Associates http://www.proedinc.com	Grades 2–12	Reading	Group/ Individual; 30 mins.
WRMT-R Woodcock Reading Mastery Test (3rd edition, 1998)	American Guidance Service http://www.agsnet.com	Ages 5–75	Reading	Individual; 30–45 mins.

Informal

This section is divided into two parts. In the first, we discuss measures to use in authentic reading and writing situations for obtaining in-depth information about what students know about words and how they learn about words. In the second, we provide practical formats for constructing assessments; most of these can be directly connected to classroom instructional decision making. The range of formats enables teachers to differentiate or adjust instruction as they see what students can and cannot do. Our goal is to present ideas that teachers can use to learn more about students' strengths and needs—and then to build on what they learn in order to help students expand their vocabulary knowledge.

Authentic Measures

There are many ways that teachers can get a better picture of what words students know and how students approach word learning. We discuss below the use of interviews and observations, rubrics and checklists, instructional strategies, and self-evaluation tasks.

Interviews and observations Classroom teachers, reading specialists, and special educators can get important information about students' vocabulary knowledge by taking the time to talk to students about what they have read and what they do when they come to unknown words. Harmon (1998) investigated the strategies and perceptions of four middle-school learners who were asked to identify unfamiliar words in materials they were reading. She found that they had various strategies, including using (1) word-level clues (trying to pronounce the unfamiliar word); (2) immediate context (familiar words surrounding the unfamiliar word); and (3) extended context (sentences surrounding the word). Students also made connections beyond the text to their own knowledge and experiences and relied on syntax to construct meaning.

  We suggest that during reading conferences and guided reading, teachers talk with their students about what they do when they come to an unknown word. This is especially important for teachers working with older students who are reading texts containing many words that may be unfamiliar to them. The knowledge gained from such interviews helps teachers plan instruction that will expand students' ability to use context to figure out words.

Rubrics and checklists Using a checklist or rubric is a more formal way to gather information about what to expect of students at specific grade levels. For example, Dickinson, McCabe, and Sprague (2001) developed the Teacher Rating of Oral Language and Literacy for assessing several aspects of literacy development in Grades

K–3, including oral vocabulary. Vacca and Vacca (2005) provide a sample checklist for observing reading and study behavior in a content area. The vocabulary sections of this checklist help teachers determine whether students have a good grasp of technical terms in the subject, can work out the meaning of an unknown word through context or structural analysis, know how to use a dictionary, see relationships among key terms, and are interested in the derivation of technical terms (p. 47).

Instructional strategies as assessment tools Instructional strategies can be useful to teachers as assessment tools, such as the Vocabulary Self-Selection Strategy (Haggard, 1986). Students select from their reading words that they feel are important. Then, working in groups, members nominate one word for in-depth investigation. The group tries to determine the word's meanings and discuss why their classmates should know the word. This encourages students to become aware of their own vocabulary learning and that of their fellow students. (See Chapter 2 for more on the Vocabulary Self-Selection Strategy.)

Semantic Feature Analysis (Pittelman et al., 1991) requires students to reduce a large number of conceptually related terms to a basic grid. For example, when learning about different types of rocks (for example, marble, sandstone, pumice) students can create an organizer comparing features such as appearance, feel, and color. The finished product allows teachers to evaluate students' understandings of similarities and differences between conceptually connected vocabulary words. (See Chapter 4 for more on the Semantic Feature Analysis.)

Self-evaluation tasks By having students rank their degree of word knowledge (Blachowicz and Fisher, 1996), teachers not only learn more about their students' self-assessed abilities, but also can determine words for future instruction. Self-evaluation tasks can be used at all grade levels. For example, Allison gives a knowledge rating chart to her graduate students to fill out anonymously the week before the reading assignment and discussion on assessment. A sampling of terms she includes in the chart is listed in Figure 9.2. She asks students to indicate their level of knowledge of the assessment terms. This informal measure helps her tailor her lectures and discussions on assessment to meet her students' needs.

	I know it well.	I recognize it as having something to do with . . .	I've heard it but don't know what it means.	I've never seen it.
Informal Reading Inventory				
High-Stakes Testing				
Miscue Analysis				
Kid Watching				
Percentiles				
Reliability				
Rubric				
Running Records				
Validity				

Figure 9.2: Sample Knowledge Rating Chart

Formats for Testing

Teachers who are interested in constructing their own assessments can use the formats we describe below. We've organized them into the following categories: contextual, applicational definition, contextual and definitional combined, morphological, and relational/categorical. The tasks under each of the five formats do not represent every alternative; also, many of the tasks, with modifications, can be applied across all five formats.

Contextual

Students use context clues to identify words. A word of caution, though: some contexts do not provide enough information to identify words, especially for students whose knowledge of the topic is limited. As described in Chapter 1, context clues are best used to determine the meaning of high-utility words. Using context clues for other types of words is certainly inadequate when struggling readers' language problems (or lack of access to print) limit their ability to build enough information about a topic through context alone. The teacher can design a context assessment so that the degree of difficulty varies, depending upon the abilities or skills of the test takers. Examples follow.

Choice

Students select the word that best fits the context.

> The wealthy man in the _____ vehicle zoomed past the other cars quickly.
>
> a. automobile
>
> b. luxurious
>
> c. swiftly
>
> d. blue

Modification options: To reduce the difficulty, limit responses to two or three choices. To increase it, make the correct answer less obvious. For example, in the item above, you could change choice *a* to "horse-drawn" and choice *c* to "dilapidated." Have groups of students discuss their choices and their rationales for them.

Cloze

Students supply the missing word in the sentence.

> In science class, the students studied about warm-blooded and cold-blooded _____.

Modification option: Provide a word bank (*mammals, biologists, whales*).

Generate

Students construct a sentence using the word correctly.

> Use the word <u>stately</u> in a sentence.

Applicational Definition

Having students apply definitional knowledge is an important method of vocabulary assessment. But, again, be aware that the depth to which students can define, explain, and provide examples for a specific word may differ. As explained in Chapters 1, 5, and

8, for students to demonstrate the deepest level of understanding, assessments must require them to make inferences about the ways in which they can determine the meaning of a word in speaking and writing. For example, students' answers must reflect an analysis, synthesis, or evaluative application of that word's meaning to events that occur in their lives. Students must demonstrate that they have moved beyond merely memorizing the definition. The following methods provide ways of reaching this end.

Retell

Rather than having students merely write a definition of a new term in their own words, students place the word—*gigantic*, for example—on a continuum of synonyms so that they must use their analysis of the word's meaning in the personal context of similar words that they already use automatically. For instance, students can create an organizer like this:

big > large > huge > gigantic

Modification option: Have students compare their continuums of meaning, select the one that most vividly displays the many word choices and their ordering of density in meaning, and, as a group, compose a rich definition of that word.

Synonyms

Students provide a synonym as a means of defining the word, through the use of analogies, similes, and metaphors (as described in Chapters 5 and 8). In so doing, the student has to think about the vocabulary term in an analytical manner and connect features within a word's meaning to features in the meanings of more familiar words.

Gigantic is like _____ .

Modification option: Provide words from which students can choose to complete the analogy. Ask them, "Which of these words means about the same as *gigantic* (thumbs up for those with which you agree): *mammoth, enormous, tiny, huge, diminutive.*"

Examples

Students provide an example or non-example as a means of defining the word, which enables them to analyze the degrees of meaning and the scope of meaning within a word. (See Chapters 6 and 7 for more information on Example and Non-Example.)

Give me an example of something gigantic. What is a non-example? (Give me an example of something that is not gigantic.)

Modification option: Provide choices of examples and non-examples, such as, Which of these is gigantic: an elephant, an ant, a dinosaur, a skyscraper, a squirrel?

Drawing or Dramatization

Students draw a picture or act out a scenario to represent a word's meaning. The depiction must contain elements that exist in the student's own life, so that evaluative thinking is used in the process of generating the meaning.

> Draw a picture to illustrate the meaning of <u>gregarious</u> as it may occur at our school and describe the event in either a paragraph or as a caption of a picture or cartoon.

Modification option: Have students work with several classmates to draw the picture or to develop a scenario, and then enact the scenario in a charades-like format. To score a point for a correct answer, a team must use the words being enacted in sentences that accurately reflect the meaning conveyed in the scenario.

Contextual and Definitional Combined

Teachers often use a combination of contextual and definitional informal testing formats when introducing or discussing words with students. Examples follow.

Definitions

Students are provided with a sentence and select the best definition based on words in context.

> One of these days, Cara's father is going to <u>erupt</u> if he needs to keep reminding his daughter to pick up after herself.
>
> a. listen attentively
>
> b. throw forth lava
>
> c. become furious
>
> d. look bewildered

Modification option: To reduce the difficulty, limit responses to two or three choices. To increase the difficulty, make the correct answer less obvious. For example, choice *a* could be changed to "quit listening."

Morphological

Teaching students to understand word structure and word-part meanings should be a vital part of the reading curriculum from even the earliest grades. When students are able to search for and identify meanings in word parts, they are better equipped to figure out the meanings of unknown words on their own. By assessing students' morphological knowledge, teachers can gain a better idea of their instructional needs.

Morphological Identification

Students read or listen to a series of words and determine the prefix or root and, based on the examples provided, try to determine its meaning.

> vision, invisible, visor (vis = see)

Modification option: Have students sort cards into categories based on similarities in prefixes, suffixes, and root words.

Morphological Closure

Students read or listen to a series of words and complete the series. For example, students who know that *-ology* means "study of" can fill in the correct words in the following series of sentences.

> The study of planets is _____. (astrology)
>
> The study of living things is _____. (biology)
>
> The study of ancient things is _____. (paleontology)
>
> The study of rocks is _____. (geology)

Relational/Categorical

We ask students to predict in language arts, hypothesize in science, and estimate in math. Conceptually, predicting, hypothesizing, and estimating are the same task, yet we use three different words to describe it. What these words have in common is the notion of guessing. Teaching students to recognize the relationships between known and unknown words is an important concept—especially in promoting independent vocabulary learning. The following techniques can be useful in assessing students' knowledge of words at several levels.

Analogy

Students provide the next word in a series of connected terms.

Kid is to goat as calf is to _____. (cow)

Harrisburg is to Pennsylvania as Lincoln is to _____. (Nebraska)

Modification options: Provide choices. Harrisburg is to Pennsylvania as Lincoln is to (a.) California, (b.) Nebraska, (c.) Hawaii. Groups of students may discuss and then select answers. Have students compose their own analogies.

Graphic Organizer

Students construct a semantic web and must explain (orally or in writing) their way into and out of the center (the key word). This can be helpful for assessing knowledge or understanding of a concept word in the content areas.

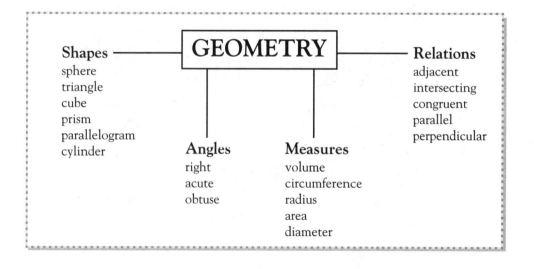

Oddity

Students hear or read attributes of a noun and determine which word doesn't belong.

house—wood, concrete, car, shingles

river—whitewater, parachute, eddy, paddle

Brainstorming

Students list as many words within a given category as possible in one minute. For example, they might brainstorm words whose meanings relate to size (for example, *big, little, enormous, tiny, large, petite, miniature, bulky*), feelings, a location, or time. Afterward, students must generate three or four categories in which to slot each of the words.

Modification option: Have students brainstorm lists of words after providing them with the set of three or four categories.

Identify words associated with school. Use the following categories to help spur your thinking: (a) supplies/materials; (b) academic subjects; and (c) clubs and associations.

Summary

Assessing vocabulary, like vocabulary knowledge itself, is complex. In this chapter, we discussed what teachers need to know if they are going to understand what the results of various assessments mean. We also described some general principles of assessing vocabulary that are critical in developing, selecting, and interpreting assessment results. Having a goal for assessment and realizing the limits of what an assessment reveals about students' in-depth understanding of a word or words are important concepts to think about when you're selecting or designing an assessment tool. In this chapter, we also provided specific examples of formal or standardized measures and described various informal tools and formats that can help you get a more complete picture of students' in-depth knowledge of words.

Discussion Questions and Teaching Activities

1. Compare your past vocabulary assessment practices with the ones present-ed in this chapter. How will the evaluative measures in this chapter increase your ability to diagnose students' individual vocabulary needs?

2. Administer one formal assessment and one informal assessment. What diagnostic information did you derive from each of these measures?

CHAPTER TEN

Preparing Today's Generation of
Students for Tomorrow

Arthur L. Costa, California State University, Sacramento, Emeritus, and **Rebecca Reagan,** educational consultant

> "The limits of my language are the limits of my mind. All I know is what I have words for."
>
> —Ludwig Wittgenstein

 nowing they are about to hear the assignment, Beth and Lisa are focused on the teacher, whom they wish to please. They have enjoyed the unit on the Civil War they have been studying. Working interdependently in groups has been not only a learning experience, but also fun. Beth was the leader of the group and sometimes used words that Lisa really didn't understand, but Lisa wouldn't dream of asking her best friend and next-door neighbor what they meant. They shared a birthday month and a first name—Elizabeth. However, Lisa had gotten very good at pretending to know what Beth knew.

Mr. Puente began to give the assignment. "Boys and girls, today you are going to have the opportunity to show me your knowledge about two of the great men who lived during the Civil War. We have been talking and reading about Abraham Lincoln and Frederick Douglass. Think about what you have learned. You are going to compare these two men. You may choose to write an essay or you may want to write a poem. However, you need to think about what you are going write so it will show what you know. Get out a blank piece of paper and begin."

Mr. Puente leads his sixth graders to develop a deeper understanding of the word *prejudice* by using the questioning strategies covered in this chapter.

Beth smiled broadly. She couldn't wait to get started and pulled out her paper and her thesaurus, too. As Lisa slowly brought a piece of paper to the top of the desk, her heart pounded. As usual, the blank page instilled fear in her.

The next day the assignment was due. Beth proudly placed her paper on top of the stack while Lisa, having struggled with the assignment, quickly placed hers on the bottom, as if it were searing her hand.

The most Lisa could write was this:

> Frederick Douglass was black.
> Abraham Lincoln was white.
> They both didn't like slavery.

Applying her knowledge and experience with a diamante poem, Beth wrote:

> Lincoln
>
> Self-taught, Clever
>
> Working, Helping, Freeing
>
> White House, Ford's Theater,
> Newspaper, Orator
>
> Speaking, Buying, Fighting
>
> Bold, Determined
>
> Douglass

Comparing the richness, complexity, eloquence, and depth of thought in these two pieces of writing, their differences become obvious. These two students began life on a level playing field and their innate intelligence was in the same range. Both were born into middle-class, loving families. Beth was bathed in language from birth by being read to every day, talked to constantly about what she was seeing when she was traveling in the car, and taken to the local zoo, science museum, and other places of interest. All the while she was encouraged to learn new words, to identify objects, and to understand vocabulary that she encountered everywhere.

In contrast, Lisa's home was bereft of language. Her parents watched TV almost every night and hoped that she would go to sleep as soon as they put her to bed with her bottle. In the front seat of the car they listened to the radio, talked to each other, or conversed by cell phone. Although they did take her to some local places of interest, they failed to reflect on and derive meaning from these experiences. In other words, Lisa was not immersed in language—most of her vocabulary was related to her survival.

We see too many Lisas in the Generation Y. How do we as educators (teachers, counselors, administrators) and family (parents, grandparents, brothers, sisters, and other caregivers) enhance the language of our youth both in and out of school? That is what this chapter is about. We will address these major questions:

♦ Why do the vocabulary and language skills of today's generation need to be enhanced?

♦ What vocabulary and language skills should be taught to prepare today's generation for the future?

Why Do the Vocabulary and Language Skills of Today's Generation Need to Be Enhanced?

From the moment they're born, children are learning. Developing most rapidly from birth to 3 years of age, a child's brain absorbs massive amounts of information and stimulation. Deep inside a baby's developing brain, tiny neuro-circuits search for pathways to connect cells. Every taste, every touch, every interaction helps or hinders this process. Whenever a child is exposed to positive experiences such as music, laughter, hugging, smiling, playing, and listening to loving voices, these connections form at an astonishing rate. Eventually these neuro-circuits will help the child speak, solve problems, and learn. But for that to happen, the circuits need to make good connections, and such connections depend on the quality of a child's earliest experiences. The more adults speak, sing, and read to the child, the faster the child's brain develops and the more a child learns. Positive interactions with humans and the environment result in the development of sound circuitry.

From birth, children begin to imitate sounds, then words, phrases, and thought patterns of the significant adults in their lives. As a result of these interactions, they develop the foundations of thought that endure throughout their lifetimes. Embedded in the vocabulary, inflections, and syntax of the language of adults are the cognitive processes and cultural values that are learned by children. Like the two sides of a coin, language and thought are entwined and inseparable. Exposure to rich, fluent, varied, and complex language and thought enable children to handle complex thinking processes as they mature (Costa, 2001).

Home life, however, isn't what it used to be. In the past three decades there has been a significant transformation of the American family and the culture of youth. Growing up in an era of immediate gratification and bombardment with visual and oral stimuli, the environment of the Generation Y child is characterized by an increased amount of time spent passively watching television, playing video games, listening to four-second sound bites, surfing the Internet, and communicating in chat rooms with abbreviated text messaging. Some students believe that writing is no longer necessary because technology has made it obsolete.

For several reasons, the amount of face-to-face interaction in many modern families has been vastly curtailed. By the time many low-income children start school, their verbal skills are already underdeveloped, due to malnutrition, poor prenatal care, and the limited way their parents talk to them. Preschool teachers may try to build children's vocabularies through word games, field trips, and parent workshops, but they find it difficult to close the gap between a child's expected and actual literacy performance. These efforts may often fail because the children have missed out on hearing millions of words in their first years of life (Costa & Garmston, 2005).

Harried family life often lacks meaningful verbal interaction. What talk there is is often bereft of complexity or deep meaning and takes the form of interactions such as: "How was school?" "Okay." "What did you learn?" "Nothing." It frequently consists of terse commands: "Go to bed." "Do your homework." "Stop teasing your sister." "Eat your dinner."

Students use vague and imprecise language to describe objects or events with words such as *weird, nice,* or *okay.* They identify specific objects with nondescriptive words such as *stuff, junk,* and *things.* They use vague nouns and pronouns: "*They* told me to do it." "*Everybody* has one." "*Teachers* don't understand me." They use nonspecific verbs: "Let's *do* it." and unqualified comparatives: "This soda is *better;* I like it *more.*"

Success in school and future careers is dependent upon skillful language usage. Potential employers will judge applicants by their written and verbal skills. When employers hear such grammatical errors as "Me and him went to the ballgame," "We ain't got no . . . ," and "Them guys," it creates a negative image in comparison with other candidates whose language is more refined. Today's youth will succeed or fail depending on their dialogical skills whether within their careers, organizations, communities, marriages, or families—that is to say, their life (Scott, 2002).

Not only is oral vocabulary important, but with the emergence of the Internet, writing has become the quintessential skill for communication. The ability to express one's thoughts in writing is an essential part of being educated (Allan, 2003). In recognition of the importance of students, being able to write with some degree of skill, many state tests require open-ended responses or essays as part of the criteria for assessing achievement. State curricula, as usual, follow the required elements of testing—instead of preceding them (McGrath, 2004).

When children enter school lacking the complexity of vocabulary and thought needed to master academic demands, they are essentially already starting out learning-impaired.

What Vocabulary and Language Skills Should Be Taught to Prepare Today's Generation for the Future?

New goals are needed for contributing to, participating in, and even surviving the remainder of the twenty-first century and on into the twenty-second century (Eisner, 2003). They include

♦ **collaboration**—the ability to work with others, particularly with those who are culturally different;

♦ **judgment**—the ability to give reasons for the choices we make;

♦ **critical thinking**—the ability to critique and to enjoy exploring and applying ideas; and

♦ **meaningful literacy**—the ability to encode or decode meaning in any of the symbolic forms used in the culture.

Each of these goals has tremendous linguistic implications, and to meet them, educators and the community alike must attend to students' verbal, linguistic, and cognitive needs.

In this section, we will explore how each of these goals applies to vocabulary instruction and gives you strategies to use in the classroom to improve your students' language skills.

The Vocabulary and Language of Collaboration

Probably the foremost skill needed by Generation Y students as they face the future is the ability to think in concert with others—to view themselves as interdependent and thus to become sensitive to the needs of others. Problem solving has typically become so complex that no one person can do it alone. One does not usually have access to all the data needed to make critical decisions; no one person can consider as many alternatives as several people can. Cooperative humans realize that all of us together are more powerful, intellectually and/or physically, than any individual alone.

> "A unique relationship develops among team members who enter into dialogue regularly. They develop a deep trust that cannot help but carry over to discussions. They develop a richer understanding of the uniqueness of each person's point of view."
>
> —Peter Senge

When working in groups, each member must be able to justify ideas to others and to test the feasibility of their solutions. Through verbal interaction, the group and the individual continue to grow. Learning the art of compromise is a lifelong process that involves listening, consensus seeking, giving up an idea to work with someone else's, empathy, compassion, leadership, supportiveness, altruism—all behaviors of cooperative human beings.

The Verbal Skills of Collaborative Groups

Of all the attributes of effective thinkers universally and cross-culturally, the capacity for dialogue is paramount (Bowers, 1987). However, it is probably the least taught skill in school. Dialogue is central to the resolution of any problem or disagreement. Because many people have not learned the verbal discipline of engaging in collaborative dialogue, they resort to other means—bullying, separation, divorce, or abusiveness in settling domestic disputes; terrorism among religious factions; street gang violence; hate crimes; wars among nations; and ethnic cleansing among cultural groups as their way of solving problems.

A culture is a group of people thinking together. It builds as meanings are shared. As a cultural group becomes more skillful in dialogue, the values of respect, empathy, and caring begin to pervade its value system, practices, and beliefs. It is through dialogue that issues are illuminated, problems solved, and differences accommodated. It builds an atmosphere of trust in human relationships, trust in the processes of interaction and trust throughout the culture. Dialogue is the process of creating a shared vision. David Perkins (2002) points out that organizations function and grow through conversations, and the quality of those conversations determines how smart your organization is. Thinking interdependently in cooperative groups provides students with opportunities to monitor and reflect on their dialogue.

At least 50 percent of any dialogue is listening. Many adults say they are listening but actually they are rehearsing inside their head what they will say next. Effective listeners set aside certain unproductive mental patterns that may block their listening capabilities. These include making value judgments, solving the speaker's problem, giving advice, and telling stories about themselves rather than sustaining their mental focus on the speaker (Costa & Garmston, 2004).

Humans, as social beings, mature intellectually in reciprocal relationships. Collaboratively, people generate and discuss ideas by eliciting thinking that surpasses their own individual efforts. Together and privately, they express different perspectives, agree and disagree, point out and resolve discrepancies, and weigh alternatives. Because the intellect grows through this process, collegial interaction is a crucial factor in the intellectual life of the school.

Baker, Costa, and Shalit (1997) identify eight collaborative competencies that may serve as standards that are understood, agreed upon, adopted, monitored, and assessed by each contributing member of a group. They are the glue that enables groups to engage in productive and satisfying discourse.

1. **Pausing.** Taking turns is the ultimate in impulse control. In a discourse, space is given for each person to talk. Time is allowed before responding to or asking a question, which allows for more complex thinking, enhances all forms of discourse, and produces better decision making. Pausing is the tool that group members use to respectfully listen to each other.

2. **Paraphrasing.** This competency lets others know that you are listening, that you understand or are trying to understand, and that you care. An effective paraphrase expresses empathy by reflecting both the feelings and the content of the message. Paraphrasing may be

   ♦ an acknowledgment and reflection of emotions.
   Example: "You're frustrated (annoyed, elated, and so on) . . . "

♦ a restatement in your own words.
Example: ". . . because you've not completed all you set out to accomplish."

♦ a short synthesis of a long communication.
Example: "So you're finished with your statement."

Focused on the speaker, the listener often starts a paraphrase with "you." Examples:

"You're suggesting . . . "	"You're thinking . . . "
"I understand that you . . . "	"You're wondering . . . "
"You're feeling . . . "	"You're hoping . . . "
"So your idea is that . . . "	"Your goal is to . . . "

3. **Probing and clarifying.** This is an effective inquiry skill to use when the speaker uses vocabulary, a vague concept, or terminology that is not fully understood by the listener. It helps the listener to understand the speaker. In groups, it increases precision of thinking by clarifying understandings, terminology, and interpretations.

Clarifying requires the listener to constantly monitor the clearness of meaning inside his or her own mind and, if there are gaps or vagueness, seek further information. Some examples follow:

♦ "Could you explain to us what you mean by 'charisma'?"

♦ "What you are saying is that you'd rather work by yourself than in a group. Is that correct?"

♦ "Go over that one more time, Shelley. I'm not sure I understand you."

♦ "You say you are studying the situation. Tell us just exactly what you do when you 'study' something."

♦ "Explain to us the steps you took to arrive at that answer."

4. **Putting ideas on and pulling them off the table.** Groups are most productive when everyone shares their thoughts, dreams, mistakes, assumptions, and opinions. When they offer ideas, opinions, information, and positions, they attempt to keep their suggestions relevant to the topic at hand. Because there are times when continuing to advocate a position might block the group's functioning, group members also volunteer to withdraw their ideas. This creates an atmosphere of give-and-take in which a group member recognizes that his or her idea is worthy of consideration.

5. **Paying attention to self and others.** Meaningful dialogue emerges when each group member is sensitive to and conscious of the subtle cues inside themselves and within the group, such as body language, facial expression, and grumbling. Paying attention to learning styles, modalities, and beliefs of group members when planning for, facilitating, and participating in meetings enhances group members' understanding of one another as they work together.

6. **Presuming "good intentions."** People operate from their own point of view and therefore, we should assume that they act with positive intentions. This assumption promotes meaningful dialogue. Because discussions contain overt and covert messages, meanings may be misinterpreted. The subtle (and often not-so-subtle) way in which we embed presuppositions in our language can be hurtful or helpful to others. The deliberate use of positive presuppositions assumes and encourages positive actions (Costa & Garmston, 2004). An example is a question like "What goals do you have in mind for your project?" It presupposes that the reader has goals and that they are in his or her mind. Thus the reader is a planned, thoughtful, and mindful person.

7. **Providing data.** Groups that communicate well act on information rather than on hearsay, rumor, or speculation. Reliable data serve as the energy sources for group action and learning. Seeking, generating, and gathering data from group members as well as from a variety of other primary and secondary sources enhances individual and group decision making.

8. **Pursuing a balance between advocacy and inquiry.** Advocating a position, as well as inquiring into another's position, assists the group to continue learning. Senge and his colleagues (1994) suggest that balancing advocacy and inquiry is critical in order for an organization to grow, learn, and perform.

What Can Teachers and Other Adults Do to Enhance the Language of Collaboration Among Generation Y Students?

In employing the competencies described above, teachers should cluster students in trios or pairs to think together. The group mind illuminates issues, solves problems, and accommodates differences. The group builds an atmosphere of trust in human relationships, trust in the processes of interaction, and trust throughout the classroom. Using these skills to make decisions, solve problems, and generate ideas facilitates the creation of a shared vision among all who participate.

Classroom time should be allocated for describing, practicing, identifying, and reflecting on the use of these skills, for drawing connections between their use and the group's productiveness, and for planning for improving students' vocabulary and usage of these skills. Teachers should encourage individuals and groups of students to monitor and assess their own vocabulary and use of these eight language skills. During and upon completion of class and cooperative group meetings, process observers provide feedback to the group about its performance. The group discusses the feedback and plans strategies for individual and group improvement. Such work will enhance students' vocabulary, their thinking, and their level of trust. As a consequence, individuals will grow intellectually and develop communication skills that will transfer beyond the classroom. The synergy produced through dialogue might be referred to as communion: fellowship, participation, friendship, growing and learning together, and love.

The Effect of Judgment on Vocabulary and Language

Generation Y is confronted with myriad choices, more so than previous generations, because of the immediacy of the Internet, the globalization of television, transportability of cell phones, and the speed of computer technology. While our ability to access massive amounts of information has exploded, there has not been a corresponding increase in our ability to interpret, evaluate, and make judgments about the adequacy, reliability, and truthfulness of such information.

Good judgment requires a set of well-defined values and accurate information.

> "Here are the three great questions which in life we have over and over again to answer: Is it right or wrong? Is it true or false? Is it beautiful or ugly? Our education ought to help us to answer these questions."
>
> —John Lubbock

Acquiring those and an effective vocabulary are part of a child's maturation processes. Generation Y students who want immediate results often take the first option that comes to them. They fail to assess the consequences of a variety of options and judge them according to an objective standard. Defending the choices that they make is even more complex and demands specificity of vocabulary. The ability to evaluate choices requires skillful thinking that they will need in school and in daily life.

Three basic but increasingly complex questions face Generation Y as it confronts the burgeoning number of confounding choices in its future:

- What makes something true?

- What makes something fair and good?

- What makes something beautiful?

Even if these questions aren't explicitly raised with students, the rationale behind students' decision-making process must be explored: Why did you make that choice? On what basis? What were your criteria? What evidence do you have? What indicators support your conclusion? Responding to these types of questions and providing the rationale and evidence to support their answers build students' vocabulary and life-success skills.

What Can Teachers and Other Adults Do to Enhance Vocabulary and Judgment Among Generation Y Students?

Educators and parents should ensure that the curriculum offers opportunities in the arts, the social sciences, and math and science. These are the disciplines that provide maximum opportunities for students to encounter judgments about beauty, fairness, and truth. Here are four ways parents and teachers can develop the vocabulary skills of judgment making:

- Capitalize on situations at home and school.

- Encourage dialogue and discussion.

- Provide opportunities for persuasive writing.

- Encourage reflecting and transferring through journals and dialogues.

Capitalize on situations at home and school. As day-to-day problems arise in schools and classrooms—discipline problems, planning school events, making arrangements for field trips, beautifying the school, and so on—teachers, administrators, and parents can seize these opportunities to help students make and support judgments.

Encourage dialogue and discussion. Dialogue and discussion are necessary skills for successful Generation Y students. The purpose of dialogue is to understand; the purpose of discussion is to persuade or convince. Groups hold discussions for the primary intent that each member present data, knowledge, positions, rationales, assumptions, ideas, or issues. Groups hold dialogues with the primary intent of expanding the permutations and possibilities of the ideas, knowledge, and issues in order to discover new solutions (Baker et al., 1997). Show students examples and non-examples of the eight collaborative competencies on pages 195–197, which will enable them to make their dialogues more positive and productive.

Provide opportunities for persuasive writing. By practicing authentic persuasion through writing, students learn that it isn't enough to give vague reasons for why a certain choice was or should be made. Instead, they must defend their reasoning with skilled strategies defined by a thinking map like the one below (Swartz & Parks, 1994).

> What makes a decision necessary?
>
> What are my options?
>
> What are the likely consequences of each option?
>
> How important are the consequences?
>
> Which option is best in the light of the consequences?

The goal of such a thinking map is for students to internalize a skillful and careful way to make sound judgments.

The following letter was written by a fifth grader using the thinking map above in conjunction with the novel *Shiloh* by Phyllis Reynolds Naylor (2000). The students were asked to make a decision faced by a character in the book and then write a persuasive letter to that character recommending the best option (Swartz, Kiser, & Reagan 1999).

Dear Mrs. Preston:

    You have discovered Marty's secret. He is keeping the dog Shiloh from Judd because he fears that Judd will kill it. You are faced with a tough choice. The purpose of this letter is to recommend what I think you should do. It may seem to you that you have to decide whether to tell Marty's father or not. However, there are many options other than just those two. You could keep Marty's secret and tell no one, make Marty take Shiloh back to Judd and not tell your husband, or take Shiloh back to the house and show him to Marty's father.

    If you and Marty take Shiloh back to Judd and do not tell Pa that you found him, there are several negative consequences and not too many positive ones. Most likely your husband would find out. After all he is a postman and they visit with everyone. He feels very strongly about the fact that Shiloh belongs to Judd and he would be embarrassed in front of Judd. Being so mean and cruel, Judd might have Marty arrested, although he often breaks the law by killing deer out of season. Judd might even kill Shiloh. He has a history of abusing his dogs and has threatened to break Shiloh's legs if he found him.

    Another option you might consider is to keep Marty's secret and tell no one. It is obvious that you believe that telling the truth is extremely important. It is part of your deep faith in God. When you made Marty tell the truth about eating Dara Lynn's treat, you showed how you felt about lying. Omission is another form of lying. You might even feel so guilty that it would change your relationship with your husband and family. Pa also might find out since he often goes hunting. He would probably be mad at you at first, but you seem to have a strong marriage so he most likely will forgive you. However, there would be some pretty miserable moments first. Guilt is hard to live with.

    Probably the best option of the three is to take Shiloh back to the house, show it to Marty's father and explain the situation to him as best you can. You have a very good relationship with your husband and he listens to you. Even though he feels strongly about property, he might help to think of another solution besides giving the dog back to Judd. Because you have told the truth, you would not feel guilty. Marty would see that the truth is very important because you were a good role model. Although Shiloh might have to go back to Judd, Marty's father might be more understanding about the situation and he might tell Judd that he is going to be watching to see if he hurts Shiloh.

    If you look at these three options, each has both positive and negative consequences. Because you value the truth so highly and more good things can come out of taking Shiloh back to the house and talking to Marty's father, that is the option that I recommend to you. It will keep the trusting relationship that you have with your husband and show Marty that truth is of great value. Thank you for your consideration and attention. Please think carefully before you make a decision. The future of your family could depend on it.

Sincerely,

Encourage reflecting and transferring through journals and dialogues. Upon the completion of learning activities, time should be provided to reflect on, evaluate, and learn from the judgment-making process. This might be done in journals and/or dialogues. Students may reflect on which dispositions and skills they employed in making the judgment, what this experience has taught them about themselves, and the effectiveness of their vocabularies to address their responsibilities in the world.

As part of the reflection process, students should explore how what they've learned can be carried forth and applied in other settings in school and in life, work, home, and the community. Students should be invited to reflect on which behaviors they may want to modify, strengthen, or even extinguish to better achieve success in the future. This bridging or transferring is essential in order for learning to be cemented and internalized. Prompt this reflection and transfer by asking:

> As you reflect on the process of decision making, what insights have you gained?

> As you encounter these types of decisions in the future, How can you use more powerful words to build deeper reflections?

Parents and teachers can encourage students to engage in the language of judgment when they ask for explicit reasons for the choices children make and good reasons for the things children want, and when they listen carefully for accurate language—options and consequences.

The Effect of Judgment, Vocabulary, and Language Development on Critical Thinking

Critical thinking roughly means reasonable and reflective thinking focused on deciding what to believe or do (Ennis, 2001). While critical thinking is a composite of many discrete thinking skills, complex mental strategies, and intellectual dispositions, in this section we shall address three linguistic components of critical thinking: (1) the explicit teaching and labeling of thinking-skills terminology in order to become aware of, communicate, and dialogue about our mental processes; (2) the "inner language" of metacognition; and (3) the vocabulary used in questioning and problem posing.

> "Judge a man by his questions rather than by his answers."
>
> —Voltaire

What Can Teachers and Other Adults Do to Enhance the Explicit Language of Thinking Among Generation Y Students?

Educators often assume that students know how to think critically. They are asked daily by the teacher or the instructional materials, for example, to summarize, to draw conclusions, to infer, to categorize, or to compare. Yet these very same cognitive processes are often not presented as essential skills to be taught. Students may be at a loss when the task is to *classify* a word list, to *infer* the author's intent in a reading passage, or to *draw conclusions* from a set of data.

Teachers can use language carefully, with syntax, vocabulary, and inflection that stimulate, engage, and instill desired cognitive processes in students. By consciously employing cognitive terminology, teachers can ensure that students will become familiar with its uses. They can formulate questions to cause students to exercise certain cognitive functions and can provide data that students must interpret for themselves. Requiring students to answer using explicit vocabulary, instead of general terms, will generate in them greater and more effective language. If adults monitor their own language and strive to use "thinking" terms in the day-to-day interactions of the home and classroom, it will foster children's linguistic skills and ultimately their academic success. For example:

Instead of saying:	Use thinking terms by saying:
"Let's look at these two pictures."	"Let's compare these two pictures."
"What do you think will happen when . . . ?"	"What do you predict will happen when . . . ?"
"How can you put these things into groups . . . ?"	"How can you classify . . . ?"
"Let's work this problem."	"Let's analyze this problem."
"What did you think of this story?"	"What conclusions can you draw about this story?"
"How can you explain . . . ?"	"What hypotheses do you have that might explain . . . ?"
"How do you know that's true?"	"What evidence do you have to support . . . ?
"How else could you use this?"	"How could you apply this?"

As children hear these terms in everyday use and experience the cognitive processes that accompany them, they will internalize the words and use them as part of their own vocabulary. Teachers will also want to give specific instruction in those cognitive functions so that students possess the experience along with the terminology (Costa & Marzano, 2001).

The Inner Language of Metacognition

Metacognition is the unique human capacity to know what we know and what we don't know. It is our ability to plan a strategy for producing the information we need, to be conscious of our own steps during the act of problem solving, and to reflect on and evaluate the productiveness of our own thinking.

> "When the mind is thinking it is talking to itself."
>
> —Plato

The major components of metacognition are (1) developing a plan of action; (2) maintaining that plan in mind over a period of time; and (3) reflecting on and evaluating the plan upon its completion. Planning a strategy makes it possible to keep track of the steps in the sequence for the duration of the activity. It helps us make temporal and comparative judgments as we act, assess our readiness for more or different activities, and monitor our interpretations, perceptions, decisions, and behaviors. Superior teachers do this daily: they develop a teaching strategy for a lesson, keeping it in mind throughout the lesson, then reflect upon it to evaluate its effectiveness.

Metacognition means becoming increasingly aware of one's actions and the effect of those actions on others and on the environment by

- forming internal questions as one searches for information and meaning, developing mental maps or plans of action;

- mentally rehearsing prior to performance;

- monitoring those plans as they are employed—being conscious of the need for midcourse correction if a plan is not meeting expectations;

- reflecting on a plan upon completion for the purpose of self-evaluation; and

- editing mental pictures for improved performance (Costa & Garmston, 2004).

Generation Y students often do not take the time to wonder why they are doing what they are doing. They seldom question themselves about their own learning strategies or evaluate the efficiency of their own performance. Some Generation Y students have virtually no idea of what they should do when they confront a problem and are often unable to explain their decision-making strategies. When teachers ask, "How did you solve that problem; what strategies did you have in mind?" or "Tell us what went on in your head to come up with that conclusion," students often respond by saying, "I don't know, I just did it."

What Can Teachers and Other Adults Do to Enhance Metacognition Among Generation Y Students?

Thinking about thinking begets more thinking. Having children describe the mental processes they are using, the data they need, and the plans they are formulating causes them to think about their own thinking—to metacogitate. When teachers invite students to describe their thought processes, they cause the covert thinking skills that students are experiencing to become overt. Teachers can invite metacognition with such questions as these:

- "What steps did you take to arrive at that answer?"

- "What can you do to get started?"

- "What goes on in your head when you compare?"

- "Can you describe your plan of action?"

- "What other ways can you prove that your answer is correct?"

- "What criteria are you using to make your choice?"

As teachers probe students' thinking, they, too, become more aware of and more able to describe their own thinking processes, and they'll be able to communicate those processes more effectively to others (Costa, 2001).

Questioning and Problem Posing

Another key component of critical thinking is the disposition for questioning and problem posing. Long considered a domain of mathematics and science, problem solving now permeates the curriculum. Many schools have listened to a business world that has begun to look at a prospective employee's ability to state and formulate possible solutions to a problem as an essential qualification.

A distinguishing characteristic between humans and other forms of life is our inclination and ability to search for problems to solve. Effective problem solvers know how to ask questions to fill in the gaps between what they know and what they don't. They are inclined to ask a range of questions that, for example,

♦ request data to support others' conclusions and assumptions.
Examples: "What evidence do you have?" "How do you know that's true?" "How reliable is this data source?"

♦ seek alternative points of view.
Examples: "From whose viewpoint are we seeing, reading, or hearing?" "From what angle, what perspective, are we viewing this situation?"

♦ search for causal connections and relationships.
Examples: "How are these people (events, situations) related to each other?" "What produced this connection?"

♦ suggest hypothetical problems (what-if questions).
Examples: "What do you think would happen if . . . ?" "If that is true, then what might happen when . . . ?"

Inquirers recognize discrepancies and phenomena in their environment and probe into their causes: "Why do cats purr?" "How high can birds fly?" "Why does the hair on my head grow so fast, while the hair on my arms and legs grows so slowly?" "What would happen if we put the saltwater fish in a freshwater aquarium?" "What are some alternative solutions to international conflicts other than wars?"

Some Generation Y students, however, may be unaware of the functions, classes, syntax, or intentions in questions. They may not realize that questions vary in complexity, structure, and purpose. They may pose simple questions intending to derive maximal results. When confronted with a discrepancy, they may lack the vocabulary as well as an overall strategy for searching and finding a solution.

What Can Teachers and Other Adults Do to Develop Questioning and Problem Posing Among Generation Y Students?

Careful, intentional, and productive questioning is one of the most powerful teaching tools for developing students' vocabulary and language fluency. Through their questioning strategies, teachers engage and transform the mind. When a teacher begins a question with, "Who can tell me . . . " there is an immediate signal that only certain students can answer the question. If, on the other hand, a teacher begins a question with, "What do we know about . . . " or "How might we . . . " the signal is that "we"—all of us—probably have something to offer. If a teacher poses questions he already knows the answer to, there is a tendency for students to "guess what's in the teacher's head," and search for conformity or agreement by offering a single-word answer. When neither the teacher nor the students know the answer to a question, then a sincere and collaborative inquiry occurs—a search together for approaches and solutions. Students focus on developing strategies to resolve the problem and generate alternative answers to the question, rather than on conforming and producing an answer that will be confirmed or negated by someone of higher authority. Following are several criteria that teachers and other adults may want to keep in mind as they design and ask questions intended to activate and engage more effective language and cognition (Costa & Kallick, 2000).

Powerful questions are open-ended.

Plurals are used to invite multiple rather than singular concepts:

"What are some of your goals?"

"What ideas do you have?"

"What alternatives are you considering?"

Words are selected to express tentativeness:

"What conclusions might you draw?"

"What may indicate his acceptance?"

"What hunches do you have to explain this situation?"

Powerful questions use invitational stems that signal and enable the desired cognitive process to be performed.

"As you evaluate . . . "   "As you reflect on . . . "

"As you consider . . . "   "As you plan for . . . "

Powerful questions assume capability and empowerment.

"What are some of the benefits you will derive from engaging in this activity?"

"As you anticipate your project, what are some indicators that you will use to know that you are progressing and succeeding?"

Powerful questions promote specific, complex thinking skills at various levels of complexity.

Level of Complexity	Vocabulary Thinking Skills	
Input	Recall	Define
	Describe	Identify
	Name	List
Process	Compare/Contrast	Summarize
	Sequence	Infer
	Analyze	Synthesize
Output	Predict	Speculate
	Evaluate	Imagine
	Envision	Hypothesize

Some examples of questions incorporating the above criteria follow:

♦ "How would you compare this project with others you have done?"

♦ "How might you sequence these events in such a way as to . . . ?"

♦ "In what ways might your emotions have influenced your decisions about . . . ?"

♦ "As you consider your alternatives, what seems most promising?"

♦ "What are some of the goals that you have in mind for this meeting?"

♦ "What lessons or insights will you carry forward to future situations?"

The Effect of Judgment, Vocabulary, and Language Development on Meaningful Literacy Achievement

The language of literacy—the foundations on which learning takes place—has at least three components: (1) reading with understanding and discrimination, (2) writing with clarity and precision, and (3) speaking with specificity about what is read and written. Each of these components is firmly rooted in the thinking that must take place before, during, and after reading, writing, and speaking. In other words, the language of literacy becomes the language of thinking.

Reading With Understanding and Discrimination

It has been said that knowledge is power. To empower students, teachers must help them to become discriminating readers. Good readers have the ability to discriminate text by using

> "Reading is a basic tool in the living of a good life."
> —Mortimer Adler

- ♦ phonemic awareness, the ability to hear the individual sounds of a word;

- ♦ phonics, the relationships between the letters of written language and the individual sounds of spoken language;

- ♦ fluency, the ability to read a text accurately, quickly, and with expression;

- ♦ language and vocabulary, the ability to communicate ideas using a vast body of words, symbols, signs, sounds, and gestures; and

- ♦ listening, the ability to give attention with the ears to make sense of speech.

It is not enough for students to be able to read the words and sentences of text. They must also be able to think about and understand the nuances of language, the way words can be used to create bias, and how facts can be manipulated to look accurate (Billmeyer, 2004). Additional skills they need include:

- ♦ comprehension, the ability to understand the meaning of the individual words and to grasp the overall meaning of the story or passage; and

- ♦ critical thinking, the ability to evaluate and analyze evidence to make informed decisions and to draw logical conclusions.

Teaching students to draw conclusions and make inferences based on actual evidence is essential. A thoughtful, discriminating reader asks:

- Are there loaded words in this text that are intended to influence my thinking?

- Where can I verify the accuracy of what I am reading?

- Does the author have a stake in the matter?

Vocabulary gives power to the discriminating reader. Critical readers who question and take time to answer those questions are powerful consumers of text.

A lifelong reader truly enjoys the skillful use of expressive vocabulary and understands its meanings (Reagan, 2001). Simile, metaphor, humor, and hyperbole are just a few of the ways to enhance language. Generation Y students who have the skills to unlock a metaphor certainly have advantages over those who do not. Lyrical language has a beauty that transports readers to events and places beyond experience. Understanding this language is reading at its zenith.

Writing with Clarity and Precision

It is vital that students think not only about what they are going to write and the purpose for which they are writing (authentic writing—not writing designed to please the teacher) but also about how they will deliver their thinking to their audience—which in turn determines the vocabulary that they use in their writing. Students must learn that specificity of vocabulary can condense lengthy passages into more readable ones. This specificity generates precise communication between speaker and listener—or writer and reader.

> **"To communicate, put your words in order; give them a purpose; use them to persuade, to instruct, to discover, to seduce."**
>
> —William Safire

A good writer should never be without a thesaurus! But this is not enough. Synonyms or antonyms for a word each have their own nuances of meaning—they are not necessarily interchangeable. Words provide different functions in different contexts, so care must be taken to substitute words that can perform the same function. Just try replacing a noun with a verb or adjective to see what we mean. A thesaurus is vital, but so is a good dictionary. It follows, of course, that students have to be taught the skills to use them.

Emphasize clear writing and precise language by requiring sound evidence. Anyone can put something in writing and call it true—or on video for that matter. It is only through our ability to recognize the bias that can be created through the use of particular words or phrases that we can fairly interpret what we read and hear. This is one of the great problems that citizens in the twenty-first century will confront—the use of vocabulary to sway opinion in a way that does not openly confront an issue, but manipulates ideas.

Speaking With Specificity About What Is Read and Written

Effective communicators strive to speak accurately by using precise language, defining terms, and using correct names and categorical labels and analogies. They strive to avoid generalizations, and distortions. Instead they support their statements with explanations, comparisons, quantification, and evidence.

> "To talk well and eloquently is a very great art, but an equally great one is to know the right moment to stop."
>
> —Wolfgang Amadeus Mozart

Language refinement plays a critical role in enhancing our cognitive maps and our ability to think critically, which is the basis for efficacious action. Enriching the complexity and specificity of vocabulary produces effective thinking.

Effective communicators are characterized by their ability to be specific, to refrain from generalization, and to support their arguments with valid data. Oral language, however, is often filled with omissions, generalizations, and vaguenesses (Laborde, 1984). Some examples:

- universals such as "always," "never," "all," and "everybody"

- vague action verbs such as "know about," "understand," "appreciate"

- comparators such as "better," "newer," "cheaper," "more nutritious"

- unreferenced pronouns such as "they," "them," "we"

- unspecified groups such as "the teachers," "parents," "things"

- assumed rules or traditions such as "ought," "should," or "must"

What Can Teachers and Other Adults Do to Enhance Meaningful Vocabulary?

Teachers should encourage parents to set aside a few minutes each day to make reading aloud an exciting routine. Parents should read with expression in their voice to bring the story to life. Librarians and teachers can help parents select books that encourage children to talk—elaborating, comparing, and creating. In addition to stories, parents can recite or sing nursery rhymes, chants, and children's songs. With students in grades 3 and up, poetry and lyrics to popular songs can be used. Young children often request stories to be repeated, and parents should read books to them again and again. Teachers and parents should also read the books their children are reading. Exchanging ideas about characters, plot, setting, and the author's point of view often becomes dinner or classroom conversation. What better way to tell young people that you recognize their worth than to take time to read what interests them?

By being alert to vague or unspecified terms the students use in oral and written communication, teachers can help them better define those terms, become more specific about their actions, make precise comparisons, use accurate descriptors, and supply sounder reasons and rationales for their assumptions, conclusions, and generalizations. Here's how:

When students say	The teacher may respond by saying
"He *never* listens to me."	"Never?" "Never, ever?"
"*Everybody* has one."	"Everybody?" "Who, exactly?"
"*Things* go better with . . ."	"Which things, specifically?"
"Things *go* better with . . ."	"Go? Go how, specifically?"
"Things go *better* with . . ."	"Better than what?"
"You *shouldn't* do that . . ."	"What would happen if you did?"
"The *teachers* . . ."	"Which teachers, specifically?"
"I want them to *understand* . . ."	"What exactly will they be doing if they understand . . . ?"
"This cereal is more nutritious."	"More nutritious than what?"

Summary

Teachers that enable and empower learners are those who don't just encourage the explicit language of thinking—they make it part of their mission. Students who have to defend their ideas with evidence and accuracy are better prepared to communicate in an environment filled with information. The key is not only being able to ask specific questions but also having the vocabulary and skills necessary to seek those types of questions.

The future of today's Generation Y youth will be complex, ambiguous, global, technological, and problematic. They will need strong verbal and written vocabulary and cognitive processes to participate fully in society. They will need to learn the language of collaboration, judgment, critical thinking and literacy to become productive contributors to their community, quality producers, and skillful thinkers. They will need to continually develop these competencies throughout their lifetime. The journey starts in the home and continues in school.

Imitation and emulation are the most basic forms of learning. Teachers, parents, and administrators must realize the importance of displaying desirable vocabulary skills in the presence of learners. In day-to-day life, when problems arise in schools, classrooms, and homes, Generation Y children must see and hear these significant adults employing the same language patterns that they value in their children and students. If we want our

> "Parents who use good communication skills are, at the same time, teaching their children to use good skills. When parents use angry or hostile words, their children do, too. Often parents cause the very behaviors they don't want in their children. In short, they reap what they sow."
>
> —Joe Hasenstab, president, Performance Learning Systems

students to read, then they must see us read; if we want our children to speak with clarity, fluency, and precision, then they must hear us speak with clarity, fluency, and precision. If we want our students to write persuasively, then they must see us write persuasively and informatively. Without this consistency, there is likely to be a credibility gap.

As Alan Kay (1990) stated, "The best way to predict the future is to invent it." If we want a future that is much more thoughtful, vastly more cooperative, greatly more compassionate, and a lot more loving, then we have to invent it. The future is in our schools and classrooms today. We must seek, nurture, and celebrate that future with effective vocabulary and skillful dialogue among children, students, and families, and among citizens around the world.

Discussion Questions and Teaching Activities

1. In what ways are Generation Y students different from students of the past? What changes will have to be made in your teaching of vocabulary in order to respond positively to their unique learning needs?

2. Plan a lesson in which you use the metacognitive, questioning, and problem-solving instructional ideas presented by the authors. Invite a colleague to watch you teach the lesson or videotape it. After the lesson, analyze how well you met your objectives. Compare your assessment to your colleague's. Discuss ways your instructional actions could be improved to enhance your students' learning.

References Cited

Allan, R. (2003, Summer). Expanding writing's role in learning. *Curriculum Update*, Volume 11. Association for Supervision and Curriculum Development.

American Educational Research Association. (2004, Winter). English-language learners: Boosting academic achievement. *Research Points: Essential Information for Educational Policy, 2*, 1–4. Retrieved from http://www.aera.org

Anders, P. L., & Bos, C. S. (1986). Semantic feature analysis: An interactive strategy for vocabulary development and text comprehension. *Journal of Reading, 29*, 610–616.

Anderson, R., & Henne, R. (1993, December). *Collaborative, integrated reading and writing instruction*. Paper presented at the annual meeting of the National Reading Conference, Charleston, SC.

Anderson, R. C., & Freebody, P. (1981). Vocabulary knowledge. In J. Guthrie (Ed.), *Comprehension and teaching: Research reviews* (pp. 77–117). Newark, DE: International Reading Association.

Anderson, R. C., & Freebody, P. (1983). Vocabulary knowledge. In H. Singer & R. Ruddell (Eds.), *Theoretical models and processes of reading* (3rd ed., pp. 343–71). Newark, DE: International Reading Association.

Anderson, R. C., & Nagy, W. E. (1992, Winter). The vocabulary conundrum. *American Educator*, 14–18, 44–47.

Baker, W., Costa, A., & Shalit, S. (1997). The Norms of collaboration: Attaining communicative competence. In A. Costa and R. Liebmann (Eds.), *The process-centered school: Sustaining a renaissance community* (pp. 91–142). Thousand Oaks, CA: Corwin Press.

Baumann, J. F., Edwards, E. C., Boland, E., Olejnik, S., & Kame'enui, E. J. (2003). Vocabulary tricks: Effects of instruction in morphology and context on fifth-grade students' ability to derive and infer word meaning. *American Educational Research Journal, 40*, 447–494.

Baumann, J., Kame'enui, E., & Ash, G. (2003). Research on teaching vocabulary: Voltaire redux. In J. Flood, D. Lapp., J. R. Squire, & J. Jensen (Eds.), *Handbook of research on teaching the English language arts* (2nd ed., pp. 4–14). Mahwah, NJ: Erlbaum.

Bean, T. W. (1981). Comprehension strategies: What makes them tick? In E. K. Dishner, T. W. Bean, & J. E. Readence (Eds.), *Reading in the content areas: Improving classroom instruction* (pp. 188–191). Dubuque, IA: Kendall/Hunt.

Bear, D. R., Invernizzi, M., Templeton, S., & Johnston, F. (2004). *Words their way: Word study for phonics, vocabulary, and spelling instruction* (3rd ed.). Upper Saddle River, NJ: Prentice-Hall.

Beck, I., & McKeown, M. (1991). Conditions of vocabulary acquisition. In R. Barr, M. Kamil, P. Mosenthal, & P. D. Pearson (Eds.), *Handbook of reading research* (Vol. 2, pp. 789–814). White Plains, NY: Longman.

Beck, I. L., McKeown, M. G., & Kucan, L. (2002). *Bringing words to life: Robust vocabulary instruction*. New York: Guilford Press.

Beck, I. L., McKeown, M. G., & McCaslin, E. S. (1983). Vocabulary development: All contexts are not created equal. *Elementary School Journal, 83*, 177–181.

Beck. I. L., McKeown, M. G., & Omanson, R. C. (1987). The effects and uses of diverse vocabulary instruction techniques. In M. G. McKeown & M. E. Curtis (Eds.), *The nature of vocabulary acquisition* (pp. 147–163). Hillsdale, NJ: Erlbaum.

Beck, I. L, Perfetti, C.A., & McKeown, M. G. (1982). The effects of long-term vocabulary instruction on lexical access and reading comprehension. *Journal of Educational Psychology, 74*, 506–521.

Bennett-Armistead, V. S., Duke, N. K., & Moses, A. M. (2005). *Literacy and the youngest learner: Best practices for educators of children from birth to 5*. New York: Scholastic.

Biemiller, A. (2001). Teaching reading and language to the disadvantaged: What we have learned from field research. *Harvard Educational Review, 47*, 518–543.

Biemiller, A. (2004). Teaching vocabulary in the primary grades: Vocabulary instruction needed. In J. Baumann & E. Kame'enui (Eds.), *Vocabulary instruction: Research to practice* (pp.28–40). Mahwah, NJ: Erlbaum.

Biemiller, A., & Slonium, M. (2001). Estimating root word vocabulary growth in normative and advantaged populations: Evidence for a common sequence of vocabulary acquisition. *Journal of Educational Psychology, 93*, 498–520.

Billmeyer, R. (2004). *Strategic reading in the content areas*. Omaha, NE: Dayspring Printing.

Blachowicz, C., & Fisher, P. (1996). *Teaching vocabulary in all classrooms*. Columbus, OH: Merrill.

Blachowicz, C., & Fisher, P. J. (2002). *Teaching vocabulary in all classrooms*. Upper Saddle River, NJ: Merrill Prentice Hall.

Blachowicz, C. L. Z. & Fisher, P. (2000). Vocabulary instruction. In M. L. Kamil, P. B. Mosenthal, P. D. Pearson, & R. Barr (Eds.), *Handbook of reading research* (Vol. 3, pp. 502–523). Mahwah, NJ: Erlbaum.

Block, C. C. (2004). *Teaching comprehension: The comprehension process approach.* Boston, MA: Allyn & Bacon.

Block, C. C., & Israel, S. (2004). The ABCs of performing highly-effective think alouds. *The Reading Teacher, 58,* 154–167.

Block, C. C., & Mangieri, J. N. (1995/1996). *Reason to read: Thinking strategies for life through literature* (Vols. 1–3). Boston, MA: Pearson.

Block, C. C., & Mangieri, J. N. (2003). *Exemplary literacy teachers: Literacy success in grades K–5.* New York: Guilford Press.

Block, C. C., & Mangieri, J. N. (2005a). *Powerful Vocabulary for Reading Success: Grades 3–6.* New York: Scholastic.

Block, C. C., & Mangieri, J. N. (2005b). *A research study to investigate the effect of the powerful vocabulary for reading success program on student vocabulary and comprehension achievement* (Research Report 2963–005). Charlotte, NC: Institute for Literacy Enhancement.

Block, C. C., & Mangieri, J. N. (2005c). *National study of the effects of research-based vocabulary instruction on students' literacy achievement and attitude toward reading.* Charlotte, NC: Institute for Literacy Enhancement.

Block, C. C., & Reed, K. M. (2004). *Trade books: How they significantly increase students' vocabulary comprehension, fluency, and positive attitudes toward reading.* (Research Report 1739-004.) Charlotte, NC: Institute for Literacy Enhancement.

Block, C. C., Rodgers, L., & Johnson, R. (2004). *Teaching comprehension in kindergarten through grade 3: Building success for all students.* New York: Guilford Press.

Boehm, A. (2001). *Boehm Test of Basic Concepts* (3rd ed.) San Antonio, TX: Harcourt.

Bowers, C. A. (1987) *The promise of theory: Education and the politics of cultural change* (pp. 31–48). New York: Teachers College Press.

Brabham, E. G., & Lynch-Brown, C. (2002). Effects of teachers' reading aloud styles on vocabulary acquisition and comprehension of students in the early elementary grades. *Journal of Educational Psychology, 94,* 465–473.

Brassell, D., & Flood, J. (2004). *Vocabulary strategies every teacher needs to know.* San Diego, CA: Academic Professional Development.

Bromley, K. (2002). *Stretching students' vocabulary.* New York: Scholastic.

Brown, J., Fischo, V., & Hanna, G. (1993). *Nelson-Denny Reading Test.* Itasca, IL: Riverside.

Brown, V., Hammill, D., & Wiederholt, L. (1995). *Test of Reading Comprehension* (3rd ed.) Austin, TX: Pro-Ed.

Buis, K. (2005). *Making words stick.* Markham, Ontario, Canada: Pembroke.

Calkins, L. M. (2001). *The art of teaching reading.* New York: Longman.

Carlisle, J. (2003). Morphology matters in learning to read: A commentary. *Reading Psychology, 24,* 291–322.

Carlson, N. S. (1958, 1990). *The family under the bridge.* New York: Scholastic.

Carroll, J. B., Davies, P., & Richman, B. (1971). *Word frequency book.* New York: American Heritage.

Cecil, N. L. (2004). *Activities for a comprehensive approach to literacy.* Scottsdale, AZ: Holcomb Hathaway.

Chall, J. S., Jacobs, V. A., & Baldwin, L. E. (1990). *The reading crisis: Why poor children fall behind.* Cambridge, MA: Harvard University Press.

Chrisp, P. (2001). *Dinosaur detectives.* London: Dorling Kindersley.

Clay, M. M. (1998). *By different paths to common outcomes.* Portland, ME: Stenhouse.

Corson, D. (1989). Adolescent lexical differences in Australia and England by social group. *Journal of Educational Research, 82* (3), 146–157.

Costa, A. (2001). Mediating the metacognitive. In A. Costa (Ed.), *Developing minds: A resource book for teaching thinking* (pp. 408–412). Alexandria, VA: Association for Supervision and Curriculum Development.

Costa, A., & Garmston, R. (2004). *Cognitive coaching: A foundation for renaissance schools* (pp. 147–172). Norwood, MA: Christopher Gordon Publishers.

Costa, A. & Garmston, R. (2005). *Cognitive coaching foundation seminar learning guide* (6th ed., revised by C. Hayes and J. Ellison). Englewood, CO: Center for Cognitive Coaching. Norwood, MA: Christopher Gordon.

Costa, A. & Kallick, B. (2000) *Activating and engaging habits of mind* (p. 34–45). Alexandria, VA: Association for Supervision and Curriculum Development.

Costa, A., & Marzano, R. (2001). Teaching the language of thinking. In A. Costa (Ed.), *Developing minds: A resource book for teaching thinking* (pp. 379–383). Alexandria, VA: Association for Supervision and Curriculum Development.

Cronin, D. (2000). *Click clack moo: Cows that type.* New York: Simon & Schuster.

Cunningham, A. E., & Stanovich, K. E. (1998, Spring–Summer). What reading does for the mind. *American Educator*, 8–15.

Cunningham, J. W., Cunningham, P. M., & Arthur, V. (1981). *Middle and secondary school reading.* New York: Longman.

Cunningham, P. M., & Cunningham, J. W. (1992). Making words: Enhancing the invented spelling–decoding connection. *The Reading Teacher, 46*, 106–115.

Cunningham, P., & Hall, D. (1994a). *Making big words: Multilevel hands-on spelling and phonics activities.* Frank Schaffer.

Cunningham, P.,& Hall, D. (1994b). *Making multisyllabic words.* Frank Schaffer.

Cunningham, P., & Hall, D. (1994c). *Making words: Multilevel words.* Frank Schaffer.

Cunningham, P. M., & Hall, D. P. (1998). *Month-by-month phonics for upper grades.* Greensboro, NC: Carson-Dellosa.

Cunningham, P. M., Hall, D. P., & Defee, M. (1991). Nonability-grouped, multilevel instruction: A year in a first-grade classroom. *The Reading Teacher, 44*, 106–115.

Cunningham, P. M., Hall, D. P., & Defee, M. (1998). Nonability-grouped, multilevel instruction: Eight years later. *The Reading Teacher, 51*, 652–664.

Dale, E. (1965). Vocabulary measurement: Techniques and major findings. *Elementary English, 42*, 895–901.

Dale, E., & O'Rourke, J. (1986). *The living word vocabulary.* Chicago: World Book/Childcraft International.

Dale, E., O'Rourke, J., & Bamman, H. A. (1971). *Techniques of teaching vocabulary.* Palo Alto, CA: Field Educational Publications.

Daneman, M. (1991). Individual differences in reading skills. In R. Barr, M. L. Kamil, P. B. Mosenthal, & P. D. Pearson (Eds.), *Handbook of reading research* (Vol. 2, pp. 512–538). White Plains, NY: Longman.

Davis, F. B. (1943). Fundamental factors in comprehension of reading. *Psychometrika, 9*, 185–197.

Davis, F. B. (1968). Research in comprehension in reading. *Reading Research Quarterly, 3*, 499–544.

De Temple, J., & Snow, C. E. (2003). Learning words from books. In A. van Kleeck, S. A. Stahl, & E. B. Bauer (Eds.), *On reading books to children* (pp. 16–36). Mahwah, NJ: Erlbaum.

Dickinson, D. K., McCabe, A., & Sprague, K. (2001). *Teacher rating of oral language and literacy (TROLL): A research-based tool* (CIERA Report No. 3-016). Ann Arbor, MI: Center for the Improvement of Reading Achievement.

Dickinson, D., & Smith, M. (1994). Long-term effects of preschool teachers' book readings on low-income children's vocabulary and story comprehension. *Reading Research Quarterly, 29*, 104–122.

Dickinson, D. K., & Tabors, P. O. (Eds.). (2001). *Building literacy with language.* Baltimore: Paul H. Brookes.

Dorris, M. (1999). *Morning girl.* New York: Hyperion.

Duke, N. (2000). For the rich it's richer: print environments and experiences offered to first-grade students in very low- and very high-SES school districts. *American Educational Research Journal, 37*, 456–457.

Dunn, L.M., & Dunn, L.M. (1997). *Peabody Picture Vocabulary Test* (revised, 3rd ed.) Circle Pines, MN: American Guidance Service.

Dykstra, R., & Bond, W. (1966-1967). National first and second grade study: Examining the effects of various methods on student reading achievement. *Reading Research Quarterly, 16*, 1–19, reprinted in 46, 7–26.

Eisner, E. (2003). Preparing for today and tomorrow. *Educational Leadership, 61* (4), 6–11.

Ennis, R. (2001). Goals for critical thinking curriculum and its assessment. In A. L. Costa (Ed.), *Developing minds: A resource book for teaching thinking* (3rd ed., pp. 44–46) Alexandria, VA: Association for Supervision and Curriculum Development.

Fitzgerald, J., & Graves, M. F. (2004). *Scaffolding reading experiences for English-language learners.* Norwood, MA: Christopher-Gordon.

Flood, J., Lapp, D., & Flood, S. (2005). Vocabulary instruction. In C. C. Cummins (Ed.), *Reading first: A simple guide to a complex issue.* Newark, DE: International Reading Association.

Frasier, D. (2000). *Miss Alaineus: A vocabulary disaster*. New York: Harcourt.

Frayer, D. A., Frederick, W. D., & Klausmeier, H. J. (1969). *A schema for testing the level of cognitive mastery*. Madison, WI: Wisconsin Center for Education Research.

Freedman, R. (1987). *Lincoln: A photobiography*. New York: Clarion Books/Ticknor & Fields.

Fry, E. B. (2004). *The vocabulary teacher's book of lists*. Indianapolis, IN: Jossey-Bass.

Fukkink, R. G., & de Glopper, K. (1998). Effects of instruction in deriving word meanings from context: A meta-analysis. *Review of Educational Research, 68*, 450–469.

García, G. E. (1991). Factors influencing the English reading test performance of Spanish-speaking Hispanic children. *Reading Research Quarterly, 26*, 371–392.

García, G. E. (1998). Mexican-American bilingual students' metacognitive reading strategies: What's transferred, unique, problematic? *National Reading Conference Yearbook, 47*, 253–263.

García, G. E., & Nagy, W. (1993). Latino students' concept of cognates. In D. J. Leu & C. K. Kinzer (Eds.), *Examining central issues in literacy research, theory, and practice: Forty-second yearbook of the National Reading Conference* (pp. 367–373). Chicago: National Reading Conference.

Gardner, H. (1999). *Intelligence reframed: Multiple intelligences for the 21st century*. New York: Basic Books.

Goodman, L. (2001). A tool for learning: Vocabulary self-awareness. In C. Blanchfield (Ed.), *Creative vocabulary: Strategies for teaching vocabulary in grades K–12*. Fresno, CA: San Joaquin Valley Writing Project.

Goodman, Y. M. (1978). Kid watching: an alternative to testing. *National Elementary Principals Journal, 57*, 41–45.

Gordon, C., & Pearson, P. D., (1983). *The effects of instruction in metacomprehension and inferencing on children's comprehension abilities* (Tech. rep. 269). Urbana: University of Illinois, Center for the Study of Reading.

Gough, P. B., Alford, J. A., & Holly-Wilcox, P. (1981). Words and contexts. In O.L. Tzeng & H. Signer (Eds.), *Perception of print: Reading research in experimental psychology*. Hillsdale, NJ: Erlbaum.

Graves, M. (2000). A vocabulary program to complement and bolster a middle-grade comprehension program. In B. M. Taylor, M. F. Graves, & P. van den Broek (Eds.), *Reading for meaning: Fostering comprehension in the middle grades* (pp. 116–135). New York: Teachers College Press/Newark, DE: International Reading Association.

Graves, M. F. (in press). *Vocabulary learning and instruction*. New York: Teachers College Press.

Graves, M. F. (1986) Vocabulary learning and instruction. In E.Z. Rothkopf (Ed.), *Review of research in education* (Vol.13), pp. 49–89). Washington, DC: American Educational Research Association.

Graves, M., Juel, C., & Graves, B. B. (1998). *Teaching reading in the 21st century*. Des Moines, IA: Allyn and Bacon.

Graves, M. F., & Slater, W. H. (in press). Vocabulary instruction in content areas. In D. Lapp, J. Flood, & N. Farnan (Eds.), *Content reading and learning: Instructional strategies*. Mahwah, NJ: Erlbaum.

Graves, M. F., Slater, W. H., & White, T. G. (1996). Vocabulary instruction in content areas. In D. Lapp, J. Flood, & N. Farnan (Eds.), *Content area reading and learning: Instructional strategies* (2nd ed., pp. 261–275). Mahwah, NJ: Erlbaum.

Graves, M. F., & Watts-Taffe, S. M. (2002). The place of word consciousness in a research-based vocabulary program. In S. J. Samuels & A. E. Farstrup (Eds.), *What research has to say about reading instruction* (3rd ed., pp. 140–165). Newark, DE: International Reading Association.

Grolier Educational. (2002). *Vietnam: A portrait of the country through its festivals and traditions*. Danbury, CT: Author.

Haggard, M. R. (1982). The vocabulary self-selection strategy: An active approach to word learning. *Journal of Reading, 26*, 203–207.

Haggard, M. R. (1986). The vocabulary self-selection strategy: Using student interest and world knowledge to enhance vocabulary growth. *Journal of Reading, 29*, 634–642.

Hallahan, D. P., & Kauffman, J. M. (2003). *Exceptional learners: Introduction to special education* (9th ed.). New York: Allyn & Bacon.

Harmon, J. M. (1998). Constructing word meaning: Strategies and perceptions of four middle school learners. *Journal of Literacy Research, 30*, 561–599.

Harmon, J. M. (1999). Initial encounters with unfamiliar words in independent reading. *Research in the teaching of English, 33*, 304–338.

Hart, B., & Risley, T.R. (1995). *Meaningful differences in the everyday experiences of young American children*. Baltimore: Paul H. Brookes.

Hart, B., & Risley, T. R. (2003, Spring). The early catastrophe: The 30 million word gap. *American Educator, 27*, 4–9.

Hirsch, E. D. Jr. (2001). *Overcoming the language gap: Make better use of the literacy time block (the core curriculum)*. Washington, DC: American Federation of Teachers.

Jenkins, J. R., & Dixon, R. (1983). Vocabulary learning. *Contemporary Educational Psychology, 8*, 237–260.

Jespersen, O. (1983). *Growth and structure of the English language* (9th ed.). Garden City, NY: Doubleday.

Johns, J. L. & Berglund, R. L. (2002). *Strategies for content area learning*. Dubuque, IA: Kendall Hunt.

Johnson, D. J., Johnson, B. V. H., & Schlichting, K. (2004). Logology: Word and language play. In J. F. Baumann & E. J. Kame'enui (Eds.) *Vocabulary instruction: Research to practice* (pp. 179–200). New York: Guilford Press.

Johnson, P., & Costello, P. (2005). Theory and research into practice: Principles of literacy assessment. *Reading Research Quarterly, 40*, 256–267.

Just, M. A., & Carpenter, P. A. (1985). *The psychology of reading and language comprehension*. Boston, MA: Allyn & Bacon.

Kame'enui, E. J., Dixon, R. C., & Carmine, D. W. (1987). Issues in design of vocabulary instruction. In M. G. McKeown & M. E. Curtis (Eds.), *The nature of vocabulary acquisition* (pp. 129–145). Hillsdale, NJ: Erlbaum.

Karlsen, B., & Gardner, E. (2001). *Stanford Diagnostic Reading Test* (4th ed.). San Antonio, TX: Harcourt.

Kay, A. (1990, April). "The best way to predict the future is to invent it." Keynote presentation at the Annual Conference of the Association for Supervision and Curriculum Development, San Francisco.

Kuhn, M. R., & Stahl, S. A. (1998). Teaching students to learn word meanings from context: A synthesis and some questions. *Journal of Literacy Research, 30*, 119–138.

Laborde, G. (1984). *Influencing with integrity*. Palo Alto, CA: Syntony Press.

Lapp, D., Flood, J., Brock, C., & Fisher, D. (in press). *Teaching reading to every child* (4th ed.). Mahwah, NJ: Erlbaum.

Lederer, R. (1988). *Get thee to a punnery*. Charleston, SC: Wyrick and Company.

Lenski, S. D., Wham, M. A., & Johns, J. L. (2003). *Reading and learning strategies: Middle grades through high school* (2nd ed.). Dubuque, IA: Kendall Hunt.

Levorato, M. C., & Cacciari, C. (1995). The effects of different tasks on the comprehension and production of idioms in children. *Journal of Experimental Child Psychology, 60*, 261–283.

Lewis, R. B., & Doorlag, D. H. (2003). *Teaching special students in general education classrooms*. Upper Saddle River, NJ: Merrill Prentice Hall.

Lipson, M., & Wixson, K. (2003). *Assessment and instruction of reading and writing difficulties* (3rd ed.) Boston: Allyn & Bacon.

MacGinitie, W., MacGinitie, R., Maria, K., & Dreyer, L. (2000). *Gates-MacGinitie Reading Tests* (4th ed.), Itasca, IL: Riverside.

Mangieri, J. N. (1972). *Difficulty of learning basic sight words*. Unpublished Dissertation, University of Pittsburgh.

Mangieri, J. N.; Bader, L., & Walker, J. (1987). *Elementary reading: A comprehensive approach*. Columbus, OH: Merrill.

Manuel, K. (2002). Teaching information literacy to Generation Y. *Journal of Library Administration, 36*, 195–217.

Maria, K. (1990). *Reading comprehension instruction: Issues and strategies*. Parkton, MD: York Press.

Mason, J. A., Stahl, S. A., Au, K. H., & Hermann, P. A. (2003). Reading: Children's developing knowledge of words. In J. Flood, D. Lapp, J. R. Squire, & J. M. Jensen (Eds.), *Handbook of research on teaching the English language arts* (2nd ed., pp. 914–930). Mahwah, NJ: Erlbaum.

McCandliss, B., Beck, I. L., Sandak, R., & Perfetti, C. (2003). Focusing attention on decoding for children with poor reading skills: Design and preliminary tests of the word building intervention, *Scientific Studies in Reading, 7*, 75–104.

McCormick, S. (1995). *Instructing students who have literacy problems* (2nd ed.), Englewood Cliffs, NJ: Merrill.

McGinley, W. J. & Denner, P. R. (1987). Story impressions: A prereading/writing activity. *Journal of Reading, 31*, 248–254.

McGrath, C. (2004, November 7). The new SAT: Writing to the Test. New York: *The New York Times*. Retrieved Nov. 7, 2004, http://www.nytimes.com/2004/11/07 education/edlife/117CHI.html

McKeown, M. G., Beck, I. L., Omanson, R. C., & Perfetti, C. A. (1983). The effects of long-term vocabulary instruction on reading comprehension: A replication. *Journal of Reading Behavior, 15*, 3–18.

Mead, M. (1954, September). The gifted child in the American culture today. *Journal of Teacher Education*, 211–212.

Nagy, W., & Scott, J. A. (2004). Vocabulary processes. In M. L. Kamil, P. B. Mosenthal, P. D. Pearson, & R. Barr (Eds.), *Handbook of reading research* (Vol. 3, pp. 269–284). Mahwah, NJ: Erlbaum.

Nagy, W. E. (1988). *Teaching vocabulary to improve reading comprehension*. Urbana, IL: National Council of Teachers of English/Newark, DE: International Reading Association.

Nagy, W. E., & Anderson, R. C. (1984). How many words are there in printed school English? *Reading Research Quarterly, 19*, 303–330.

Nagy, W. E., Anderson, R., & Hermann, P. (1987). Learning vocabulary from context during normal reading. *American Educational Research Journal, 24*, 237–270.

Nagy, W. E., Diakidoy, I. N., & Anderson, R. C. (1993). The acquisition of morphology: Learning the contributions of suffixes to the meanings of derivatives. *Journal of Reading Behavior, 25*, 155–170.

Nagy, W. E., & Hermann, P. A. (1987). Breadth and depth of vocabulary knowledge: Implications for acquisition instruction. In M. C. McKeown & M. E. Curtis (Eds.), *The nature of vocabulary acquisition* (pp. 19–35). Hillsdale, NJ: Erlbaum.

Nagy, W. E., Hermann, P. A., & Anderson, R. C. (1985). Learning words from context. *Reading Research Quarterly, 20*, 233–253.

Nation, I. S. P. (2001). *Learning vocabulary in another language*. Cambridge, England: Cambridge University Press.

National Institute of Child Health and Human Development (2000). *Report of the National Reading Panel: Teaching children to read: An evidence-based assessment of the scientific research literature on reading and its implications for reading instruction* (NIH Publication No. 00-4769). Washington, DC: U.S. Government Printing Office.

National Reading Panel. (2000). *Teaching children to read: An evidence-based assessment of the scientific research literature on reading and its implications for reading instruction: Report of the subgroups* (NIH Publication No.00-4754). Washington, DC: National Institute of Child Health and Human Development.

National Reading Panel. (2001). *Report of review of reading research to National Institute of Child Health and Human Development*. Washington, DC: National Institute of Child Health and Human Development.

Naylor, P. R. (2000). *Shiloh*. New York: Aladdin.

Newcomer, P. I., & Hammill, D. D. (1997). *Test of Language Development—Primary* (3rd ed.), Austin, TX: Pro-Ed.

O'Neill, M. (1989). *Hailstones and halibut bones: Adventures in color*. New York: Doubleday

Oswald, R., & Rasinski, T. (2002). Making and writing words in a second grade classroom. In W. Linek, et al. (Eds.) *Celebrating the voices of literacy: Yearbook of the College Reading Association* (pp. 108–116). Readyville, TN: College Reading Association.

Palinscar, A. S. & Klenk, L. (1992). Fostering literacy learning in supportive contexts. *Journal of Learning Disabilities, 25*, 211–225, 229.

Palinscar, A. S., (1986). The role of dialogue in providing scaffolded instruction. *Educational Psychologist, 21*, 117–175.

Pariza, J. L. (2002). A description of vocabulary learning in at-risk college freshmen cooperatively engaged in generative study of self-selected words. *Dissertation Abstracts International*, 2002 416–459. (UMI 3055459)

Park, B. (1993). *Junie B. Jones and a little monkey business*. New York: Random House.

Parrish, P. (1963). *Amelia Bedelia*. New York: HarperCollins.

Patterson, K., Grenny, J., McMillan, R., and Switzler, A. (2002). *Crucial conversations: Tools for talking when stakes are high*. New York: McGraw-Hill.

Pearson Education. (1999). *Longman American idioms dictionary*. Essex, England: Author.

Perkins, D. (2002). *King Arthur's round table*. New York: Wiley.

Pittelman, S. D., Heimlich, J. E., Berglund, R. L, & French, M. P. (1991). *Semantic feature analysis: Classroom applications*. Newark, DE: International Reading Association.

Ponterotto, D. (1994). Metaphors we can learn by: How insights from cognitive linguistics research can improve the teaching/learning of figurative language. *Forum, 32*. Retrieved October 17, 2004, from http://exchanges.state.gov/forum/vols/vol32/no3/p2.htm

Rasinski, T. V. (1999a). Making and writing words. *Reading Online*. Retrieved April 13, 2005, from http://www.readingonline.org/articles/words/rasinski.html

Rasinski, T. V. (1999b). Making and writing words using letter patterns. *Reading Online*. Retrieved April 15, 2005, from http://www.readingonline.org/articles/rasinski/MWW_LP.html

Rasinski, T. V. (2001). *Making and writing words*. Greensboro, NC: Carson-Dellosa.

Rasinski, T., & Oswald, R. (in press). The effects of making and writing words among grade-two students. *Reading and Writing Quarterly*.

Rathvon, N. (2004). *Early reading assessment: A practitioner's guide*. New York: Guilford Press.

Readence, J. E., Bean, T. T. W., & Baldwin, R. S. (1998). *Content area literacy: An integrated approach* (6th ed.). Dubuque, IA: Kendall/Hunt.

Readence, J. E., Bean, T. W., & Baldwin, R. S. (2004). *Content area literacy* (8th ed.). Dubuque, IA: Kendall/Hunt.

Reagan, R. (2001). Developing a lifetime of literacy. In A. L. Costa (Ed.), *Developing minds* (3rd ed, pp. 347–362). Alexandria, VA: Association for Supervision and Curriculum Development.

Richek, M. A. (2005). Words are wonderful: Interactive, time-efficient strategies to teach the meaning of words. *The Reading Teacher, 58*, 414–425.

Richek, M. A., Caldwell, J., Jennings, J., & Lerner, J. W. (2002). *Reading problems: Assessment and teaching strategies* (4th ed.). Boston: Allyn & Bacon.

Robb, L. (2000). *Teaching reading in middle school*. NY: Scholastic.

Roswell, F., & Chall, J. (1992). *Diagnostic assessments of reading with trial teaching*. Itasca, IL: Riverside.

Schmitt, N. (2000). *Vocabulary in language teaching*. Cambridge, England: Cambridge University Press.

Scott, J., Jamieson-Noel, D., & Asselin, M. (2003). Vocabulary instruction throughout the school day in 23 Canadian upper-elementary classrooms. *The Elementary School Journal, 103*, 269–286.

Scott, J. A., & Nagy, W. E. (1997). Understanding the definitions of unfamiliar verbs. *Reading Research Quarterly, 32*, 184–200.

Scott, J. A., & Nagy, W. E. (2004). Developing word consciousness. In J. F. Baumann & E. J. Kame'enui, (Eds.), *Vocabulary instruction: Research to practice* (pp. 201–217). New York: Guilford Press.

Scott, S. (2002). *Fierce conversations*. New York: Penguin Putnam.

Searfoss, L. W., & Readence, J. E. (1989). *Helping children learn to read* (2nd ed.). Englewood Cliffs, NJ: Prentice Hall.

Semali, L. (2001). Defining new literacies in curricular practice. *Reading Online, 5*(4). Retrieved Nov. 9, 2004 from http://readingonline.org/newliteracies/lit_index.asp?HREF=semali1/index.html

Semel, E., Wiig, E., & Secord, W. (2003). *Clinical evaluation of language fundamentals* (4th ed.). San Antonio, TX: Harcourt.

Senge, P., Ross, R., Smith, B., Roberts, C., & Kleiner, A. (1994). *The fifth discipline fieldbook*. New York: Doubleday/Currency.

Shanahan, T. (in press). Relations among oral language, reading, and writing development. In C. MacArthur, S. Graham, & J. Fitzgerald (Eds.), *Handbook of writing research*. New York: Guilford Press.

Shand, M. (1993). *The role of vocabulary in developing reading disabilities* (Tech. Rep. No. 576). Urbana IL: Center for the Study of Reading.

Singer, H. A. (1965). A developmental model of speed of reading in grades 3 through 6. *Reading Research Quarterly, 1*, 29–49.

Smith, M. K. (2002) Howard Gardner and multiple intelligences. *Encyclopedia of informal education*. Retrieved Feb. 14, 2004, from http://www.infed.org/thinkers/gardner.htm

Smith, M. K. (1941). Measurement of the size of general vocabulary through the elementary grades and high school. *General Psychological Monographs, 24*, 311–345.

Soule, S. (2001, September). Will they engage? Political knowledge, participation and attitudes of Generations X and Y. Paper presented at the German and American Conference "Active Participation or a Retreat to Privacy." Retrieved Oct. 15, 2004, from http://www.civiced.org/research_engage.pdf

Stahl, S. A. (1985). To teach a word well: A framework for vocabulary instruction. *Reading World, 24*, 16–17.

Stahl, S. (1986). The principles of effective vocabulary instruction. *Journal of Reading, 29*, 662–668.

Stahl, S. (1998). Four questions about vocabulary. In C. R. Hynd. (Ed.), *Learning from text across conceptual domains* (pp. 73–94). Mahwah, NJ: Erlbaum.

Stahl, S. A., Duffy-Hester, A. M., & Stahl, K. A. D. (1998). Everything you wanted to know about phonics (but were afraid to ask). *Reading Research Quarterly, 33*, 338–355.

Stahl, S. A., & Fairbanks, M. M. (1986). The effects of vocabulary instruction: A model-based meta-analysis. *Review of Educational Research, 56*, 72–110.

Stahl, S., & Kapinus, B. (2001). *Word power: What every educator needs to know about vocabulary.* Washington, DC: NEA Professional Library.

Stahl, S. A., & Nagy, W. E. (in press). *Teaching word meanings.* Mahwah, NJ: Erlbaum.

Stahl, S. A., & Shiel, T. G. (1992). Teaching meaning vocabulary: Productive approaches for poor readers. *Reading and Writing Quarterly, 8*, 223–241.

Stanovich, K. E. (1986). Matthew effects in reading: Some consequences of individual differences in the acquisition of literacy. *Reading Research Quarterly, 21*, 360–401.

Stauffer, R. G. (1942). A study of prefixes in the Thorndike list to establish a list of prefixes that should be taught in the elementary school. *Journal of Educational Research, 35*, 453–458.

Steinbeck, J. (1945). *The Pearl.* New York: Penguin Books.

Sternberg, R. J. (1983). Most vocabulary is learned from context. In M. G. McKeown & M. E. Curtis (Eds.), *The nature of vocabulary acquisition* (pp. 89–105). Hillsdale, NJ: Erlbaum.

Swartz, R., Kiser, M., & Reagan, R. (1999). *Teaching critical and creative thinking in language arts grades 5 & 6.* Pacific Grove, CA: Critical Thinking Books and Software.

Swartz, R., & Parks, S. (1994). *Infusing critical and creative thinking into elementary instruction: A lesson design handbook.* Pacific Grove, CA: Critical Thinking Books and Software.

Terban, M. (1996). *Dictionary of idioms: More than 600 phrases, sayings, and expressions.* New York: Scholastic Reference.

Thorndike, E. L. (1917). Reading as reasoning: A study of mistakes in paragraph reading. *The Journal of Educational Psychology, 8*, 323–332.

Thorndike, E. L. (1932). *The teacher's word book of 20,000 words.* New York: Teachers College Press.

Thorndike, E.L., & Barnhart, C.L. (1993). *Thorndike Barnhart Dictionary.* Glenview, IL: Scott Foresman.

Tierney, R. J., Readence, J. E., & Dishner, E. K. (1995). *Reading strategies and practices* (4th ed.). Boston: Allyn & Bacon.

Tompkins, G. E., & Blanchfield, C. (Eds.). (2004). *Teaching vocabulary: 50 creative strategies, grades K–12.* Upper Saddle River, NJ: Pearson Education, Inc.

Torgeson, J. (2004, November). Vocabulary instruction: The new emphasis for the 21st century. Keynote address at the Iowa State Reading First Conference, Boise City, IA.

Vacca, R. T., & Vacca, J. L. (2005). *Content area reading: Literacy and learning across the curriculum* (8th ed.). New York: Longman.

Verhallen, R. T., & Schoonen, R. (1993). Vocabulary knowledge of monolingual and bilingual children. *Applied Linguistics, 14*, 344–363.

Wallace, G., & Hammill, D. (2002). *Comprehensive receptive and expressive vocabulary* (2nd ed.). Austin, TX: Pro-Ed.

White, T. G., Graves, M. F., & Slater, W. H. (1990). Growth of reading vocabulary in diverse elementary schools. *Journal of Educational Psychology, 82*, 281–290.

White, T. G., Sowell, J., & Yanagihara, A. (1989). Teaching elementary students to use word-part clues. *The Reading Teacher, 42*, 302–308.

Williams, K. T. (1997). *Expressive Vocabulary Test.* Circle Pines, MN: American Guidance Service.

Wood, K. D. (2002). Differentiating reading and writing lessons to promote content learning. In C. C. Block, L. B. Gambrell, & M. Pressley (Eds.), *Improving comprehension* (pp. 155–180). San Francisco: Jossey-Bass.

Woodcock, R. W. (1987–1988). *Woodcock Reading Mastery Tests—Revised/Normative* (3rd ed.). Circle Pines, MN: American Guidance Service.

Index

A

Alford, J. A., 10
Allan, R., 193
American Educational Research Association (AERA), 122
Anders, P. L., 57
Anderson, R. C., 20—21, 56, 77, 98, 100—102, 166, 170
Arthur, V., 57, 110
Ash, G., 98, 102
Asselin, M., 104
assessment, 10
  analogy, 185—86
  applicational definition, 181—83
  authentic measures, 171—74, 178—80
  comprehension connection, 173
  contextual, 180—81
  contextual and definitional combined, 183
  degrees/stages of word knowledge, 102
  depth of understanding, 172
  formal measures, 173—77
  formative, 174
  formats for testing, 180—86
  Gates MacGinitie Reading Test, 171
  goals and purposes, 171
  heterogeneity, 168
  high-utility words, 169
  incrementality, 167
  inferential thinking, 13
  informal measures, 173—74, 178—80
  interrelatedness, 168
  morphological, 184
  multidimensionality, 167—68
  polysemy, 167
  professional texts on specific tests, 175
  relational/categorical, 184
  root words and word etymology, 170
  self-evaluation tasks, 179—80
  Semantic Feature Analysis, 71
  specific subject words, 169
  standardized tests (chart), 176—77
  strategies as tools for, 179
  summative, 174
  Teacher Rating of Oral Language and Literacy, 178—79
  word-learning tasks, 168
  word parts and structures, 170
  words students should know, 168—70
Au, K. H., 22
authentic measures of assessment, 171—74, 178—80

B

Baker, W., 195, 200
Baldwin, L. E., 101
Baldwin, R. S., 57, 64, 110, 155
Bamman, H. A., 102, 103, 167
Baumann, J. F., 167, 170
Bean, T. W., 57, 64, 110, 155
Bear, D. R., 81
Beck, I. L., 8, 10, 13, 16, 39, 56, 77, 98, 100, 102—104, 125, 136, 166, 174
Bennett-Armistead, V. S., 6
Berglund, R. L., 57, 85, 179
Biemiller, A., 10, 170
Billmeyer, R., 209

Blachowicz, C., 27, 56—57, 77, 97, 102, 179
Blanchfield, C., 149, 153, 157
Block, C. C., 8, 10, 12—13, 15, 17, 21, 121, 168
Boland, E., 170
Boland's Key Word Collection strategy, 157
Bond, W., 10
Bos, C. S., 57
Bowers, C. A., 194
Brabham, E. G., 10
Brassell, D., 57, 104, 110, 113, 117
Brock, C., 104
Bromley, K., 20—21
Buis, K., 117

C

Cacciari, C., 84
Caldwell, J., 175
Calkins, L. M., 113
Carlisle, J., 170
Carmine, D. W., 77
Carroll, J. B., 106
Cecil, N. L., 154, 159
Chall, J. S., 101
classroom tips, 83, 88, 95, 136
Clay, M. M., 172
collaboration, 193—98
content-area words
  assessment (vocabulary), 71
  Contextual Redefinition, 57, 64—67, 72—73, 110—113
  prior knowledge, 56
  research, 56—57, 68
  Semantic Feature Analysis, 57, 68—72
  Vocabulary Self-Awareness Chart, 57—64, 72—73
context, learning through
  assessment, 180—81
  comprehension and vocabulary, 20—21
context clues, using, 22—25
  reading (time spent), 21
  research, 13, 20—23
  Vocabulary Cloze Procedure, 22, 25—27, 35, 181
  Vocabulary Self-Selection Strategy, 22, 28—35
  see also content-area words
Corson, D., 101
Costa, A., 192, 195, 197, 200, 204—205, 207
Costello, P., 173—74
critical thinking, 193, 202—208
Cunningham, A. E., 21
Cunningham, J. W., 38, 40, 57, 110
Cunningham, P. M., 38, 40, 57, 110, 117, 170

D

Dale, E., 77, 102—103, 106, 167, 169
Daneman, M., 98
Davies, P., 106
Davis, F. B., 77, 98, 117
Defee, M., 39
de Glopper, K., 22

Denner, P. R., 107
De Temple, J., 124
Dewitz, P., 133
Diakidoy, I. N., 170
Dickinson, D. K., 10, 12, 16, 178
Dishner, E. K., 57, 110, 113
Dixon, R. C., 77, 101
Doorlag, D. H., 140
Dreyer, L., 171
Duffy-Hester, A. M., 39
Duke, N. K., 6, 100
Dykstra, R., 10

E

Edwards, E. C., 170
Eisner, E., 193
English-language learners (ELLs)
  classroom tips, 136
  fostering word consciousness, 122, 132—36
  idioms, 76, 84, 133—36
  interactive oral reading, 123—24
  Latin-Greek derivations, 50
  Paired Question technique, 120—21
  Prefix Removal and Replacement Strategy, 132
  prefixes, 128—32
  providing rich and varied language experiences, 122—24
  research, 122—23
  teaching individual words, 122, 125—28
  teaching word-learning strategies, 122, 128—32
Ennis, R., 202

F

Fairbanks, M. M., 101—102
Fisher, D., 104
Fisher, P. J., 27, 56—57, 77, 97, 102, 179
Fitzgerald, J., 122
Flood, J., 57, 104, 110, 113, 117
Flood, S., 104
formal measures of assessment, 173—77
  see also tests, assessment
Frayer, D. A., 113, 125
Frayer steps/method, 125—28
Frederick, W. D., 113, 125
Freebody, P., 56, 77
French, M. P., 57, 179
Fry, E. B., 10
Fukkink, R. G., 22
future, preparing students for the
  collaboration, 193—98
  critical thinking, 193, 202—208
  dialogue, 194—97, 200, 202
  enhancing skills, need for, 191—93
  judgment, effect of, 193, 198—202
  meaningful literacy achievement, 193, 209—12
  metacognition, 204—205
  questioning and problem posing, 206—208
  "thinking" terms, 203

THE VOCABULARY-ENRICHED CLASSROOM

G

García, G. E., 122—123
Gardner, H., 141—42
Garmston, R., 192, 195, 197, 204
Generation "Y," 143—45, 156—57,
191—92, 194, 198—200, 205—207,
212—213 *see also* future, preparing students for the
gifted students
bodily-kinesthetic intelligence,
152—53
characteristics, 140—42
definition, 140
interpersonal intelligence, 156—58
intrapersonal intelligence, 158—59
linguistic intelligence, 146—49
logical-mathematical intelligence,
150—51
multiple intelligences, 140—42, 145,
161
musical intelligence, 151—52
naturalist intelligence, 160—61
periodicals that publish student
work, 163
relationship between spelling and
vocabulary, 138—40
spatial intelligence, 153—55
techniques and NRP strategies list,
144—45
Goodman, L., 57—58
Goodman, Y. M., 172
Gough, P. B., 10
Graves, B. B., 104
Graves, M. F., 20—22, 76, 98, 101—
105, 110, 122, 125, 128, 132—33,
136—37, 168

H

Haggard, M. R., 28, 179
Hall, D. P., 39, 117, 170
Hallahan, D. P., 140
Harmon, J. M., 21, 178
Hart, B., 10, 20, 122
Heimlich, J. E., 57, 179
Henne, R., 98
Hermann, P. A., 20, 22, 101, 137
high-frequency words, 103—106 *see
also* word tiers
high-utility words, 10—11, 103—106,
169 *see also* word tiers
Hirsch, E. D. Jr., 10
Holly-Wilcox, P., 10
homophones, idioms, and figurative
language
classroom tips, 83, 88, 95, 136
definitions, 78, 82, 89, 133
Discover the Author's Connection,
91—95
ELLs and, 76, 84, 133—36
homophone sets, 78—79
Homophone Win, Lose, or Draw,
81—83
Idiom Board, 134—35
Idiom Four Square, 85—88
introduction of, 80—81, 84—85,
89—91
research, 76—77, 97

I

important/useful words, 11, 16—17,

106 *see also* word tiers
individual words, teaching, 122, 125—
28
informal measures of assessment, 171—
74, 178—80
instruction
additive methods, 77
assessment, and, 164—187
content-area, 57, 64, 67, 72
daily, 11
ELLs, for, 118—137
exemplary literacy instruction, 10—
15
generative methods, 77, 97
gifted students, for, 138—163
instructional activities, 12
preparing students for the future,
188—213
struggling readers, 98—117
word building in curriculum, 39
word-learning beliefs, 16—17
word-meaning, clues, 14—15
see also context; strategies
interactive oral reading (defined),
123—24
Invernizzi, M., 81
Israel, S., 15

J

Jacobs, V. A., 101
Jamieson-Noel, D., 104
Jenkins, J. R., 101
Jennings, J., 175
Jespersen, O., 76
Johns, J. L., 85
Johnson, B. V. H., 84
Johnson, D. J., 84
Johnson, P., 173—74
Johnston, F., 81
Juel, C., 104
judgment, effect of, 193, 198—202

K

Kaatz, D., 88
Kallick, B., 207
Kame'enui, E. J., 77, 170
Kapinus, B., 113
Kaplan-Schwarz, E., 88
Kauffman, J. M., 140
Kay, A., 213
Kiser, M., 200
Klausmeier, H. J., 113, 125
Kleiner, A., 197
Klenk, L., 100
Kucan, L., 10, 13, 16, 98, 100, 102—
104, 125, 136, 166, 174
Kuhn, M. R., 22

L

Laborde, G., 211
language experiences, 122—24
Lapp, D., 104
Latin and Greek derivations, 50—52
Lederer, R., 136
Lenski, S. D., 85
Lerner, J. W., 175
Levorato, M. C., 84
Lewis, R. B., 140
Lipson, M., 117, 175
low-frequency words, 103

Lynch-Brown, C., 10

M

MacGinitie, R., 171
MacGinitie, W., 171
Making Words/Making and Writing
Words, 38—46, 53
Mangieri, J. N., 8, 10, 12—13, 15—17,
21, 121, 168
Manuel, K., 143, 145
Maria, K., 100, 171
Marzano, R., 204
Mason, J. A., 22
McCabe, A., 178
McCandliss, B., 39
McCaslin, E. S., 100
McCormick, S., 174—175
McGinley, W. J., 107
McGrath, C., 193
McKeown, M. G., 8, 10, 13, 16, 56, 77,
98, 100, 102—104, 125, 136, 166,
174
Mead, M., 143
meaningful literacy achievement, 193,
209—12
Moses, A. M., 6
multiple intelligences, 140—42, 145
bodily-kinesthetic, 152—53
interpersonal, 156—58
intrapersonal, 158—59
linguistic, 146—49
logical-mathematical, 150—51
musical, 151—52
naturalist, 160—61
spatial, 153—55

N

Nagy, W. E., 20—21, 56, 77, 88, 98,
100—103, 117, 122—23, 125, 132,
136—37, 166—68, 170
Nation, I. S. P., 122
National Institute of Child Health and
Human Development (NICHD), 20
National Reading Panel, 11—13, 16,
38, 57, 98, 101, 144, 166
Nifty Thrifty Fifty, 170

O

Olejnik, S., 170
Omanson, R. C., 77, 104
O'Rourke, J., 102—103, 106, 167, 169
Oswald, R., 39

P

Palinscar, A. S., 100
Pariza, J. L., 77
Parks, S., 200
Peck, G., 95
Peltzer's Building Vocabulary
Comprehension through
Dramatization strategy, 158
Perfetti, C. A., 10, 39, 77, 98
Pittelman, S. D., 57, 179
planning vocabulary instruction *see*
assessment
Ponterotto, D., 89—90
prefixes, focusing on, 128—32

R

Rasinski, T. V., 39—40, 46
Rathvon, N., 175
Readence, J. E., 57, 64, 110, 113, 116, 155
Reagan, R., 200, 210
Reed, K. M., 13
Rennie, H., 83
reproducibles
  Class Words: Vocabulary Self-Selection Strategy Sheet, 31—32
  Contextual Redefinition chart, 111—12
  Idiom Four Square, 86
  Making and Writing Words, 41—42
  My Words: Vocabulary Self-Selection Strategy Sheet, 29—30
  Vocabulary Self-Awareness Chart, 58—61, 63
research
  assessment, 10, 13
  content-area learning, 56—57, 68
  context, 20—21
  daily instruction, 11
  ELLs, 122
  exemplary literacy instruction, 10—15
  gifted students NRP techniques and strategies list, 144—45
  high-utility words, 10—11
  homophones, idioms, and figurative language, 76—77, 97
  important/useful words, 11, 16—17
  multimodal learning, 12
  multiple exposures to words, 12—13
  struggling readers, 98—101
  Think Alouds, 15
  word-learning beliefs, 16—17
  word-meaning clues/vocabulary-building strategies, 14—15
  word retention, 12, 16
Richek, M. A., 107, 175
Richman, B., 106
Risley, T. R., 10, 20, 122
Robb, L., 21
Roberts, C., 197
Ross, R., 197

S

Sandak, R., 39
Schlichting, K., 84
Schmitt, N., 122
Schoonen, R., 122
Scott, J. A., 56, 77, 103—104, 132, 166—68, 193
Searfoss, L. W., 116
Secord, W., 175
selecting words, 103—106, 168—170
Semali, L., 143
Semel, E., 175
Senge, P., 194, 197
Shalit, S., 195
Shanahan, T., 122
Shand, M., 98
Shiel, T. G., 169
Singer, H. A., 117
Slater, W. H., 101, 105, 122
Slonium, M., 10, 170
Smith, B., 197
Smith, M. K., 12, 100—101, 141

Snow, C. E., 124
sorting words, 103—106 see also word tiers
Soule, S., 143
Sowell, J., 128
Sprague, K., 178
Stahl, K. A. D., 39
Stahl, S. A., 13, 21—22, 39, 77, 88, 101—102, 113, 125, 136, 169, 172
Stanovich, K. E., 21
Stauffer, R. G., 128
Sternberg, R. J., 20, 123
strategies, 14—16
  assessment tools, as, 179
  Boland's Key Word Collection, 157
  context clues, 22—25
  Contextual Redefinition, 57, 64—67, 72—73, 110—13
  Discover the Author's Connection, 91—95
  ELLs, for, 128—32
  Example and Non-Example, 113—17, 127
  Homophone Win, Lose, or Draw, 81—83, 96
  Idiom Four Square, 85—88
  intelligences, for differing, 145—61
  Prefix Removal and Replacement Strategy, 132
  Semantic Feature Analysis, 57, 68—73, 179
  Text Impressions (Story Impressions/Semantic Impressions), 107—110
  Vocabulary Cloze Procedure, 22, 25—27
  Vocabulary Self-Awareness Chart, 57—64, 72—73
  Vocabulary Self-Selection Strategy, 22, 28—35, 179
  word building, 36—53
  word clusters, 149
struggling readers, 21
  Contextual Redefinition, 110—113
  definition, 100
  degrees/stages of word knowledge, 102
  Example and Non-Example, 113—17
  research, 98—101
  selecting words, 103—106
  Text Impressions (Story Impressions/Semantic Impressions), 107—110
Swartz, R., 200

T

Tabors, P. O., 10, 16
technical vocabulary (specific domain), 103—104 see also word tiers
Templeton, S., 81
Terban, M., 84
tests, assessment
  Clinical Evaluation of Language Fundamentals, 175
  formal, 173—75
  Gates MacGinitie Reading Test, 171
  Peabody Picture Vocabulary Test, 175
  standardized tests chart, 176—77

Think Alouds, 15, 23—25
Thorndike, E. L., 77, 128
Tierney, R. J., 57, 110, 113
Tompkins, G. E., 149, 153, 157
Tompkins's Word Clusters Strategy, 149
Tompkins's Where in the World, 153
Torgeson, J., 8

V

Vacca, J. L., 179
Vacca, R. T., 179
Verhallen, R. T., 122
vocabulary-building strategies see strategies
Vocabulary Cloze Procedure, 22, 25—27
vocabulary development, 10
  complexity, five aspects of, 167—168
  degrees/stages of word knowledge, 102
  expressive, 166
  factors that affect, 100—101
  need for enhancing skills, 191—93
  receptive, 166
  research, 10—15
spelling and, 138—40
vocabulary logs, 34
Vocabulary Self-Selection Strategy, 22, 28—35, 179

W

Watts-Taffe, S. M., 21—22, 76, 132—133
Wham, M. A., 85
White, T. G., 101, 105, 128
Wiig, E., 175
Wixson, K., 117, 175
Wood, K. D., 72
Word Building
  curriculum, in, 39
  definition, 38
  example, 36, 40, 42—46
  Greek and Latin roots, 50—53
  improving reading, 39
  Making and Writing Words, 40—46, 53
  Making Words, 38—40, 53
  Word Ladders, 46—49, 53
  word-learning beliefs, 16—17
word families (defined), 102
Word Ladders, 46—49, 53
word lists, 11, 128, 169—170
word-meaning clues, 14—16
word selection, 103—106, 168—70
word tiers, 104—117
writing, 123, 149, 156, 200—202, 210—211

Y

Yanagihara, A., 128